THE IDEAL MAN

The Tragedy of Jim Thompson and the American Way of War

Joshua Kurlantzick

WILEY

John Wiley & Sons, Inc.

For Caleb

Published by John Wiley & Sons, Inc., Hoboken, New Jersey
Published simultaneously in Canada

For general information about our other products and services, please contact our Customer Care Department within the United States at (800) 762-2974, outside the United States at (317) 572-3993 or fax (317) 572-4002.

Wiley also publishes its books in a variety of electronic formats and by print-on-demand. Some content that appears in standard print versions of this book may not be available in other formats. For more information about Wiley products, visit us at www.wiley.com.

Library of Congress Cataloging-in-Publication Data:
Kurlantzick, Joshua, date.
  The ideal man : the tragedy of Jim Thompson and the American way of war / Joshua Kurlantzick.
    p. cm.
  Includes bibliographical references and index.
  ISBN 978-0-470-08621-6 (hardback); ISBN 978-1-118-09809-7 (ebk.);
  ISBN 978-1-118-09810-3 (ebk.); ISBN 978-1-118-09811-0 (ebk.)
  1. Thompson, Jim, b. 1906. 2. Silk industry—Thailand. 3. Businessmen—Thailand—Biography. 4. Businessmen—United States—Biography. 5. Disappeared persons—Malaysia—Biography. 6. Cold War. 7. United States—Foreign relations—1945–1989. I. Title.
  HD9926.T52K87 2011

  338.7'67739092—dc23

  [B]

2011034994

Printed in the United States of America

10 9 8 7 6 5 4 3 2 1

Contents

Preface

When I first moved to Bangkok, in the late 1990s, I quickly became disillusioned by how familiar Thailand seemed. The downtown business district could have been Boston, New York, or Singapore, all glass-and-steel towers, shopping malls, chain restaurants, and yuppies sipping five-dollar lattes at Starbucks. At night, I'd relax by watching the latest episodes of *Sex in the City* on cable television, and in the morning I'd catch up on the latest headlines, online, in the *New York Times* and the *Washington Post*.

When I met longtime expatriates in Bangkok, they told tales from a bygone era, before the city had become so homogenized and before the world paid close attention to Southeast Asia. As the launching pad for U.S. military actions during the Vietnam War, Thailand had been transformed from an isolated, exotic nation into the center of American Cold War strategy, a bulwark against the tide of communism that seemed to be moving, inexorably, east and south after the stunning communist takeover in mainland China in 1949. At that time, even tiny Laos, a country of only a few million people surrounded by Thailand, Cambodia, and Vietnam, became a theater for superpower conflict, so much so that early in the Kennedy administration the young president was convinced that Laos had become America's biggest foreign policy challenge.

It's a common phenomenon in many countries for the older generations of foreign residents to tell the younger generations that they missed out on the authentic experience—the classic tale of "you should have been here when." In the case of Thailand, and indeed much of Southeast Asia, which has gone through such rapid modernization, the old hands actually had a point. By the time I got there, Thailand had pretty much dropped out of global consciousness, except as a pleasant tourist destination, a source of fiery cuisine, and a code word for sordid male pleasures. Living in Bangkok, I enjoyed eating homemade curries and learning the impossibly tough tonal language, but I didn't think that monumental history was being made around me.

However, back in the 1950s and 1960s, when the United States made Southeast Asia its top priority in the world, the story was much different. Harry Truman had struck the first blow, declaring that Thailand was the only independent nation in Southeast Asia, and it would be where the United States would make a stand against communism. John F. Kennedy, in one of his early foreign policy speeches, upped the ante, declaring Laos, which faced a communist insurgency, one of the biggest security challenges in the world. Kennedy soon began pouring American advisers into Indochina. Lyndon Johnson and Richard Nixon went much further, committing American ground forces to Indochina and making Thailand into a staging area for the massive U.S. involvement in the war.

The Indochina war thrust Thailand into the center of world events, but for many Americans who focused on Thailand, it also became a canvas for ideological conflict. For some American advisers who had worked with anticolonial nationalist movements in Southeast Asia during World War II, the United States could best serve the region—and its own interests—by maintaining alliances with the men and women fighting to free themselves from French, British, and Dutch colonial rule. Franklin Roosevelt, after all, had promised an end to colonialism and a new day of self-determination for all men, and upholding those promises would gain the United States the friendship of Southeast Asia's peoples indefinitely.

For others, the Southeast Asian nationalists, including Vietnam's Ho Chi Minh, were a dangerous cocktail, flirting with socialism and communism and threatening to destabilize the region by wiping out entire political orders. The United States should support stability and development, the thinking went, even if that meant picking conservative dictators rather than gambling on left-leaning men who might be Democrats. As the Cold War grew hotter, this debate would consume American foreign policy, determine the course of the Indochina war, and boost and destroy the careers of many American advisers, spies, and politicians.

Asia was beginning to modernize, its young "tiger economies" (economies that undergo rapid growth) just starting to become the export powerhouses they would turn into, eventually dominating world manufacturing. With the United States dominating the world economy after World War II, newly wealthy Americans had started to travel much farther from home, their jets and cruise ships descending upon Asian ports like Bangkok. A fascination with the Orient rippled through American middlebrow and highbrow culture, from *The King and I*, the story of Thailand's King Rama IV that turned into a Broadway smash, to *Time* magazine, founded by the son of missionaries in China and dedicated to shifting Middle America's worldview from Europe to the Far East.[1]

Nevertheless, in the 1950s and 1960s, monks still wandered the streets of Bangkok in the morning to beg for rice from shopkeepers. Canals still crisscrossed the city, which was once called the Venice of the East. You could still walk many Bangkok side streets rather than sit in unmoving traffic so dense it made Los Angeles look like a driving paradise.

The more I learned about Thailand in the 1950s and 1960s, the more I became obsessed with the story of one man from that time. Jim Thompson had first come to the country in the waning days of World War II; he had changed himself from an American society dilettante back in New York into an Asian legend—as a spy, a silk magnate, and a man who had gained access to Thai worlds that foreigners never saw. Thompson stood for one side of *the* foreign policy question, the Cold War. He was willing to gamble on democracy in Southeast Asia, and he ultimately paid a price for his gambling.

Even decades later, with Thompson long gone, idle talk at Bangkok dinner parties turned to his life, perhaps because Thompson, like every foreigner who shows up in a new place, had tried, in ways large and small, to reinvent himself, to remake his life into something a little more poetic and a little more meaningful. He had succeeded wildly in this reinvention, unlike many others who had failed.

Perhaps, too, we saw in him the idealism of a relatively young man who had been dropped into a foreign country with vast needs and suddenly understood the privilege he'd been born into. Perhaps we recognized in Thompson's later years, as he became more disillusioned with U.S. policy in Asia, the alienation that develops when you live away from home for so long and wind up a stranger in your own culture yet have never been fully accepted in your adopted home. Perhaps we saw in the ideological conflicts of the Cold War a reflection of the sharp ideological conflicts of today, often as black and white as in the McCarthy era. Or maybe, decades after Thompson's time, we just realized that his life made for a great story to retell.

1

Staring out across the Bangkok canal, where women washed themselves wrapped in modest sarongs and long-tailed boats floated by carrying crates of mangoes and tiny red chilies, Denis Horgan couldn't believe his luck.

A twenty-five-year-old Irish American from South Boston with a boxer's jaw and sharp blue eyes, Horgan had for years feared being sent to Vietnam. Back home, in his working-class neighborhood, most people disdained the Vietnam objectors who demonstrated in Harvard Yard, and since it was only early 1967, the antiwar movement had not yet built up its roar and fury. So Horgan kept his mouth shut at home, but he knew his mind. "I didn't know what we were doing there, and I certainly didn't want to fight," he said.

When Horgan finally was drafted, he didn't flee, but he snagged an assignment almost as perfect, and one that would transform his life. He was detailed as aide to Brigadier General Ed Black, commander of the headquarters of U.S. forces in Thailand, where the U.S. military launched its bombing raids into Indochina, planned its overall war strategy, and generally enjoyed all the luxuries of life unavailable in places like Danang or Cam Ranh.[1]

In the early days of the Vietnam War, back during the Eisenhower and Kennedy administrations, the Americans serving in Thailand had come to the country on tourist visas and kept a low profile, for fear that the Thai public, so proud that its nation had never been colonized, would resent a U.S. Army presence. But by 1967, with the United States lavishing so much aid on Thailand, the Americans and the Thais had dropped that pretense, and now thousands of GIs arrived in the country every month. By 1968, the United States would have forty-six thousand troops in Thailand, housed on bases around the country.[2]

Still, Thailand wasn't Vietnam. Instead of having firefights with the Viet Cong, Black and Horgan roamed the dusty, baked-earth Thai Northeast, site of most U.S. bases. In the Northeast, the two men toured U.S. Army outposts, shared banquets of sticky rice and grilled catfish hosted for them by village leaders, and made sure that the general found courts in every small Thai town so he could get in his regular tennis game.

Most weekends, the general and his young aide, like most men detailed to the Northeast, came to Bangkok. The Thai capital still seemed exotic to anyone who arrived from the United States. Three-wheeled pedicabs jostled for road space in the potholed streets with vendors hawking dried squid and creamy banana leaf curries and crunchy fried locusts. Monks' chanting rang out in the morning from the courtyards of temples glittering with gems inlaid in the spires.

But Bangkok was becoming more Americanized, and you could grab a real, juicy burger and a Coke over on Sukhumwit Road and then head over to Petchaburi Road's go-go bars to run through the street of brothels. By 1967, Bangkok already had such a reputation for male pleasure that the U.S. military routinely sent men exhausted from tours in Vietnam to the city for R & R tours, and *Time* magazine wrote, in a lengthy article on the country, "Any jewelry store on Oriental Avenue has star rubies for the asking. . . . Equally abundant are instantly available women."[3] The bars filled up with young Thai women from the countryside with sweet round faces and hard, flinty eyes; they latched on to the GIs' clothing as the men walked past, the start of a long night of negotiation.

Barhopping for girls wasn't Ed Black's style. Generals didn't do that, at least not where enlisted men could see them, and being a general had always been Ed Black's dream. A squat-shouldered, square-jawed man with hair brushed straight back, and with a nose that seemed to have been flattened against his face, Black stood spine-stiffeningly straight and looked like the answer to a casting call from an army recruitment advertisement. Even now, in his sixties, the general completed his daily regimen of push-ups every night, no matter where he and Horgan bunked.

The army had been his life since he had enlisted more than twenty years earlier, in the days before World War II. The general hadn't risen as quickly as he had hoped—his blunt speaking style and love of press conferences didn't exactly endear him to the higher brass, and Horgan sometimes wondered if the general had picked him as an aide just because Horgan had once worked as a journalist—but Black had now made it to a command in a real hot war. He had a wife, who would join him in Thailand, but for now he was alone in the country, his time filled only with the lives of other men and the vast details of managing a massive military buildup.[4]

Without bars on the agenda, when the general and his aide came to Bangkok, they stayed instead at the antique teakwood mansion of Jim Thompson, one of Black's oldest friends. This weekend, like most, the routine at Thompson's residence varied little. As the sun began to set in the soupy, hundred-degree Bangkok heat, Jim Thompson arrived home from his silk shop over at the Suriwong Road business district, and Black and Horgan joined a seemingly endless parade of guests for a tour of the house and of Thompson's enormous art collection, for scotches on the veranda, and then for dinner.

Horgan did not have much familiarity with American high society, but he knew enough to know that he should be impressed by Thompson's guests: Eleanor Roosevelt, the du Ponts, Truman Capote, various counts and countesses, and marquises. Each time Horgan showed up at Jim's house with the general, some other famous person would be joining them for dinner.

As the dinner crowd sat down on the terrace—passing through rooms surrounded by bronze Buddha heads, Ming bowls, and Burmese tapestries inlaid with gold leaf—the out-of-town visitors, always overdressed for the Bangkok weather, oohed over Thompson's food and offered quick, uncomfortable bows back to the retinue of servants who saluted Thompson and his guests with the hands-together Thai gesture known as the *wai*. Black and Horgan knew that dinner would just be ordinary curries and steamed rice, bought by the houseboy Yee from some street vendors nearby for less than twenty-five cents a dish.

Still, no one really came to Jim Thompson's house for the food. They came for Jim Thompson. By 1967, Jim Thompson did not just manage his extravagant house; he was the curator of another exhibit: his own legend. The best-known American in Asia, he lived the life that all these visitors to his house wished for. Now sixty years old, Jim was not very physically memorable upon first meeting: a soft putty chin, a permanently tanned and creased face from years in the Thai sun, thinning sandy hair, an eggplant nose and a high brow, bright blue eyes, a simple white shirt and khakis, and delicate soft hands—usually wrapped around a cigarette, against his doctor's advice.

Unlike some expatriates, he never boasted, or at least it did not seem like boasting. The scion of an old, wealthy Delaware family, raised alongside the du Ponts and the Rockefellers, Jim still spoke with a clipped, boarding-school accent, and he still knew that it was bad manners to tout your money, your connections, and your adventures; perhaps his life as a spy had made him naturally secretive, too. Thompson might actually have loved flattery, but when people praised him, he played it off with a shrug; when they oohed over his antiques, he told some story about how he'd been lucky and found this or that priceless statue in some secondhand market.[5]

When guests arrived, Thompson welcomed them with a studied informality, calling out "Hallo there. . . . Come on up," from the top of the stairs.[6] Once you met Jim Thompson, you never forgot him. Everyone at dinner knew Jim's basic life story, from all the newspaper articles, television newsreels, and gossip about him.

They knew that Thompson had come to Thailand, a country now central to the Vietnam War, at the end of the Second World War as part of the predecessor of the Central Intelligence Agency. They knew, vaguely, that he'd been involved in some sort of secret missions, the type that required knowing how to dynamite railroads and parachute into war-torn territory. They knew that when Japan had surrendered, Thompson had stayed on in Bangkok as a spy; everyone knew that— he'd been working all over the region, with Thais, Lao, Cambodians, and Vietnamese.

Even after Thompson had formally resigned from America's spy service, most people in town worshiped his advice, and many assumed that he had never really left his old job. Meanwhile, even if he did still spy, his legitimate business alone, the Thai Silk Company, had made him an international celebrity. The silk king, the newspaper profiles called him—the man who had built Thai silk from a small cottage industry into a global fashion powerhouse, made Bangkok the Paris of the East, and brought glamour to this remote capital.

If the guests were lucky, Jim might take them on a quick predinner tour of his silk weavers just across the canal. They'd wander through the clusters of wooden houses filled with the endless clacking of silk shuttles moving back and forth on the looms. Conductors from the sampans (canal gondolas) called out destinations and fares, and Thompson's weavers *wai*ed Jim as though he were some kind of god. Jim just smiled back, as if he were embarrassed and thrilled all at the same time.

His guests knew that they had become part of the show. They knew that Jim entertained virtually every night, in a traditional teak-wood house that had become a combination museum and gathering place for not only socialites but also all of the generals, politicians, and world leaders who came to Bangkok to observe and analyze the American buildup in Indochina. At his home, with the dim house-lights flickering on the gold-lacquer bodhisattva statues and the sandstone Buddha heads from the twelfth century,[7] the talk always somehow turned to Jim, everyone seated around him, lobbing questions about his life, his world, and his opinions. The silk king was, of course, happy to answer.

When Jim paused, Horgan would often hear whispering back and forth between some of the female socialites in the room, wondering behind their hands why Jim had never remarried and running their fingers through their hair whenever Jim glanced over at them.

After the tourists and the countesses had returned to their hotels, promising to stop by the silk shop the next day to spend more money, Thompson, Horgan, and Black would retire to one of the alcoves off the dining room. In the sitting room, Thompson had an elaborate model of a Chinese mansion. Even at 11 p.m., Bangkok's heat could be intense, but Jim's house was shaded by feral palms grown massive under the endless sun. When Horgan walked over to the veranda, across the canal he could see families of Thai Muslims eating dinners of chicken biryani and *roti murtabak* in their houses, the men in white skullcaps and robes and the women in straight long frocks.

Jim and the general poured themselves generous scotches, and Jim lit up another cigarette. Black refused to smoke, on health grounds, but he allowed himself drinks—and Jim offered the young aide a drink as well. Now the real conversation began, really a two-man conversation. "I just sat there and listened," Horgan said. "We'd be there until one or two in the morning, but I didn't say much. What did I have to say around these two giants?"[8]

General Black couldn't care less about Jim's art, the silk company, or the latest famous person who'd dined at Jim's house. Ed Black cared about his family, his tennis game, and, above all, his job. So inevitably the conversation would drift to war—or rather, wars, the talk bouncing back and forth between the Second World War and Vietnam. Black had recruited Jim to join the spy agency during World War II, and the two men would slip into a discussion of that war with a kind of shorthand common to old buddies. Caserta, Trincomalee, Fort Monroe—Black or Thompson would only have to mention a place, and they'd both laugh at the memories without saying more, even if the names were nothing more than a spot on the map to Horgan. They never boasted about their World War II exploits, either, but they also never talked about the blood and boredom and brutality—it all sounded like a kind of honorable adventure, in their telling.

When the glasses were nearly empty, Jim would reach into a cabinet for more scotch or call out to Yee to grab another bottle and some blocks of ice. The talk would turn to Vietnam, and the whole tenor of the evening would change. Sometimes Black and Thompson would gossip about the generals in Thailand and Vietnam: who was up, who was down, when the next coup would happen in Bangkok. But Horgan always came to Bangkok prepared to hear another argument, and he was rarely disappointed.[9]

For Black, the Vietnam War truly was the critical stand against communism—and even if it wasn't, the army bosses had ordered it, so that made it right. The communists were causing problems all over the world, and they had to be dealt with; it was that simple. Jim would come right back at him. For Thompson, who'd lived through the failings of one colonialist after the next in Asia, the fighting hadn't started when the United States showed up. The conflict had been going on for decades, and American involvement would be just another episode of an outsider getting caught up in battles and games it knew nothing about, and of coming down against average people in Southeast Asia—never a position that was wise to be in.

"Look," Jim said one night, as Horgan looked on from the margins of the conversation, "this war has gone on for a long time—the Vietnamese fought the Chinese, the French, beat them both. When you go back to America, they'll still be fighting—and you'll go home, and all the trouble you've left here, it will cave in on these countries."[10]

Thompson never spoke about the consequences of his views directly in front of Horgan, but occasionally, when the aide wandered out onto the veranda for some air, he'd hear the two old friends talking in more worried tones about that. Thompson's deeply lined face looked more weary than normal. With America's staunch support for the conservative leadership in Thailand and in Vietnam, Thompson's views could put him in danger. He openly questioned the Thai leadership and worried that America's policies were hindering democracy in Southeast Asia and turning the United States into a new type of colonialist.

He'd already been investigated by the Federal Bureau of Investigation, which had quizzed everyone all the way back to his prep school buddies to find out whether he was involved in "un-American" activities. Now Thompson was receiving regular threats from Thais close to the ruling dictators who didn't appreciate a foreigner (even Jim Thompson) criticizing their rapidly expanding—and for the generals, lucrative—alliance with the U.S. military. Other foreigners in Bangkok had started shunning Thompson, fearful of whom he had offended. Business competitors had begun trying to muscle into his lucrative industry.

Occasionally, Thompson would stop Black with a slight smile and a wave of his hand. "Let's listen to this young man," he'd say, pointing to Horgan. The young aide would then try, while carefully watching the general, to express his antiwar feelings without making his boss sound like an idiot, knowing that Black viewed the antiwar movement as unpatriotic. Every time Horgan finished, Jim would flash him a small smile. Later, back in their own guest quarters on Jim's compound, Black would mutter to Horgan, "Jim has been out here so long, he doesn't get it anymore, he doesn't understand our world."[11]

To Horgan, Jim always seemed more than angry; he seemed hurt—personally hurt by the war. The general was just a visitor, passing through, happy enough in Thailand but always ready to head back home. For Jim, this *was* home—and the war, with its American GIs, American midwestern tourists, American burgers, and American-style go-go shows, was forever changing that home, and not in ways Jim welcomed. On the few occasions that Jim had traveled up-country to see Black, Horgan thought he saw the same hurt.

Once, the general had given Thompson a tour through the "Taj Mahal," the army's name for a massive sprawl of buildings in the Thai Northeast where Americans in fresh crewcuts shuttled in and out. Black had come to the area to inspect a new radar and radio station as well as a new reservoir cut into the nearby mountains. All around the base, makeshift little cafés selling Singha beer on ice and brothels doubling as barbershops had opened their doors; a few of the women from the brothels carried babies who looked like they must have had some GI genes in them. Jim diligently followed Black around the base, but when the general invited him to stay extra days, Jim quickly declined.

Thompson didn't like to get up early, but the general, true to form, never slept in, so at Jim's house Black usually cut the discussion short by 2 a.m. This particular night, the general began to yawn around 1:30 a.m., so Horgan started to pack up the small bag he always carried with him when he traveled with Black. Jim stood up and walked over to them. His voice had not risen above a mellow monotone all evening, even when he embroidered stories for his guests or seemed angry at his old friends' views. "If we keep on like this, this buildup, there won't be much left of Thailand," he said now, in the same monotone, the same clipped, boarding-school voice. "It will just disappear."[12]

That weekend would be the last time that Denis Horgan ever saw Jim Thompson. Only a few months later, Thompson would vanish. On a vacation in neighboring Malaysia, over Easter weekend in 1967, Thompson set off for a short hike in the jungle. By nightfall, he had not returned, and his friends called for a search party. Eventually, the party grew to include hundreds of local trackers, American military helicopters, and the Central Intelligence Agency—a massive rescue effort unparalleled in the region. But Jim Thompson was never found.

2

In the winter of 1940 and the spring of 1941, before Pearl Harbor, life in the Delaware National Guard wasn't exactly fast-paced. When Jim Thompson reported for duty on November 28, 1940, he found the guard, decimated by years of government ignorance and Depression-era cuts, struggling to pay its men and to keep its facilities from crumbling. On arrival day, Thompson met two other men who, like him, had enlisted just because they wanted to be ready for war with Hitler. Mostly, he told his family, he encountered men who seemed either desperate or lost: working-class family men with no job prospects who needed some cash, sons of once-prosperous Delaware families who'd lost their fortunes in the stock market crash of 1929, or drifters who'd joined the guard after failing at everything else during the 1930s.[1]

More galling, Thompson, thirty-four and just a private first-class, had to salute many of these dregs of Delaware, when he wasn't making up tasks for himself to escape the tedium. "We rise at 4:30 a.m. but there is not much to do all day, and the life is very boring," Thompson wrote to his mother.[2] He applied for an officer candidate course and eventually made noncommissioned officer, but it didn't help him to land more demanding positions in the guard.[3]

Even after the attack on Pearl Harbor shattered America's isolationism and created an immediate need for young men, Jim Thompson remained stateside. By the time of Pearl Harbor he was thirty-five years old, with a soft and slightly paunchy face, and commanding officers worried about his fitness. He camped with his battalion in Wilmington, Delaware, hardly a major German target. In January 1942, the army transferred him to Camp Davis in North Carolina to study rail transportation—another field with limited possibilities for wartime heroism—before shipping him off again, to the coastal artillery installation at Fort Monroe in Hampton, Virginia.

To friends who'd wondered back in 1940 why he had joined the decrepit guard, Thompson tried to maintain a brave face. "We think of you very often in these trying days, and know that you must be busy and doing something that is of real interest and importance," a friend from his old architectural firm wrote to him.[4]

To an outsider who'd just arrived at Fort Monroe from the grueling campaigns in the Pacific, Jim's life could not have seemed more perfect. Rather than fighting Japanese snipers or Wehrmacht gun nests, his biggest challenge was making sure that his bosses enjoyed their trips to Florida, where aide-de-camp Thompson accompanied the Fort Monroe brass for stone crabs at the Inn at Ponte Vedra Beach and walks among Miami Beach's palms.[5] He had time to grow a garden on the base and to write letters to his old secretary resolving every minute business detail from his time in New York: exactly how much to pay the insurance company, which sofa cushions to ship down from his old apartment, and so on.[6]

To himself, Jim Thompson admitted that he seemed to have found a military version of his previous life back in New York during the 1920s and 1930s, an era for him of easy pleasures, little thought, and plenty of parties: make-work jobs, always looking up to other men, fun to be around but not a man to be taken seriously, flitting from party to dinner to afternoon tea on the shockingly posh base. "There seems to be a great deal of social life on this post and it's all very civilized and unwarlike," Thompson wrote to his mother. "I don't believe I will really like it very much."[7]

By the early 1940s, Thompson had already spent a decade and a half of his life in a manner he would later bitterly say was a total waste. By the middle of the 1930s, Jim seemed to have settled into the Wilmington–New York society circuit, and perhaps somewhere in the back of his mind he realized that his life was drifting away.

Unlike some other Delaware and New York society families, the Thompsons, who'd long been part of the American aristocracy, had made it through the worst of the Depression relatively unscathed. Henry, Jim's older brother, had lost most of his assets in the 1929 crash, but overall the family's fiscal conservatism had inoculated it from the worst speculation of the 1920s and so prevented it from being wiped out in the 1930s.[8]

Still able to afford extravagance, Jim Thompson didn't hesitate to do so in New York, where he'd come to work as an architect. He flitted from debutante balls to nights at the ballet to parties at friends' apartments; he rarely allowed himself any time alone, or even to think about his life. "Jim was popular, his was a life of parties, going out. . . . He didn't seem like an intellectual person at the time," one friend of his from Depression-era New York remembered.[9]

Before the Depression, the Thompsons had established themselves alongside the du Ponts and the Rockefellers as one of the leading East Coast society families, and Thompson's mother rarely let him forget his place in society. Jim's mother, Mary Wilson Thompson, often reminded friends that she could trace her heritage all the way back to a family that came from Normandy to England with William the Conqueror, and that branches of her clan were connected to Lord Waldorf Astor, the Spendor Clays of England, and other wealthy British and American families.

After marrying Jim's father, Henry, Mary would expand the Thompson family home, in Greenville, Delaware, so that it would eventually grow into a 350-acre farm. She and her children socialized with a small group of high-class friends. "It was a very tightly controlled social circle [in Wilmington society]. . . . You were supposed to know exactly the social rules you were to follow," remembered Ann Donaldson, Jim Thompson's niece. The Thompsons went to boarding schools—Jim attended St. Paul's in New Hampshire—and then Princeton; any other option was not even considered.

Unlike some of the other Delaware matriarchs, however, Jim's mother tried to cultivate interests beyond high-society balls, dinners, and social clubs. "The Thompsons were brought up to be patriots, a kind of old-fashioned patriot, to give back to the country," said Ann. "She [Mary] was an idealist—she wanted to teach [her children] that America had been put here to help the world, to lead the world."[10]

Mary drew on a family tradition of service. Jim's grandfather, James Harrison Wilson, fought as a Union general in the Civil War. When that war ended, Wilson volunteered for some of the toughest government jobs, serving as a governor of several provinces in Cuba and in China during the Boxer Rebellion, when angry Chinese nationalists were targeting and killing foreigners. In China, Wilson demonstrated, as his grandson Jim later would, an appetite for actually trying to understand average people in the countryside. According to Wilson's biographer, the general traveled over fifteen thousand miles by horseback and cart through China, studying local culture and interviewing people across the country.[11]

The general also developed a friendship, through British society friends, with Vajiravudh, then the crown prince of Siam, as Thailand was called, and later King Rama VI. When Vajiravudh toured the United States, the general guided him, and his daughter Mary threw a party for the Thai royal at the Thompson family home in Delaware.[12] The general also displayed a streak of progressivism that would manifest itself in his grandson, launching agricultural reforms in Cuba and trying to support local governance on the island.

Mary Wilson Thompson attempted to instill grandfather's sense of duty to America in all of her children. A severe yet beautiful woman with a mouth that always looked pursed and long, birdlike fingers, she frequently described herself as "warlike," and indeed, she seemed to approach every task in life like a battle. "I grew up in a warlike atmosphere, the tales of valor and warfare," Mary remembered, adding, "Something of my father's restless energy pervades my make-up and the sound of a bugle or a drum sets my heart to beating."[13]

Jim Thompson's older siblings imbibed Mary's ethos of competition, valor, and honor. Henry, the oldest boy, asked his parents' permission to join World War I; he was not yet eighteen years old at the time. Henry joined an ambulance company in France. The oldest daughter, also named Mary, had already married by the time the United States entered the war. The second daughter, Katherine, had not married and joined Henry on the western front, serving in the Red Cross. Henry and Katherine would serve valiantly. A shell exploded near Henry's car, almost destroying the automobile and leaving shrapnel in Henry's legs and back, wounds that left him hospitalized for four months, though he eventually recovered.[14]

Mary Wilson Thompson's sense of idealism and devotion to duty did not seem to have sunk into her son Jim, at least not in the early 1930s. While others who graduated from college alongside him in 1928 soon found themselves hunting for even manual labor, Jim, who'd always taken an interest in design, had landed a job right after Princeton, through family connections, with the Fifth Avenue architectural firm of Holden McLaughlin & Associates. It didn't pay well, but Thompson could draw upon a regular allowance from his family, and the job certainly did not require long hours. "He didn't seem very adventurous, he didn't seem so ambitious," remembered one friend.

Still, by the late 1930s, on trips back to his family's estate in Delaware, Jim, unmarried and doing a job that meant little to him, seemed to be changing. Friends remembered that he would now launch into bitter monologues about the tedium of New York life. New York acquaintances noticed that the man always surrounded by friends was beginning to withdraw, turning down dates and invitations to events. He suddenly started criticizing old acquaintances for wasting their lives on parties and hunts and reading the newspapers' society pages, and he stopped talking to some old friends entirely. For the first time, too, a man whose life seemed limited to his family, his friends, and his hobbies had started to pay attention to a much wider world, to the bad news coming out almost daily from Europe.

In the late 1930s, Thompson's family did not see any American role in the looming European conflict. This isolationism was hardly a unique position: most Americans wanted nothing to do with the European war that was obviously coming. Just beginning to recover from the Depression, Americans wanted to enjoy life again, to get back to work, to forget about the world outside their borders.

From 1935 to 1939, Congress passed a series of Neutrality Acts preventing the United States from sending arms to other countries involved in wars. Always finely attuned to popular sentiment, Franklin Roosevelt won a third term in 1940 by vowing (falsely) to avoid any foreign wars, even as he quietly laid plans for America's eventual participation in the conflict. Like most wealthy, traditionally Republican families, the Thompsons had developed a visceral hatred for Roosevelt. The older Thompsons viewed any potential American involvement in a war against Hitler as Roosevelt's doing, and since Roosevelt was inherently dangerous, a war he supported must be a mistake.

Jim Thompson couldn't muster up such hatred for Roosevelt, and at family functions back in Delaware he gingerly began to defend Roosevelt's social policies and the president's liberal internationalism.

"He said all the spending of money on just consuming champagne . . . was evil, and he became rather self-righteous, as people often do who switch from being gadabouts to being very serious citizens," remembered his sister Elinor. Fighting with his family only seemed to encourage Jim to go further. In the late 1930s, almost all at once, he switched his party registration from Republican to Democrat, gave up the lease on his small but coveted New York apartment, and told his boss at the architectural firm, Arthur Holden, that he would shortly be leaving his job. Then, in October 1940, Thompson—at thirty-four already considered too old to join the military—enlisted in the Delaware National Guard. "I think he felt a tremendous urge to do something for his country," said Elinor. "He felt his life was a little hollow, that there wasn't quite the depth that he would like to find out of life and that, perhaps having a totally new experience, he would come to a deeper understanding about what life was about."

Perhaps Thompson joined up because he truly saw the great danger building up in Europe and believed that it eventually would threaten America. He wouldn't have been the only one—even as most of the United States turned away from the world, idealistic young Americans had volunteered to fight the fascists in the Spanish Civil War. Perhaps, fueled by stories of his siblings' sacrifices in World War I and his mother's patriotism, he wanted to make his own mark in the family archives.

More than any other reason, his friends remembered, Thompson seemed to have joined the guard because he wanted to get out—out of his life, out of his past, out of his job—and it was the only solution he could think of at the time. "If Jim didn't make a break then, he never would," his nephew Henry remembered. "He just knew he didn't want to be who he was anymore."[15]

Jim Thompson's daily chronicle of life on the National Guard base, the letters home to Mary Thompson, could as easily have been pages from his New York diary from the 1930s; at Fort Monroe, as aide-de-camp to the commanding officer, Thompson's life bore little resemblance to the rationing and wartime frugality of most of America. "General and Mrs Kilpatrick came and had dinner with [Thompson and his bosses] at our quarters. . . . I must say we had a very good dinner for them with a roast of lamb, artichokes, and some Viennese pancakes," Thompson told his mother. "I must stop and attempt to look busy in my office."[16]

Younger Thompson relatives destined for hard duty in places like Anzio (Italy) or Guadalcanal mocked his Fort Monroe softness. "I read of your hard rough life," Jim's nephew Henry teasingly wrote to him, from his own posting in the brutal Allied assault on Italy.[17] Jim had even picked up projects that reminded him of designing public toilets for the Delaware beaches: at Fort Monroe, his commanders, discovering Thompson's background in design, had tasked him to build a baseball diamond for the base.[18] "The life here defeats me," Thompson admitted in his most forthright war letter, to his old boss Arthur Holden. "Anyone just out of kindergarten could have done [the job]."[19]

17

By 1943, Jim Thompson had been trying for nearly two years to get out of his desk job. He had requested a transfer to air intelligence. He'd asked to be sent to Australia to work in naval supply. He'd pleaded with his bosses to give him any job that would take him to Europe, but they just transferred him to another coastal defense position. "I could blow up the War Department for my latest transfer," Thompson told Arthur Holden. "There is some possibility of my being left out [of the war entirely] on account of my advanced age," he admitted.[20]

Almost forty, still untested in a live battle, Jim Thompson seemed partly ready to finish out his time at Fort Monroe, wait for the end of the war, and return to New York and Delaware society. He wasn't going to end up dead, or even injured, at Fort Monroe—but it was a small life, a regular life, not the life Thompson had imagined for himself in his mind. "Jim had always been a happy person, a very genial person," said his nephew Henry. "He could always be very gracious, very fun, no matter what was going on, but he was having trouble even keeping up that appearance."[21]

In June 1943, Thompson seemed to assume that he'd be returning to society life. "After all these long years, I have finally persuaded somebody to marry me," Thompson wrote to his mother. "Pat and I are engaged." An accomplished horse rider and a firmly established daughter of Virginia society—she'd been introduced as a debutante in 1938—twenty-three-year-old Patricia Thraves, who had been dating Jim for less than a year before the engagement, seemed like a proper match, but because of wartime travel restrictions, Jim and Pat would be married at noon in a brief ceremony at the base without any of his family present and with his commanding officer serving as best man. "She is just the kind of person you have always wanted me to marry," Thompson told his mother.[22] Later, when Mary finally met Pat, she would offer her son's new bride a diamond bracelet and pin that had been in the family for generations.[23]

Pat Thraves didn't bring just breeding to the marriage. A former model with the famous Powers agency and more than a decade younger than Jim Thompson, she was considered by many men at

Fort Monroe to be among the most beautiful women in Virginia, with her swept-back dirty blond hair, narrow angular face, and full glossy lips.[24] "She is not only lovely looking, but a most capable, talented person and I am terribly happy about the whole thing," Thompson wrote to Arthur Holden.[25]

Yet even in the days just after his marriage, Jim Thompson apparently had regrets. He and Pat had hardly spent enough time together to know how they would make a life or how she would even handle his tough and politically active family. "Remember that Pat is very young and don't say anything harsh or critical to her. . . . I don't want her to be scared of my family," Thompson told his mother.[26]

He'd had few conversations with Pat about her plans in life, her dreams, and whether they extended at all beyond society life. His letters about Pat began to sound as if he were trying to convince himself about the decision he'd made, and in the convincing his writing could turn condescending, as though he were talking of a child or a prize mare rather than a wife. "She [Pat] has been very well brought up, I am sure, as she is so neat, capable, and efficient," Thompson wrote his mother. "She has all sorts of talents."[27]

A deeper fear gnawed at Thompson, too. Half his life was over. Every day men from his base, from Princeton, and from his own family were making names for themselves in Europe and the Pacific; every day, he had to watch as men passed through Fort Monroe on their way to campaigns that would be remembered in U.S. history, while he designed baseball fields and planned social hours for sodden generals not trusted to lead commands in Europe.

His close friend Ed Black, an officer he'd met on the base, sensed Jim's frustration, his worry that he'd miss the last chance in life to achieve something meaningful before settling down. In the fall of 1943, Black suggested that Thompson apply to join the Office of Strategic Services (OSS), the wartime intelligence service that seemed to be writing job applications devised to find Jim Thompson.[28] OSS preferred Ivy League men, from the right families, smart and gregarious, and a bit older than the average army officer; when OSS looked for female employees, its commanders hunted through the Social Register.[29]

Pushed by Black, who'd already joined OSS himself, Thompson traveled to the intelligence service headquarters in Washington and applied for jobs in espionage, communications, and demolition in Europe. On December 4, 1943, the War Department ordered him "relieved from assignment and duty with the Chesapeake Bay sector . . . [to be] assigned to the Office of Strategic Services."[30] Jim Thompson finally had his war.

3

Although most Americans viewed December 7, 1941, as the beginning of World War II, China had been fighting off Japan for nearly a decade by the time of Pearl Harbor, and Britain and France had declared war on Germany in 1939. In the years before America entered the battle, Franklin Roosevelt had publicly promised to keep the United States out, but he knew that America would eventually take the side of the Western powers.

Among Roosevelt's many worries about his unprepared, isolationist, and exhausted country was that the United States possessed so little intelligence about the strategy and planning of the fascist nations. By mid-1940, the Nazis' blitzkrieg offensives had already overwhelmed Poland, the Low Countries (Belgium, Luxembourg, and the Netherlands), Denmark, Norway, and France. In the Balkans, Czechoslovakia (today's Czech Republic and Slovakia), and Austria, German intelligence had skillfully infiltrated local fascist organizations and used them as fifth columns, allowing the Nazis to make the argument that the populations in these countries actually desired German rule and, once the Germans had arrived, to help ensure the Nazis' total dominance of local politics.

The fragmented and weak American intelligence-gathering operation that did exist—in the army, the FBI, and other government agencies—was, even in the best of times, "poorly and inadequately informed," according to John Gade, an American diplomat who had proposed a "central intelligence agency" to Roosevelt's predecessor, Herbert Hoover. "We were amateurs [compared to Britain and France] where they were past masters," Gade complained.[1]

Constrained by American popular sentiment about the war in Europe, an ingrained American fear of bureaucracy, and a sentiment that intelligence work and sabotage were somehow un-American, Roosevelt had to move gingerly in establishing a U.S. intelligence service that could eventually penetrate enemy communications, conduct acts of sabotage and guerrilla warfare, or whip up propaganda campaigns. In July 1941, the president launched the intelligence operation, giving it the bland title Office of the Coordinator of Information.

His choice to run the new operation, though, was anything but bland: Colonel William "Wild Bill" Donovan, a bombastic Irish Catholic World War I hero with a swept-back mane of silver hair, a prominent New York politician and lawyer, and a tireless man with deep connections in official Washington's cloakrooms and corridors. He had a tendency to lead from the front that would endear him to his wartime employees, many of whom came to worship the boss. On D-Day, when the American military command had barred any senior officials from landing with the front-line troops, Donovan ignored the command and convinced one landing craft to drop him at Utah Beach, where he huddled under machine-gun fire and then climbed up the seawall, oblivious to German snipers.

"I never felt that Donovan was afraid of anything," remembered one OSS employee who served in the Far East.[2] "It was like he was so excited to do whatever job was next, to jump into it, that there was no time for fear."

Though Donovan, a lifelong Republican, opposed the New Deal, he admired Roosevelt's internationalism and desire to prepare the United States, as much as possible, for war. With the president's backing, in 1940 Donovan had traveled through Europe and the Middle East, carefully observing the talents—and the flaws—of the Nazi and

British intelligence services and quietly recruiting locals who might eventually serve as American agents. "His sixty days on the ground [in this mission] were an unending procession of generals, admirals, air marshals, spies, politicians, sheikhs, priests, mullahs, princes, colonels, and kings," wrote Donovan biographer Anthony Cave Brown.[3]

The Americans lagged far behind the Europeans. In his initial report on the U.S. overseas intelligence assets, Donovan presented the president with a thin accounting: a few expatriate Americans dabbling in espionage in occupied France and Bulgaria, an assistant museum curator in Iran who might be recruited, and a man traveling to Africa, ostensibly to study gorillas, who could observe German espionage and military activity.[4] It wasn't exactly an inspiring outfit.

Donovan, who in World War I had led New York's "Fighting 69th" regiment, burned with ambition to push the United States—and himself—into this new global conflict. Donovan, said Secretary of War Henry Stimson in August 1940, "was determined to get into the war some way or other."[5] Returning to Washington from his travels, Donovan, an optimist who never believed there was a project he could not master, pushed to set up an American equivalent of the British service. With the 1940 presidential election behind him, Roosevelt agreed. Wild Bill was in.

Donovan came from a humble background, born to first-generation Irish immigrants and educated at Niagara University and Columbia Law School. However, later in politics and corporate life, he had developed, with the fervor of a convert, a powerful belief in the intelligence and cunning of America's upper class, the Ivy League sons and Smith College daughters. The belief, Donovan's biographer wrote, "was essentially tribal": men and women who came from the same schools, the same clubs, and the same social circles would be less likely to betray one another or their country.[6]

For the Office of the Coordinator of Information, whose name would be changed in June 1942 to the Office of Strategic Services, with its mission greatly expanded, Donovan recruited according to his belief. His agents sought out men in Yale's Skull and Bones, at Princeton's eating clubs, and at Wall Street's finance houses. Donovan created in the OSS the atmosphere of an elite men's club not so different from those all-male Ivy League secret societies, and OSS men would develop a fierce loyalty to their boss far beyond what the average infantryman felt for generals like Dwight Eisenhower or Omar Bradley.

Despite his Republican politics and military background, Donovan had an ingrained animosity toward authority, which he seemed to view as constantly preventing him from embarking on whatever cause or adventure he desired at the time. He wound up creating a very left-wing and informal organization, the informality bolstered by the chaotic nature of America's decision to enter a world war for which, despite Roosevelt's efforts, it was utterly unprepared. The Ivy Leaguers Donovan recruited tended toward liberal politics, and OSS's morale operations branch, which churned out print and radio propaganda, hired Hollywood and Broadway writers with communist backgrounds without a second thought.[7] Wild Bill made few rules for any of them, encouraging OSS men to think for themselves and act quickly—sometimes far too quickly in a business where lives were at stake. "Woe to the officer who turned down a project because on its face it seemed ridiculous, or at least unusual," remembered one former OSS officer.[8]

OSS men greeted senior officers by their first names, and seeing anyone salute at headquarters was a rare event; in the field, OSS agents grew long mustaches or scruffy beards if they wanted.[9] Many OSS officers, who'd come over from army jobs they hated, took every opportunity to remind their colleagues that they were no longer in the army; OSS officers sometimes made decisions on critical matters by taking roll call votes, a practice that chain-of-command generals like Douglas MacArthur hardly would have condoned.[10] "Enlisted men and officers would mix freely—officers would talk to you like an ordinary person, and we wouldn't wear stripes. We were just one band," remembered one OSS employee who served in Asia.[11]

With his connections to Roosevelt, Donovan also secured virtually unlimited budgets for his organization, allowing its operatives to live lavishly, to throw massive parties in their European residences, and to conceive of ever more complicated schemes, often with no one from headquarters to tell them no. "OSS agents bought or hired planes, automobiles, office equipment, houses, printing plants—anything they needed or thought they did," said one critic of the agency.[12]

When the organization eventually sent operatives into Thailand, some of the men stayed at Suan Kularb Palace, a wedding cake confection of marble pillars and tiger-skin rugs, teak-paneled walls and sweeping tile roofs inlaid with gems.[13] In their palace quarters, the OSS men drank coffee brought to them on silver trays by Thai manservants who bowed and then scurried away, walking backward into the palace's bowels as if the OSSers were kings.[14] "This fabulous life continues," wrote one of the OSS men in Bangkok, Dilworth Brinton, who complained that he would come home fat from all his lavish meals.[15]

The OSS also stood out in wartime for its intense idealism and anticolonialism. In the Atlantic Charter of 1941, Roosevelt had promised "the right of all peoples to choose the form of government under which they will live," interpreted by many around the world as a call for the end of colonial rule after the war was over. The president did have little tolerance for imperialism, and he was personally committed to ending colonialism, which he thought had added to European rivalries and made war more likely among the European powers.

Roosevelt's ally, Winston Churchill, might have gone along with the Atlantic Charter at the time—a necessary promise, given that it would be hard to recruit men from places like India to fight if they believed they'd return, after the war, to being colonial subjects—but the following year he vowed that he had not become prime minister in order to oversee the dissolution of the British Empire. Most American commanders in the field, and certainly the average infantrymen, paid little attention to any debate about the future of Europe's colonies after the world war—not when pressing matters like preparing invasions of Italy and France were at hand.

But in the OSS, full of New Deal liberals, the sentiment was much different. The spy organization would become probably the clearest representation of Roosevelt's anticolonial attitudes, shared completely by Donovan. Richard Harris Smith, a biographer of the OSS, found that "a sampling of thousands of intelligence analyses produced by the OSS Research Branch reveals certain recurrent themes: democratic, social, progressive reform."[16]

"Donovan recruited idealists, he recruited people who'd thought a lot about the world, and then we worked very closely with British intelligence," said one former OSS staffer who served in Asia. "We saw how the British acted [toward their colonies.] In OSS, we'd talk about how the colonial rulers were there perpetuating this caste system in the colonies. Sometimes it seemed like spent we'd spend most of our time arguing with the Brits rather than trying to fight Japan."[17]

Unlike regular infantrymen, too, the OSS agents worked closely with, and developed real affection for, nationalist resistance fighters. "Living and working behind the lines with dedicated guerrillas . . . these OSS officers found real meaning in the Roosevelt slogans of the Atlantic Charter," Smith wrote. Often operating alone and in places far behind enemy lines, the OSS men served as the face of the United States, and their declarations became like American pronouncements—which only made them more idealistic. "Here, I was America," one OSS officer wrote, according to Smith. "I had a message . . . to a long-suffering people."[18]

"We believed we had an idea," another OSS officer remembered. "We believed it was a good one, we worked hard for it."[19]

The OSS sought out any anticolonial guerrilla fighters they could use against the Germans and Japanese, paying little attention to these men's political beliefs, even when they veered far to the left. OSS agents worked with the Viet Minh guerrilla fighters led by Ho Chi Minh, Josip Broz Tito's partisans in Yugoslavia, and Mao's Chinese communists at their northern China base in Henan, and they often developed intense admiration for these fighters. When Ho was stricken with malaria and dysentery and nearly died in the Vietnamese jungle, the OSS flew in a medic who injected him with quinine and other drugs, probably saving his life.[20]

The thankful Vietnamese leader offered OSS agents, who dressed in Vietnamese guerrilla clothing and ate the Vietnamese diet of rice and bamboo shoots, locally brewed aphrodisiacs and their pick of Vietnamese women who'd arrived from Hanoi. The OSS provided arms to Ho's guerrillas and, as World War II ended, OSS officers would march into Hanoi alongside the Viet Minh as Ho's army took control of what would become North Vietnam.[21]

The informality bordering on insubordination, the elite background, the massive budgets, the fanciful schemes—none of this endeared the OSS to the other branches of the American armed forces, whose men were slogging across African deserts or crawling up Pacific island beaches rather than figuring out which exiled royals to invite for dinner to their parties in London. "Oh So Social,"[22] army grunts called the OSS—an organization of effete rich boys playing at spies. In the Pacific, theater commander MacArthur barred the OSS from operating in the Philippines and tried to keep them out of other areas under his control, with less success. Many commanders in Europe tried to do the same.

There *were* plenty of rich boys in the OSS: Paul Mellon, from the famous Mellon banking family, served in OSS special operations in London; J. P. Morgan's son handled funding for clandestine operations in London; and the Rockefellers' Standard Oil Company gave Donovan officers for sabotage in Romania's oil fields.[23] But by the end of 1943, the organization could boast real triumphs, too. The OSS had penetrated the Vatican's upper echelons and used the Holy See's embassy in Tokyo to provide American forces with high-level information on strategic bombing targets in Japan.[24] It had built close links to the Italian antifascist resistance, ties that would become essential after the Allied landings in Italy. Its propaganda campaigns in the Balkans had helped to convince Hitler that the Allies might fight there, and thus tied down many of the fuehrer's divisions in an area where the United States and Britain actually had no designs.[25]

The regular army's disdain for the OSS only further united Donovan's men and added to their fame and glamour as renegades, men who would fight not only Hitler and Hirohito but also their own army commanders if they had to, not caring who they offended. "We didn't have any doubt that we had the best jobs in the war," remembered one OSS intelligence officer. "We had free rein, no one looked over our shoulder. It wasn't like [the often tedious life in *The] Spy Who Came in from the Cold*, it was like James Bond."[26]

A small industry of fawning press articles chronicled the OSS's glamour and successful operations, only adding to the organization's mystique; OSS operatives in Europe and Asia amassed mistresses from local high society. Parachuting into France, the OSS men became "kings of their particular castles. They were men of position and power . . . had money to spend and lived well from sources so hidden that even scavenging Nazis could not locate the supply," wrote one biographer.[27]

As the OSS expanded its operations, it had to ramp up its staff, and by 1943 Donovan could no longer rely upon Yale, Princeton, and Harvard and major corporations to fill a wartime intelligence agency that had outposts all over the globe. Donovan's outfit wanted to keep its tribal nature, but now it also recruited more from within other military branches: current OSS men would search for acquaintances with the right background, decision-making skills, and somewhat reckless desire to make their mark. Often, these would be men who had expected a great adventure from the war and found only great drudgery.

Certainly, the Chesapeake coastal defense sector qualified, to most of its men, as great drudgery. Still, Jim Thompson hadn't gotten in OSS easily, despite his money and his family ties. And after the transfer finally came through—after four years of preparing to defend Delaware and North Carolina and Virginia from German battleships that never arrived, four years of stifled desires to do something, anything other than what he was doing—Jim Thompson could hardly contain his glee. In letters home to his mother, he warned her that soon he might not be able to tell his family where he was posted or where he was headed, but for now, it was enough to know he'd gotten out of coastal defense.

Pat Thraves did not seem so thrilled. She too had wanted to join the war effort, to serve in the Women's Army Corps or the Women Airforce Service Pilots. Her new husband convinced her not to join up, and even though she agreed to stay home, she seemed to resent Jim's glamorous assignment. With Thompson headed for OSS training, she dutifully sewed all his clothes and made his uniforms gleam, but a frost had developed between them, and in his first days at OSS headquarters, before shipping out to training, Thompson barely spoke with Pat.[28] And by the time Jim Thompson finished his wartime OSS service, his young wife had simply given up on him.

4

From the day he arrived for OSS training at Catalina Island, off the coast of Southern California, Jim Thompson felt at home. The men around him had prepped at St. Paul's and Andover and gone to college at Yale and Princeton, but no one knew Jim from his time in New York or cared what he'd done before he arrived at Catalina. No one heard his name and immediately knew about his brother who was decorated in the Great War, his dad the Princeton trustee, or his mom the political warrior.

In several of the training courses, Thompson never even learned the names of the other men, since OSS regulations at times prevented them from disclosing anything about their pasts.[1] All that the other OSS trainees cared about was whether Thompson could read the map that would get them through survival training, coax a light out of the supposedly waterproof matches, or figure out which wild grasses to eat so they'd get something thick in their bellies during survival camp.[2]

Never a fitness fanatic—he enjoyed swimming, but mostly so he could tan, and he couldn't go an hour without burning a cigarette down to a stub—Thompson pushed himself at OSS training into the best shape of his life. His natural charm and social breeding had helped him to excel in the training courses on espionage, but his physical skills impressed as well. On Catalina Island, the men assigned to his group for survival training had worried at first about Thompson's bony arms and putty face, but when they were dropped onto the three-day survival course with nothing but a six-inch knife and a small waterproof cylinder containing matches, Thompson, who'd spent years hunting in the Delaware woods, kept them alive. He organized a hunt for wild pigs on the island and foraged for abalone in the ocean. When one of the men in his group ate wild mushrooms that made him vomit so fiercely the man could no longer walk, doubled over in pain and dehydrated, Thompson pulled him up hills and through the rest of the survival course.[3]

Trapped in coastal defense for so long, Thompson, now a major after his OSS training, had no interest in a post at Washington headquarters. "I would much rather go now than be sent over when the war is over, with an army of occupation," he wrote to his mother.[4] In March 1944, with the backing of Ed Black, who worked in the OSS station in London, planning resistance operations in France and ultimately the D-Day landings, Thompson obtained one of the most coveted and dangerous jobs in the OSS.[5]

Transferred into the North African and then the Mediterranean theaters of war, Thompson moved from Algeria to Morocco to Italy to France, where he served as an intelligence officer with the advance units of the Seventh Army.[6] In France, Thompson's unit would launch some thirty missions, trying to build up the French Resistance. In the summer and fall of 1944, the unit coordinated plans for a post–D-Day landing in southern France, code-named Operation Dragoon.[7]

Just before the invasion, the OSS men, together with the French Resistance fighters, snuck up and attacked the German coastal defense. This attack opened up the beaches to Allied troops coming ashore, who could wade in without having to face the meat grinder of machine guns and coastal artillery that greeted the infantrymen on D-Day.

An advance intelligence man didn't just fight, though. He was expected to almost perform miracles: one day he might have to slip behind enemy lines to meet with guerrillas who could link up with the Allied forces, and the next he would have to sabotage enemy transportation and communication links or survey the landscape behind enemy positions.

Most OSS commandos got along easily, with little of the resentment between officers and enlisted men in the regular army. Thompson's liberal politics, which had isolated him back at home, fit in with the OSS men all around him. "We'd have guys singing the [Communist] Internationale anthem, no one cared," said one former OSS officer who knew Thompson.[8] And Thompson's facade of permanent amiability, which had made him both popular and somewhat unknowable in New York and Delaware, now allowed him to charm, plot, and backstab other men, all at the same time.[9]

Thompson excelled at the job, as he'd never done before in his life, apparently drawing the attention of Bill Donovan himself.[10] Unlike many OSS officers, who just developed schemes but rarely followed through, Thompson was a methodical worker—as he'd never been at school or in architecture—and seemed able to plan steps ahead.

As the Allied forces were about to land in southern France, the OSS commandos—with Thompson probably one of the leaders—dropped behind enemy lines and marched through the night, weighed down by bags full of explosives, detonating devices, and other hardware. When they reached four bridges, they blew them up, then melted back into the woods to ambush German troops rushing to meet the Allied forces.[11]

Later, as the Allies advanced farther, the OSS men scouted ahead of the infantry, ranging behind enemy lines in the hilly and wooded French countryside, moving house to house, resistance cell to resistance cell, until they found small bridges where the Germans could still cross. Under fire, the OSS men and their French allies blew up one bridge after the next, forcing German troops to retreat and earning the OSS, often maligned by army grunts, the respect of the Dragoon men.[12] By the end of the war, Thompson himself had won five Bronze Stars and other medals for exemplary service in three theaters of the conflict.[13]

While performing heroically, Thompson also managed to alienate most of his superior officers. Finally a success, no longer living off of other men, Thompson could turn harshly on anyone he thought was slacking, unprepared, or incompetent—especially younger men of higher rank. "This officer has wide experience [but] he would run down his superiors and equals in rank which [he] believed too high," one senior officer wrote in a report on Thompson.[14]

But even as Jim Thompson made a home for himself at the OSS, his home life was crumbling. The wedding to Pat had been hasty, even by wartime standards, and with her new husband gone so quickly, tall and blond Pat Thraves, used to being the center of attention, found herself surrounded by other men. One man, Jim Murphy, pursued her diligently. With a husband she still did not know well, and soldiers returning home full of stories of the French, British, and Italian girls they'd bedded, Pat became convinced that Jim, who refused to give her details of his OSS life and who sent back letters so vague as to be useless, was cheating on her.[15]

"The girl has the idea that everyone is evil and does not trust Jim to be faithful to her," wrote one of Thompson's acquaintances, the Thailand scholar Kenneth Landon. "Tough on Jim. She needs a psychoanalyst or a paddling or both."[16] Scared of the future and suspicious of her new husband, Pat Thraves started to accept Murphy's invitations.

While Jim Thompson moved from front to front in Europe, in Thailand the OSS was building perhaps its most daring operation of the entire war. Thai politics, like those of most of its neighbors, had been turbulent even before the Second World War. In 1932, after centuries of absolute monarchy, a group of young Thai intellectuals, many of whom had studied in Paris together in the 1920s, overthrew King Rama VII. Standing atop tanks in Bangkok and claiming that "the king has treated the people as slaves. . . . There is no country in the world that gives its royalty so much money as this," they stripped Rama VII, then living at his beach palace, called "Far from Worry," of his power. In deference to the long tradition of monarchy in their country, they allowed the king to keep his title, but he soon abdicated.[17]

Paris in the 1920s had been a petri dish for revolutionaries. After the Russian Revolution, nationalists from Thailand, Vietnam, China, Laos, and many other poor countries had come to the French capital to learn how they could adapt the ideas of Karl Marx and Leon Trotsky, Thomas Jefferson and Adam Smith, to their own cultures and their own politics. But among the revolutionaries in Paris, the Siamese—for Thailand then was called Siam—were known as the least bellicose, perhaps because they had to fight only their own system, not some colonial master, and so enjoyed the confidence that comes from knowing that their history, however brutal, was at least *their* history and not that of some European power.

The Thais' acknowledged leader, a university professor named Pridi Banomyong, with an almost square face and ears that jutted out like antennae, was careful to disassociate himself from the communists and guerrillas who were taking up arms in China and later in Vietnam. "Pridi belonged to the same political generation as Jawaharlal Nehru, Sukarno, Ho Chi Minh. . . . They shared many of the same ideas on law, constitution[s], parliament[s]," wrote one of his biographers.[18] Yet the Thai leader was not a military man like Ho Chi Minh or a flashy orator like Indonesia's Sukarno, and he vehemently denied that he was a communist. He more closely resembled a school principal: an educator, a writer, a man who wanted to teach his countrymen, and an idealist. Pridi simply believed, more than anything else, that Thais deserved to be treated better.

Though not a communist, Pridi was a new kind of man in feudal Siam, where commoners had to use an entirely different vocabulary to speak with the royal family, and a group of aides once let a queen drown in the Chao Praya River because they could not, by custom, even touch someone of such high status. Pridi was a real democrat, one easily recognizable to a New Deal American. "Equality will arise in rights and duties. . . . People will have equal rights in not going hungry, but not equality in the sense that if one person has a hundred baht [the Thai currency] it must be seized and shared equally among a hundred people," Pridi wrote in one manifesto.[19]

In removing the monarch, Pridi formed the country's first political party, the People's Party, and declared that the overthrow was just the first step toward a real democratization of Siam.[20] After centuries of living under monarchs who bankrupted the national treasury to pay for ever more lavish palaces—the Grand Palace in Bangkok topped even European structures like the Palace of Versailles, with walls inlaid with gems—while illiterate farmers scratched out harvests of rice in the plains of the baking-hot Northeast, Pridi seemed, to many Thais, a revelation. Under the king, educated Bangkokians would return home from universities in Europe and the United States[21] to find no jobs except working for a prince as a kind of high-class secretary.

Now, Pridi promised, Siam would become a modern country, a land governed by a constitution and laws, a place with votes for everyone, not just princes, a country where educated Thais would have real opportunity. "Those who need the help of the government will be assisted: the poor, the unemployed, the homeless, and the unfortunate," Pridi promised. He founded a progressive-minded university in Bangkok, and the students there, like many young Thais of that generation, would come to worship Pridi as more than a teacher, as a kind of secular deity. And while Pridi never gained the global fame of fellow post–World War II leaders like Mohandas Gandhi, Ho Chi Minh, or Sukarno, had he remained in power for longer and had more of a chance to put his ideas into practice, he could have gained global renown.

During the Second World War, the OSS officers who dealt with Pridi—including, eventually, Major James Thompson—came to worship the Thai leader as well. Kenneth Landon, the premier Thai expert in the U.S. government, declared that Pridi, with his democratic idealism, could prove a valuable ally to America.[22] "He is the most impressive man in Siam and one of the real statesmen of Asia," another OSS man reported after meeting the Thai leader.[23] "Pridi," Thompson later told his nephew Henry, "was one of the great men, he was someone you knew you'd remember every minute you were with him."[24]

By the early 1940s, however, another of the young Thais, a man Pridi had known for decades and who had also studied in Paris, had usurped Pridi's leadership role, foreshadowing years of battle between the two men over the future of their country. Plaek Phibulsonggram, known as Phibul, was almost Pridi's exact opposite: a lifelong army man, suspicious of democracy and comfortable with clear and direct lines of authority, and vain, charming, suave, and silkily conniving while Pridi, reserved and academic, paid little attention to his physical appearance.

A captain in the army in the 1920s, Phibul had joined the other Thai revolutionaries plotting in Paris and, later, overthrowing the absolute monarchy.[25] But while Pridi had taken inspiration from the European social democrats, Phibul looked to another ideology born on the Continent: fascism. Following Mussolini, Hitler, and Franco, as well as the fascists in Japan, Phibul was naturally drawn to the military-style order and pomp of fascism, and in the 1930s the young captain saw totalitarianism as the future of the world, triumphing over the weak Western democracies struggling through a global economic catastrophe.[26]

Phibul could not match Pridi's intellectual heft, but his close ties to the Thai military would prove far more important in the long run. As minister of defense, deputy commander of the army, and finally, in 1938, prime minister, Phibul gradually rose to supreme power, backed always by the army, who easily crushed any dissent from Pridi's circle of intellectuals. As prime minister, Phibul launched a nationalist program that resembled fascist Italy and Japan. He executed political opponents, and he launched a vicious campaign against the Chinese minority. He created young storm troops similar to the Hitler Youth, and he built up increasingly close ties to fascist Japan.[27] He did allow Pridi and his allies to retain some government posts, though.

Like the European and Japanese fascists, Phibul established a powerful propaganda wing designed to create a cult of personality around himself. Phibul's photos went up on walls everywhere in Siam, replacing old shots of the king, and at movie theaters the audiences stood up before the showings and bowed before Phibul's image, just as they once had before the king's. To cement his version of nationalism, Phibul renamed the country "Thailand," implying that this was the land of the ethnic Thais, even though Siam contained sizable numbers of minorities who were not Thai.

• • •

As Japan expanded its empire in Asia in the early days of World War II, the battle between fascism and progressive values, epitomized in Thailand by the struggle between Phibul and Pridi, seemed to be going poorly for the liberals. In late 1941 and early 1942, Japan marched through the weakly defended European colonies in Southeast Asia, proclaiming a new era of Asian brotherhood and shocking Britain, France, and the Netherlands, which had badly underestimated the Japanese Imperial Army and left only tiny garrisons in many of their colonies. In Malaya, British forces would simply turn and flee from the Japanese jungle fighters, and the Imperial Army soon captured Singapore, supposedly an impregnable island fortress.

With an openly profascist leader in charge and no colonial ruler, Thailand presented a unique opportunity for Tokyo. And within the Thai government, the two camps—Pridi's men and Phibul's—fought bitterly about how to handle the Japanese invasion that occurred shortly after Pearl Harbor. Despite Japan's stunning victories, Pridi, who'd seen the inherent strength of Western democracies, told his close friends that the Allies undoubtedly would triumph in a world war.

"My close friends and I shared the belief in democratic idealism," Pridi later said. "As the war was made by the anti-democratic side, we therefore felt we must fight for what we believed."[28] But Phibul had control of the cabinet, and despite a few isolated skirmishes between Thai troops and Japanese forces landing in the country, he ordered Thailand not to resist the Imperial Army. Soon, Thailand declared itself a military ally of Japan.[29]

For Pridi and his circle, conceding to fascist Japan was not only humiliating and contrary to their democratic revolution but also a tactical mistake, since in a postwar world won by the Allies, friends of Japan surely would be punished. So Pridi conceived of a bold plan. While remaining part of the Thai ruling elite—Pridi had become regent for the underage constitutional monarch living in exile—they would secretly work with the Allies to destroy Japan and their own prime minister.

It was probably the most audacious subterfuge in the entire world war, and a strategy that easily could have killed all the double-agent

Thai leaders, especially since neither the OSS nor the Thai politicians had much idea at first of what intelligence assets they could set up under the Japanese.[30] "Perhaps no intelligence mission ever had less to go on than this one," one of OSS's allies in the Thailand mission warned an OSS agent preparing to head to Thailand.[31]

Thailand's ambassador to Washington did not deliver the country's declaration of war on the United States; instead he told Franklin Roosevelt that the declaration did not represent the real desire of the Thai people and asked the White House for help in ousting Phibul's puppet regime.[32] Washington agreed to treat Thailand as an occupied country rather than a Japanese collaborator.

Back in Bangkok, as well as in the United States and Britain, a group of young Thais, encouraged by Pridi and later known as the Free Thai, volunteered to help the OSS penetrate Thailand, slip U.S. agents into the Japanese-occupied country, and build an underground that could smuggle out intelligence and potentially rise up to overthrow Phibul.[33] At first, the Free Thai comprised just a few dozen men who trained outside Thailand in guerrilla warfare, including with three-and-a-half-inch bazookas and single-shot guns disguised as ballpoint pens, but eventually, the underground would number some sixty thousand men training under the nose of Phibul's government.[34]

During the war, Thailand held enormous potential importance for the United States. As an ally of Japan, but still in many ways an open city, Bangkok was becoming a hive of intelligence operatives from Japan, Germany, the Soviet Union, China, and other countries. The Allies had almost no agents on the ground in the Thai capital.[35] With the old colonists pushed out of Asia, many American officials realized that once the war was over, the United States would reign supreme in the Pacific, and Thailand would prove central to Washington's Asia strategy.

In 1944, with the war against Japan still hardly won, one OSS political analyst wrote in a memo that the country's "post-war status will be the example to the rest of Asia."[36] With American assistance, Thailand, endowed with natural resources, could build the strongest, most procapitalist economy in the region. Never having been colonized, and harboring little distrust of Americans, the country could become an ally in a turbulent region—or, if necessary, a stand against the growing power of communist China. After the war, Bill Donovan, who by then had been named U.S. ambassador to Thailand, summed up the American strategy.

"The independent kingdom of Thailand occupies a position of unique importance," Donovan wrote in an essay. "It is the free world's strongest bastion in Southeast Asia."[37]

Though the idea seems lost to history, Thailand was the obvious fulcrum for lifting all of Asia into the future. To Pridi and most liberal Thais, the United States also seemed like an ideal partner for the future. "If we cooperated with the United States . . . I was certain that Thailand would regain its freedom and democracy would be restored to our country, because the United States always stood for freedom and democracy," one Free Thai guerrilla, imbued with the anticolonial spirit of Roosevelt and Donovan, told his OSS allies.[38]

"We looked up to the OSS and Donovan as a hero," remembered another Southeast Asian underground fighter.[39] In return, many OSS officers developed an intense, almost missionary love for the Free Thai, as well as a belief that America alone could help Thailand become a modern democracy. "Wherever he [Pridi] was affected I probably should never be fully objective in my writing and thinking," wrote Alexander MacDonald, an OSS friend of Thompson's who also would stay on in Thailand after the war.[40]

The Thais seemed to appreciate the informality and lack of superiority among the Americans, in contrast to the imperial— and imperious—British and French. Attempting to give a toast to some Thai guerrilla leaders in Bangkok, one OSS officer mistakenly declared, in broken Thai, "American officers hate Japanese, love Thai people. Otherwise [Americans are] no good, all the time drink whiskey, shoot craps, fornicate, masturbate."[41] This garbled speech, which quickly circulated among Thai intellectuals, apparently impressed the Thais with its willingness to poke fun at the United States itself.

The initial planning for the Free Thai guerrilla movement did not seem auspicious. After training the Thais in Ceylon, India, and the United States, two of the first agents sent into Thailand by the Allies were captured and killed by the Japanese, and other agents blacked out in the air when they tried to parachute into the country.[42]

But with a large base of support in Thailand, Pridi and his OSS allies soon rebounded, setting up twelve training camps in the Thai jungles and sneaking into Thailand a regular flow of agents, who arrived in nighttime parachute landings, in tiny submarines, and on overland hikes through the rugged mountains of French Indochina, disguised as local tribesmen with shaved heads and bare feet.[43] By early 1945, Pridi had smuggled into Thailand over twenty OSS men. A small group of the Americans holed up in the center of Bangkok in an old royal palace, which resembled a Swiss chalet topped with tall towers and surrounded with rose gardens, and packed inside with smuggled tommy guns, bazookas, and grenades, alongside rugs made of tiger and wild bearskins.[44]

From inside the palace, in a reception hall with gold roses carved into the ceiling, the OSS men received secret visits from nearly every top Thai politician, including Pridi himself. "I am sure that no secret agents trying to deliver a country from oppression ever enjoyed such palatial quarters," wrote one OSS agent.[45] The OSS agents helped to sneak Allied prisoners of war out of Thailand, radioed out intelligence reports for Allied bombers targeting Japanese military installations in Thailand,[46] and moved arms to Thai underground units just waiting for an order to rise up.

Working with this information, Allied bombers hit over fourteen hundred buildings in Bangkok. Some of the Thai guerrillas smuggled bombs and other devices of sabotage into Japanese garrisons, destroying their arms and men.[47] Eventually, as Japan's power weakened in the late stages of the war, Phibul's government fell and a more pro-Allies prime minister took over, handing the Free Thai a great triumph.

The work in Bangkok might have been dangerous and confining, but the rewards could be staggering, especially to an OSS man who'd never traveled to Asia before. The Americans who infiltrated Bangkok had to hide from Japanese patrols on the streets, but inside their walled palace, they hosted lavish banquets for local dignitaries, consumed the most gourmet Thai royal cuisine, and were eventually treated like local celebrities by a people known for their innate hospitality.

One U.S. army captain hiding in Bangkok complained in jest to his replacement, "You just wait—sixteen dishes every meal, and no exercise,"[48] and when the Americans eventually could move around the city, their Thai partners rewarded them with performances of Thai dance and massive parties full of long, formal toasts to Thailand and the United States.[49] "This fabulous life continues and we are all enjoying it immensely," one American stationed in Bangkok wrote to his family. "We are treated like royalty."[50]

As the war in Europe drew to a close, Bill Donovan began transferring many of his most skilled agents to Asia. Jim Thompson, like many OSS officers, had come to admire Donovan personally, and although the spy organization had mushroomed in size from its early days, Wild Bill still ran it like a small college club. The director and some of his senior aides pushed officers with backgrounds in Asia or language skills to transfer to Indochina or China, and Thompson's French, as well as his success in Europe, made him a natural for working with French-speaking Indochinese resistance groups based in and around Thailand.

After a short training course in California, Major Thompson sailed for Ceylon (present-day Sri Lanka), to be briefed in the political background of Indochina and the Free Thai and to master the parachute skills he'd need to sneak into Thailand's Northeast, where many of the resistance fighters operated.[51] From his OSS colleagues, he heard the legends of Pridi, of the Thais' apparent love for Americans, of Thailand's riches of tin, rubber, silk, and other resources.

Learning about the country, Thompson seemed to decide that he could put all his skills and ideals to use in Thailand. "In the OSS he could make a difference, but more so in a place like Thailand, which needed so much more help than Europe," said Charles Burwell, a wartime friend of Thompson's who later would become a business partner.[52] "If you had ambition, and you were in Thailand just after the war, it was like a blank slate for you, you could do anything, and that was attractive to him."

Thompson had other reasons for not coming back to the United States to live. Even during the war, he'd fought with his family over his political transformation—in one letter home he complained that his sister Katherine basically had stopped speaking to him[53]—and on a brief trip back to the United States in the spring of 1945, when he surprised Pat with family jewels he'd gotten from his mother, Thompson must have learned that while he hadn't cheated, his new wife had.[54] Some of Thompson's relatives were even convinced that Pat had brought her lover, Jim Murphy, to one of the Thompson family estates in Delaware, where she had passed him off as a friend and they signed the guestbook together.[55]

In the summer of 1945, after Thompson had transferred to Asia, where he dropped into Thailand just after the Japanese surrender, Pat wrote him a long letter, declaring the marriage over—she worried that Jim would never come home from the OSS, and, anyway, she'd found someone else who wanted to marry her. As he flipped through it, page after page, crying, Thompson turned to Kenneth Landon, an OSS colleague, and told him he would never return to the United States again.[56]

5

By the time that Jim Thompson reached his cramped corner of the temporary U.S. legation in Thailand each morning, a small crowd had already formed, waiting to see him. The Bangkok heat was not yet as murderous as it would be at midday, but even in the morning, the temperature approached ninety degrees Fahrenheit, and the fans in most buildings just moved the fetid air slowly around the rooms.

Bangkok's humidity carries scents very far, and Thompson could smell in the morning air a mixture of freshly cut orchids, dirty canal water, pork bones soaking in broth hawked by roadside vendors, and rotting durian, the giant, spiky Thai fruit whose insides smell like old tennis shoes. Thompson had already begun to soak through his shirt and pants, which always amused Thais, who never seemed to sweat and who enjoyed watching burly *farangs* gush all over their bodies. He looked out over one of the canals, seeing an ancient truck rumbling up a nearly deserted road.

"Bangkok was an intriguing clutter of old and new," one of Thompson's OSS friends, Alexander MacDonald, would write. "It tried on the things of modern civilization—electric power, fast automobiles, telephones, and public health campaigns—like a woman trying on hats, oftentimes giggled at their absurdity and discarded them."[1]

Outside the temporary legation, men waiting for Thompson squatted on their haunches while chewing on snacks of sour mango slices and dried pork skins. Sometimes it seemed like every one of the city's 860,000 people had shown up to see him. Thompson pushed through the waiting crowd, normally a mix of Thais, Lao, Cambodians, Vietnamese, and an occasional American, and grabbed his seat before the mob surrounded him.[2]

In the months after Japan's surrender, as Jim Thompson decided to stay on in Thailand, the OSS appointed him as intelligence officer in Bangkok. But on arriving at the makeshift embassy at Suan Kularb Palace, he soon found that he would be called on to do much more than just analyze Thai and regional politics or send a few cables back to Washington.

With the whole world recovering from war, the future of the Pacific for the taking, and the United States seemingly called upon to rebuild every part of the globe, Washington could hardly send a large new team of diplomats to Bangkok. The OSS men—Thompson and others, already on the ground in Bangkok after V-J Day—were the U.S. government in Bangkok, at least for now.

"Whatever the OSS guys thought, whatever they did, that was what happened, they were making policy," remembered Elizabeth McIntosh, the wife of Alexander MacDonald and a former OSS employee herself.[3] The OSS officers tracked down Allied prisoners of war, many of whom had nearly starved to death building and maintaining the infamous "death railway" from western Thailand to Burma. They ensured that the garrison of over a hundred thousand Japanese troops in Thailand put down its weapons and went home without reprisals. They helped Thais whose homes had been destroyed by bombs or looting to find places to sleep, solid food to eat, and access to medicine, all hard to find in postwar Bangkok.

They started setting up U.S.-backed Thai agents along Thailand's borders, equipped with radios and capable of reporting on events throughout Indochina.[4] They met American businessmen interested in investing in Thailand, who quickly learned you had to see the OSS guys if you wanted an in.[5] They carved out a bit of time at night for themselves to buy up Thai sapphires, Burmese rubies, and alligator bags at the Thieves Market near Chinatown and ship them home to mothers and wives and sisters.[6] They worked behind the scenes to make sure their Free Thai friends, now running the country, were not punished by Britain, which had wanted to treat Thailand as a conquered enemy and force it to pay reparations but had ultimately bowed to American pressure.[7] "The [Thai] cabinet is deliriously happy over US intervention with Britain over terms of settlement of peace," colleague Kenneth Landon wrote to his wife.[8]

During the war, OSS agents like Dwight Bulkeley had predicted that Thailand could become a vital U.S. ally. Now, with stratospheric American prestige in Thailand, a small group of American Thai specialists, liberals in the OSS and the State Department, were working to cement that alliance, making a democratic Thailand pivotal to the United States, now the preeminent Pacific power. They helped Pridi embark upon a goodwill tour of the United States, while Phibul prepared to face trial as a war criminal, and they set up old Free Thai recruits in key positions in the Thai police and civil service. Landon, Thompson, and others helped to make sure that Washington sold surplus military equipment to the Thais (at discount prices), they set up programs for Thai officers to come to the United States to train, and they granted Thailand millions of dollars' worth of credit for postwar rehabilitation and reconstruction programs.[9]

"The Americans hoped that the absence of a colonial background in Thailand would enable it to serve as a model to the former European colonies as they achieved their national independence," wrote one Thailand expert.[10] American officials also must have realized that in a battered world, Thailand's rubber, tin, oil, rice, and other resources would prove extremely valuable for a superpower hungry for raw materials.[11] Soon even President Truman would join in, in 1946 quietly telling the incoming U.S. ambassador to Thailand, Edwin Stanton, that the United States had a special interest in Thailand, the only independent country in the region.[12]

Soon after arriving, Stanton would drastically expand the embassy staff in Bangkok, a sign of the importance of Thailand.[13] "In Southeast Asia a whole new struggle was beginning in 1946—had begun, actually, the moment Japan laid down her arms in 1945," remembered Alexander MacDonald. "It was the people's movement for independence, and it went coursing into every part of Southeast Asia. Neighbors on all sides of Siam—Indochina, Burma, India, and Indonesia[—]were deep in it."[14]

The Thais in turn welcomed America's hand—particularly the Free Thai men now in charge, who had trained in the United States alongside OSS agents. "They Love Us in Siam," proclaimed one headline in the influential *Saturday Evening Post.*[15] (The postwar government, for a time, restored the old name of the country, since it was Phibul who had changed the name to Thailand.) And to the OSS men in Bangkok, the headline seemed absolutely true. "We had vanquished the Japanese Empire. Here we just couldn't do anything wrong," remembered one U.S. intelligence agent active in Thailand just after the war. "I can't imagine the relations we had with our Thai counterparts, that they could have been better."[16]

The Americans surely lived well. While average people in Bangkok filled up any container they could find when water from bombed-out pumping stations actually flowed, and they scrounged for backup electricity sources to get through brownouts, the parties for the Americans in Bangkok got even bigger.[17] The toasts got grander, the banquets longer, the visits to brothels even more drawn out. One American working in Thailand after the war remembered "a dinner which will live long in my memory" at the house of one Thai prince: turtle soup in fresh coconuts, lobster thermidor, goose, Thai curries, shrimp soufflé, and ice cream made from steamed bananas.[18] Thailand's major newspapers seemed to be competing to run as much news as possible about America, the global superpower—and Thailand's new friend.[19]

From his corner of Suan Kularb Palace, Jim Thompson could easily see this love and respect for America, or at least for the image of America in Thais' minds. Thais he'd met once would come in and ask him to mediate in internecine family feuds or start a business with them; if he went to every party to which he got invited, he'd have to attend three or four functions every night.[20] Thais came into the palace to drag the OSS men to local schools, where the children all wanted to see and touch them; even the teachers just wanted to grab them, to touch an American.[21]

Around noon, after a lunch of noodles quick-fried with fresh basil and the tiny chilies Thais called "rat shit," since they looked like mouse droppings, Thompson would sometimes head down to Rattanakosin, the oldest part of Bangkok, where the Grand Palace and Wat Pho temple, with its gold-plated reclining Buddha the size of a large house, abutted the Chao Praya River. Across the water you could see the Temple of the Dawn, its white porcelain central spire reflecting the midday sun.

Thompson would sit down for another long, leisurely meal with Pridi, and their conversation could range from plans for the next Thai election to hard-nosed bargaining about U.S. support for Thailand against Britain and France, which both had demands on Thai territory and assets. Even after his wartime triumph, Pridi had allowed another man, Seni Pramoj, to assume the prime ministership, but no one doubted that Pridi was the most powerful man in Thailand. His long-time enemy, Phibul, faced war crimes charges, and the young king, Ananda, heir to the monarch Pridi and Phibul had overthrown, lived in exile in Switzerland, only occasionally coming to Thailand. Pridi's allies staffed the key government departments; Pridi's missives dominated discussion within Thai government offices.[22]

Pridi wasn't only powerful; to the OSS men and the Thai liberals suddenly running the country, he was uniquely good, a new type of leader for a new world of democracy. For Jim Thompson, even more than his work in the war, Thailand seemed like the crystallization of his dreams.

"Jim was an idealist, a romantic, an anti-imperialist, and there was no more idealistic time than just after the war," remembered Rolland Bushner, who served in the U.S. embassy in Bangkok. "We had stood with the anticolonialists, the democrats, in the war, and we expected that would continue."[23]

Ann Donaldson, Thompson's niece, remembered, "When people asked him whether he'd come back to the United States, Jim would always say, 'No, there is too much to do here [in Thailand,] this is where I can make a difference.'"[24]

Shortly after the war, the United States still seemed committed to the end of imperialism and the beginning of new democracies. Washington asked Britain and the Netherlands to take U.S. markings off of the military supplies they were using to regain control of colonies like Indonesia, and it refused to allow American military ships to transport troops, arms, or equipment to Indonesia.[25] Given these signals, many nationalist leaders throughout Asia believed the United States would stand by Roosevelt's Atlantic Charter, which had promised a new era of self-determination for all men.

The belief in Pridi was not just OSS men deluding themselves. In the post–World War II elections, Pridi oversaw the largest expansion of the franchise in Thai history, the first truly democratic vote in the country.[26] "Pridi and his civilian allies succeeded to a remarkable extent, given the trying circumstances of the war and its aftermath, in running a stable, effective government," wrote Daniel Fineman, an expert on the U.S.-Thai relationship. "Pridi managed to reform the country's political system. . . . In January 1946, he oversaw open, nonpartisan partial elections and, that May, led Parliament in promulgating a new, more liberal constitution."[27]

Many of the Thais who descended on the temporary U.S. legation knew that Jim Thompson enjoyed close ties with Pridi. When they asked for Thompson's help in getting medicine, food, or the paperwork to start a new business, they knew that along with that aid might come a critical link to Pridi. But by early afternoon, most of the Thais who'd been waiting to see Thompson had either gotten in or drifted off for another day, paring down the line to see the intelligence officer to a small band of Vietnamese, Cambodians, and Lao. The Thais wanted to see Thompson, but if he didn't have time, they could find other ways to get information or access to Pridi and the government. But for the Laotian or Vietnamese insurgents living in Thailand, where they'd taken shelter and planned from during World War II, there was no one else to see but Jim Thompson.

Thompson, with his French language skills, originally had been sent to Thailand to work underground with the Vietnamese, Lao, and Cambodian nationalists fighting the Japanese and Vichy French. Even though the war with Japan had ended and these nationalists now were battling French forces trying to retake control of their colonies, Thompson's intelligence mission remained a critical part of his job. Even more than the Thais, the Lao, Cambodians, and Vietnamese brought together all of Thompson's beliefs all at once: his anti-imperialism, his desire to help the most alienated and hopeless of men, his need to have a mission that was his alone, and his paternalism.

Since no one else in the U.S. mission focused on the Lao, Cambodians, and Vietnamese—even though, one day soon, these same men would become vital to American interests—Thompson could run the operation himself. And because the Lao, Cambodians, and Vietnamese were so dependent on him to plead their cause with Washington and with the Thai government, he became, in a way, all-powerful. "Thompson wanted to help people like the Lao, the Vietnamese, even the Thais, but in the way of a father handing out presents to his children," remembered one old friend of Thompson's.[28]

Most afternoons, these nationalist fighters would come to see Thompson at Suan Kularb, but on weekends Thompson often tried to catch a flight to the Thai Northeast, where tens of thousands of Vietnamese, Lao, and Cambodians lived and where Ho Chi Minh's forces had built a sizable operation. "Bangkok has become a home away from home for revolutionary elements from various Southeast Asian colonial areas," reported one newspaper. "The Vietnamese, partisans of Ho Chi Minh's rebel government, regularly steal back across the Indochinese border. They fight the French four or five months and then return to Siam."[29]

The United States maintained good ties to these nationalists, even though in just a few years Washington would be arming the French to fight these same men and some of Thompson's ideas about the Vietnamese or Lao nationalists would appear, to American hawks, like treason.

That U.S. policy shift remained over the horizon, and for now Thompson made little effort to conceal his sympathies. He quietly met regularly with the prime minister of the Free Lao movement, who was living secretly in Bangkok, brought the leaders of the Free

Cambodian groups to meet with other American officials, and even got a clandestine rendezvous with Prince Suphanouvong, a leftist member of the Lao royal family who, during the Vietnam War, allied himself with the communists and would become known as the Red Prince.[30] In the Northeast of Thailand, where Thompson traveled with Tiang Sirikhanth, a former Free Thai and a populist sympathetic to the anti-French insurgents, Thompson assured the Indochinese insurgent leaders that they would eventually get their independence, with America's backing—a bold claim, since that was not exactly U.S. policy at the time.[31]

The more time Thompson spent watching French colonialism, the more bitter he seemed to become. Thompson denounced the unwillingness of the French to change their attitude toward these locals even after World War II.[32] France feels locals "must be browbeaten and kept in place," he complained in one secret report. "The sooner the European suckups of the State Department realize that the days of colonies are over, the better. . . . I see a great deal of the Laos, the Vietnamese, and the Indonesians here and they are a very intelligent bunch and not ones to be fooled."[33]

Thompson's solution to the fighting, clearly, would be to eventually let these people become independent, a move that France, and soon the United States, would bitterly resist, with the result of that resistance a disaster. "There is still time to save the day here [from all-out war against France,] but we would have to work fast," he warned Washington in one cable. "The hatred of the French grows continually."

Not far from the temporary U.S. legation in Bangkok, over on Rajdamnern Avenue, a wide boulevard that looked like it belonged in Paris and not Thailand, Willis Bird started his day earlier than Jim Thompson. Bird lived with a Thai woman, but his work was his life, and he never seemed happier than when he first arrived in the office for the day. Most of Bangkok shut down for good in the late afternoon—Thai businesses weren't known for their strong work ethic, and Thai culture valued *sabai*, fun and relaxation. But Bill Bird didn't care; he'd always be a puritan, even if that stood out in Bangkok. He'd stay frozen at the desk in his Rajdamnern office, in his standard work uniform of white shirt, white shorts, and white socks worn high on the calves, until 9 or 10 p.m., long after the papaya sellers outside had gone home and the last of his delivery boys on Vespas had parked their little bikes for the night.[34]

Like Jim Thompson, Willis Bird had served in the OSS, had seen opportunity in Asia after the war, and had never gone home. Jim Thompson's wife had left him; Bird decided to leave his American wife and young family to stay in Thailand and eventually marry a Thai woman who happened to be from one of the most powerful families in the country.[35]

Thompson had grown bored by architecture and parties back in New York; Bird, who in his early thirties had also been somewhat too old to enlist in World War II, had tired of a string of financial jobs at Sears and longed to work for himself. Thompson's siblings viewed him as strange and unknowable for moving to Thailand; Bird's family, remembered his son, "could never understand why he wouldn't come back to Lansdowne, Pennsylvania," Bird's hometown, instead of settling down in Thailand.[36]

The two men would spend many evenings together in the days after World War II—in such a small foreigner community, they inevitably got to know each other well, and over the coming decades, few other foreigners would have the same insight into Jim Thompson's life as Bird, since few others had been in Bangkok as long as Jim.

But for all their superficial similarities, Jim Thompson and Willis Bird didn't really have as much in common as it first appeared. Sure, Bird could seem like an idealist, too, at times. He'd served with the OSS in China, where he'd had to work with Mao's communists as well as Chiang Kai-shek's nationalist forces. Bird had developed an admiration for the communists' ability to win popular support, their discipline, and their fight to reunite their country, a version of the Southeast Asians' anticolonialism.[37] (Like most Americans working in China at that time, he also failed to see the looming totalitarianism of Mao Tse-tung.) After his time in the OSS, Bird didn't seem to have much love for the world of imperial rule: friends in Bangkok knew him as an Anglophobe and a Francophobe, rarely interested in even speaking with British or French residents of Thailand.

But Willis Bird was a hard-nosed, even cold, man, and he never doubted the real reason for staying in Thailand: business. In a post–world war economy where Thailand needed virtually every type of finished goods and Bird had connections in the United States and throughout Asia, he finally had the chance to work for himself, to be a pioneer—and to be rich in a way that never would have been possible back in America. Servants, gardens, a whole company answering to him—none of that would have been possible back at Sears, where he was working his way up the corporate ladder, waiting for a pension and a farewell party.

"One thing lacking here is what we know as capitalists," Bird wrote from Bangkok in a letter to friends in the United States. "Some day a smart American company will wake up to the opportunities here"—but for now, pioneer businessmen like Bird would thrive.[38] Bird would put in ten-hour days while most people in Bangkok turned in five, and he didn't care for the Bangkok social life, which left him more time to plan his work. Using his wartime connections with old OSS friends, now scattered around the globe, Bird would import paper, insecticides, glass, building materials, and almost anything else needed in Bangkok.[39] "The only place in the world where a guy with $5.00 cash money and a lot of gall had a chance of survival was Siam," Bird wrote to his friends.[40]

Bird had made the right decision to stay in Thailand, at least from a business perspective. With so much need and the unstable financial situation—inflation in Bangkok was running at over 100 percent annually after World War II—his business skills and access to foreign products were in demand, and he branched out into even more imported products, quickly becoming one of the largest import-export firms in Bangkok. Bird's Rajdamnern office could be as busy as Jim Thompson's enclave at the American legation, and like Thompson he soon stopped talking about returning to the United States, or even about the family he had back there, at all.

Bird's hard, cold practicality did not make him a man like Jim Thompson, beloved in high-society circles and desired for company, drinks, or dinner. "Willis Bird was always looking for the best deal," one old Thailand intelligence officer remembered. "Bill Bird was first and always about himself, about what was best for him. . . . He could read any situation and figure out what would be best for him."[41] And unlike Thompson, Bill Bird was adaptable: he might like Pridi, but if American policy changed, and Pridi was tossed aside, Bill Bird, unlike Jim Thompson, could change, too, if it was necessary to survive.

When Bill Bird turned his attention from glass and pesticides to U.S. intelligence, his plans, his practicality, and his innate sense of politics and scheming soon mattered much more. Soon he would be running his own private intelligence operation out of Bangkok, rivaling Jim Thompson for influence.

6

The border between Thailand and Laos, a country that shares a language, culture, and heritage with the Thai Northeast, has always been something of an arbitrary boundary. Crossing from Thailand into Laos, one might notice a customs post or a change in the standard of living, but the rituals, the earthy and fiery foods, and the unique tones of the northeastern Thai–Lao language—even today those have stayed basically the same.

In 1946, though, Laos remained part of French Indochina, and Jim Thompson, responsible for relations with the Lao militants fighting for their freedom, found himself spending a great deal of his time along the Thai frontier with Indochina. Arriving at the Thai border after reports that fighting was breaking out along the frontier and that men, women, and children were fleeing with their possessions into Thailand, Thompson dropped himself in the middle of a maelstrom. All along the border, Vietnamese, Cambodian, and Lao insurgents had camped out, with some fifty thousand of the fighters crossing back and forth into Thailand for safe haven.

The French, though they appeared in strong control of their Indochinese possessions, were detested and could not stop the hit-and-run attacks, a preview of their demise in Vietnam. The Lao or Cambodian fighters would launch surprise attacks on the French forces, killing twenty to thirty soldiers at a time and leaving Lao border towns in rubble, and then flee into the jungle or back across the Mekong River into Thailand.[1] As Thompson suspected, some Thai soldiers were playing a role, too, secretly arming the Lao, Cambodian, and Vietnamese fighters, and occasionally joining in the attacks.[2] Thailand had previously given up territory to the French, and it wanted to get back the border provinces it considered its own.

Provoked, the French troops, outnumbered but well armed with machine guns and artillery, were beginning to fight back, shooting their heavy weapons into Thailand as they traded fire with the fighters along their border outposts. Striking back, some Indochinese fighters began kidnapping and killing local soldiers working for the French and burning down towns inside Laos and Cambodia.[3] Thompson, and some of his Thai contacts, feared the entire border could collapse into warfare.[4]

The American legation in Bangkok, understaffed, only slowly began to realize that the entire region around it could be descending into war. And only Thompson seemed to have the connections—and the skill with the Thais, the Indochinese, and the French—to help avoid a war, at least for now. At the border, Thompson met the French and Thai officers, and then found the Indochinese resistance leaders; they knew him and trusted him. When the Lao resistance leaders needed someone to confide in, they turned to Thompson; when the Thais needed a go-between, they turned to Thompson. Thompson grew so trusted that soon he was actually helping the Thais take their claims to territory controlled by the French to the United Nations.

Rapidly gaining experience on Thailand's borders, Jim Thompson expanded his connections to the Vietnamese, Lao, and Cambodian nationalists. As the fighting wore on along the borders, he was becoming the best authority on these militants, winning their trust by walking day after day through Vietnamese refugee camps, Lao villages, and Cambodian towns just inside Thailand's borders, where these refugees had set up replicas of home, complete with stalls serving steaming bowls of pho (sticky rice) and charred pieces of gamy grilled chicken. Thompson recognized, even when some of his bosses did not, that with the Soviet Union growing more powerful, these contested countries would soon become critical.

As Thompson traveled to Thailand's borders, he laid plans to set up new information-gathering stations that would feed intelligence back to Washington, with Thompson at the hub of the network—even if he had to use his own personal money to get the intelligence operation started.[5] The network, he planned, would recruit official U.S. government staff, freelancers working as businesspeople throughout Asia, and local Southeast Asians who could be trusted—it would be a whole network of agents, the kind of peacetime intelligence operation the United States had never tried before. Soon these plans would get him in trouble: the OSS, worried that Thompson was freelancing, trying to build his own operation, would have him investigated. But for now, some of his bosses liked the idea, so much so that Thompson believed his intelligence network just might happen.

Although in person he could adopt an easily humility, Jim Thompson wasn't shy about touting his connections and qualifications to lead. "I seem to be the only person now who can cope with this business [of the Indochinese militants,]" he wrote in one cable back in Washington, after earlier warning his superiors that some of the Americans he worked with were naïve and unqualified.[6]

In another cable, Thompson boasted that the Southeast Asian militants would bare their souls to him, as they would to no other foreigner. "I have just about persuaded myself that it's much more important to keep up with the struggles of the surrounding colonies than to go back to being an architect."[7] He also saw, perhaps more than his bosses back in Washington, that these small countries in Southeast Asia soon were going to be critical to the United States. "The future of southern Asia depends on them [these Southeast Asian nationalists]," Thompson wrote his OSS superiors. "I can not only be of use to them but to our own country."[8]

· · ·

While Thompson worked Thailand's borders, apparently trying to build up his own intelligence network, in Bangkok the political situation became increasingly unstable. On the morning of June 9, 1946, a servant at Barompiman Hall in Bangkok's Grand Palace heard what seemed like a gunshot from the room of King Ananda, the young monarch who had returned, along with his brother Bhumibhol Adulyadej, from exile after the Second World War and had quickly won the affection of many Thais who saw the throne as the country's central stabilizing force.

The servant rushed into the king's bedroom, and inside he found carnage. Blood oozed from a hole in the twenty-year-old king's forehead, and he lay on his back in his blue silk pajamas on the bed, as though asleep, according to one account. Near his left hand rested a Colt .45 pistol. The royal nanny, who had raised Ananda from childhood, snatched any pieces of cloth, desperately trying to stop the bleeding, and for a few brief moments, as she touched his arm, she could feel a weak pulse in the king.

But when the nanny grabbed the king's wrist again, minutes later, the pulse appeared to have stopped.[9] Soon the royal doctor arrived, crawling on the floor toward the king, per tradition: even though the doctor now crawled toward a lifeless body, ordinary Thais had learned from a very young age that they must always keep their bodies below that of the king, since to stand above the monarch would be the ultimate insult. The royal doctor briefly examined Ananda and pronounced him dead, confirming that he could do nothing now to revive His Majesty.[10]

Even before the king's death, Pridi and the democrats ruling Thailand had not exactly had an easy time. The damaged infrastructure in Bangkok, grinding postwar inflation, and the wartime destruction of Thailand's major trading partners in Asia had constrained the economy and made it hard for many Thais to afford even staple goods. Poverty caused massive conflict: riots between Thais and ethnic Chinese immigrants in Bangkok, hated by many Thais for dominating business, had turned much of the city's Chinatown into a shooting gallery, killing hundreds.

In the postwar chaos, Thai unions launched one strike after the next, paralyzing the docks, the rice trade, and other critical industries.[11] The army, angry that Pridi's party had curtailed its power and funding, was quietly maneuvering for a way back into politics, along with its hero, Phibul, who still enjoyed plenty of powerful friends in the palace and the army. Worse, while Pridi himself enjoyed enormous popularity among average Thais, since he was truly the first politician to pay attention to their needs, Pridi's party and its allies, which had little experience governing, lacked discipline, squabbled incessantly among themselves, and grasped for any contracts, hand-outs, and outright graft.

"Pridi was trying to rebuild from a war, create a new democracy, and modernize the country all at the same time; it was basically an impossible task," remembered Rolland Bushner, who served in the U.S. embassy in Bangkok.[12]

When he heard the news of Ananda's death, Jim Thompson rushed to see Pridi. He found the normally serene and professorial Thai leader, who had survived a radical overhaul of his country's political system and World War II, anxious. Pridi seemed extremely worried, even more suspicious of other people than normal, and suddenly morose. It was, Thompson remembered, as if the Thai leader knew that all his hopes for the country and for America's new role in Asia—hopes shared by Thompson—might have died along with Ananda.

In the process of Jim Thompson's intelligence work, many of these militants had become Thompson's closest friends. Traveling to Vietnamese refugee villages in northeastern Thailand, Thompson marveled at the discipline and popularity of Ho Chi Minh's Viet Minh forces.[13]

The Vietnamese, he admitted in one classified intelligence report, were "the most industrious and best organized of all the people of Southeast Asia." They were, he wrote, dedicated fighters and, potentially, powerful allies; with a superpower rivalry emerging, Washington, working with Pridi's government, could blunt Soviet inroads in Southeast Asia by backing the Viet Minh, who desperately sought ties to America. Ho Chi Minh, Thompson wrote, "stated several times since 1946 that he will have to count mainly on the

United States. The future of Southern Asia depends on them [these Indochinese nationalists.]"[14] Pridi's government was already lending support to several Southeast Asian nationalist fighting forces.

The Viet Minh fighters, like the Cambodians and the Lao, were nationalists first, Thompson wrote—they might embrace communism to force out the French and get their country back, but only if the United States shunned them. If America embraced the Vietnamese fighters, they'd surely choose Washington over Moscow, but if the United States chose otherwise, the Vietnamese, turning to the Soviets, would develop into the harsh and fearless opponent Washington feared. In this prediction, as on many of the other central questions of U.S. policy toward Southeast Asia, a policy that ultimately would result in disaster, Thompson effectively predicted the future, but few of his superiors were willing to take his advice.

That there were communists in Vietnam could not be denied, Thompson wrote in one classified cable, but hardened Marxists were but a tiny minority of their movement, and the Vietnamese insurgents enjoyed enormous popularity. "Even many of the French themselves admit that the puppet government [in South Vietnam, backed by the French] is doomed to failure as it has little or no popular backing compared to the government of Ho Chi Minh."[15]

Thompson made his personal respect for Ho Chi Minh clear—a decision that would throw suspicion on Thompson later—by reportedly visiting the Viet Minh station in Bangkok and using the Viet Minh office to send messages and even a birthday gift to the Vietnamese leader.[16] Jim's niece Martha Galleher remembered that her uncle called Ho the "George Washington of Vietnam" and recalled that he could have served as a buffer against China.[17]

As Thompson grew closer to these Indochinese nationalists, his hatred of French colonialism hardened and curdled. "They [the French] are really a scurvy race—I hope I never have to fight another war for them—they are not worth the trouble," he wrote. "The people behind the desks in Washington would never know what is going on in Southeast Asia unless they came out here and really saw the Laos and Vietnamese and what they have to put up with [from the French.]"[18]

Thompson's constant advocacy of wholehearted U.S. backing for the Vietnamese and other insurgents, though shared by some of his colleagues in Bangkok, was not welcomed by many superiors in Washington, where the State Department was eager not to antagonize France, a country it believed most vulnerable to communist influence among the Western European powers.

"Thompson was kind of a romantic," said Bushner. "He'd get carried away advocating for these people, like the Vietnamese, like Ho Chi Minh, who was a friend of his, but he didn't understand the politics of it, that he could get in trouble for what he said."[19] Later, that romanticism would cause Thompson a great deal of trouble with his bosses and with the FBI.

Since coming to Thailand, Thompson had spent almost no time back in the United States, and even fewer days in Washington. But at the State Department, a new breed of diplomats, more attuned to Washington politics and less willing to give embassy staff on the ground a free hand, were rising up the ranks of the postwar Foreign Service, the kind of company men needed as the American policy-making apparatus grew to fit the demands of a new superpower. In the field, operatives like Thompson did not adjust easily: one of the new senior diplomats in Bangkok, Charles Yost, a suave and extremely skillful man who would eventually rise to the job of U.S. ambassador to the United Nations, reprimanded Thompson for repeatedly ignoring directions from Washington.

Yost probably wasn't just angry about Jim Thompson's political activities. Shortly after Yost arrived in Bangkok, Thompson began an intense affair with Yost's wife, Irena, a glamorous woman Yost had met while serving in Poland. It was a romance that would last for years, and at times it seemed to consume Thompson. It seems impossible to imagine that Charles Yost, who had overlapped at Princeton with Thompson and certainly would have known him, did not find out about the affair. In his growing flood of letters to Thompson's sister Elinor, who would become, through this regular correspondence, his private confessor, Thompson confided to thinking about "I" constantly.

"I am very worried about 'I' as I have never received a word from her since I have been back in this country [Thailand]," Thompson wrote to Elinor. "I don't know how tactful and discreet you can be but if you ever happen to hear anything do let me know." In another letter, Thompson worried constantly about whether Irena would ever leave her husband for him, complaining bitterly to his sister of his desperate state, always waiting to be contacted by Irena and never having any control of this secret relationship. "I haven't heard from 'I' for months. I don't know whether it's the Iron Curtain [she had visited Poland] or whether she thinks it's better to stick it out the way it is," with her husband, Thompson wrote to Elinor. "If there had not been so many complications, we would be having a wonderful life here together instead of now being at opposite ends of the earth from each other."[20]

Thompson's nephew Henry remembered that his uncle Jim desperately wanted to marry Irena Yost, to take her away from her family—he loved her far more than he had loved Pat Thraves. Thompson introduced her to his closest friends, something he hadn't done with Pat and would never do with any future girlfriend. On numerous occasions, Henry said, Jim Thompson proposed to Irena, and though she always turned him down, the fact that he couldn't have her only made Irena Yost even more desirable.[21]

Aside from Elinor, who kept Jim's secrets like a safety deposit box, Thompson family members hardly approved of the affair, and on top of their lack of interest in his life in Thailand—his brother Henry wrote him constantly asking Jim to come home—Irena drove Thompson even further from his family.[22] "A lot of people in the family didn't get the attraction—maybe they looked down on her since she was Polish or a Roman Catholic—but Jim was totally devoted, he always seemed convinced she'd eventually divorce her husband and marry him," said Thompson's nephew Henry.[23]

Thompson was bold enough to travel openly with Irena. The couple went south to the Thai beach resort of Phuket for a holiday, where they snapped photographs together, shots that Thompson kept forever in the papers in his house. Thompson even brought his lover to America with him. When Thompson brought Irena to the United States on a visit to meet his family, Jim's sister Katherine, the most puritan of the Thompson family, scolded the couple brutally.

"Katherine laid into them, asking how could they do this, when she [Irena] had a husband and a family; she made life very unpleasant for Irena," remembered Thompson's nephew.[24] Jim almost never spoke to Katherine after that.

Like Jim Thompson, Willis Bird, who still had close friends back at central intelligence in Washington, could see that, slowly, Washington was beginning to pay more attention to Southeast Asia. Bird had served in China for the OSS and had seen the Chinese civil war up close. Like most of the men who'd been there on the ground, he left China convinced that Mao's communists would triumph over the weak and corrupt armies of the U.S. ally Chiang Kai-shek, a triumph that easily could put the American Right, with its almost fanatical allegiance to Chiang, on the lookout for communists everywhere.[25]

In 1945, shortly after the end of the Second World War, the FBI arrested one of the most prominent U.S. Foreign Service "China hands," a man named John Stewart Service, who, like Bird, had served in China during the war, advocated building American ties to the Chinese communists, and harshly criticized the flaws of Chiang Kai-shek's government. After bursting into the offices of a magazine called *Amerasia*, the FBI accused Service of leaking confidential information about China to *Amerasia*, and even though he ultimately was cleared of all charges, the State Department still fired him.[26] Bird himself had not returned to the United States after the war in part for fear of being questioned about his work with Mao.[27]

Less romantic than Jim Thompson, Bird saw, too, that the conservative forces in Thailand—the army, the royalists, Phibul—still had a lot of power. If he was going to survive in Thailand, he shouldn't alienate anyone. With his meticulous files of thousands of index cards, each containing the name of and critical information on anyone who could help his business, Bird could smooth-talk anyone in the city.

"Willis Bird was a con man, but he was the best con man, he was a brilliant salesman," said one close associate.[28] With his doughy face, large round glasses, and thin mustache, Bird was not a physically intimidating man, but at dinner parties (which Bird attended mostly to find clients), while waiters in white linen suits offered heaping plates of prawn cakes and slivers of pomelo, Bird would press close to a potential client, staring at him as if he were the only person who mattered in the world. Up close, Bird seemed able to spin almost any story, melding his persona to fit whatever the other person wanted to hear. Increasingly successful, Bird expanded his Bangkok import-export business into financial services, glass, machine tools, books, and many other items.[29]

Bill Bird didn't let dangerous politics affect his nascent private intelligence operation, either. Unlike Jim Thompson, who quickly took an interest in Thai painting, textiles, and religion, Bill Bird had no desire to become more Thai, to blend into the local culture any more than necessary.[30] But Bird did dedicate himself to knowing every powerful Thai politician, no matter if they were close to the military or his old enemy Phibul.

Bird began to make himself invaluable and irreplaceable. When one senior Thai politician needed a loan of eighty thousand dollars to cover his living expenses, Bird helped to arrange the financing.[31] When army and police officers sought ways to buy new weapons, Bird contacted them and started to arrange private arms sales. When the Thai government could not get back its gold reserves from Japan, which had seized a large portion of the gold during the war, a powerful Thai general came to Bird, a man already known in Bangkok for being able to get important missions done without publicity. Working with old OSS friends, Bird quietly got the gold back, leaving the Thai government in his debt.[32]

The U.S. embassy in Bangkok took notice, too—and wasn't thrilled that Bill Bird, a man seen by many embassy employees as cold and self-interested, was taking jobs from the official intelligence agency. "We wrote one dispatch about Bird, about how Bird was compromising us," remembered one diplomat from the U.S. embassy in Bangkok. "He didn't make many friends."[33]

The king's mysterious death was the opportunity Pridi's enemies had been waiting for. A murder plot seemed extremely far-fetched. But while Pridi had served as Ananda's regent and had promoted the return of the young king to Thailand after World War II to serve as a constitutional monarch, allowing the institution to survive, he had led the 1932 revolution against the absolute monarchy, and now that history left him vulnerable.

"Pridi killed the king!" Almost as soon as reports leaked out of the palace of Ananda's death, the political opposition—allies of Phibul, military men, and archroyalists who had never accepted real democratization—began to accuse Pridi of murdering the monarch. There was no real evidence for this charge, but as one account noted, "The words [accusing Pridi] flung Bangkok into a state of seething anger, speculation, disbelief."[34]

Opposition parties paid young men to go to public places in Bangkok and publicly gossip about Pridi's guilt; royalist thugs started attacking politicians, and two leading opposition politicians, Seni and Kukrit Pramoj, quickly went to the U.S. embassy to claim that Pridi was involved in the death.[35] (The embassy staff mostly greeted their claims with skepticism.)

When the Thai police conducted an investigation of the murder, the police chief, an ally of the opposition party, handed out bribes to witnesses to finger Pridi.[36] Casual conversations in Bangkok now always seemed to turn to conspiracies around the king's death, and political infighting, which had once been done with a kind of Thai courtesy and even *sanuk*, or fun, became increasingly brutal.

With rice shortages and inflation leading to hungry crowds of unemployed men and women in the capital, it was easy to recruit a political mob for a few coins each. At cinemas in the capital, remembered Thompson's colleague Alexander MacDonald, people yelled out "Pridi killed the king!"[37] Prince Subhasvasti, one of the most articulate observers of Thai politics at the time, noted, "It was a dirty war [between parties] without any quarter given."[38]

Still, Thompson furiously tracked down any evidence or rumors about the king's death, probably looking for details that would definitively clear Pridi. Day after day, Thompson lurked around palaces, pressing sources for information or holding clandestine meetings with bored royals eager for a chance to gossip with a foreigner.

But whatever the truth was, it didn't seem to matter anymore. With stocks of surplus weapons left in Thailand by the Japanese army, political groups could easily arm themselves, and many did. When Pridi's allies held a public rally, someone detonated a bomb; when the opposition gathered for a rally of its own, someone tossed grenades into the crowd, tearing apart the leg of one leading opposition politician.[39] A prominent newspaper editor who exposed rampant government corruption was bicycling home one night when a car pulled up alongside him, and a man wielding a machine gun blasted him.[40]

Pridi himself looked, to Thompson, like he might be on the verge of a nervous breakdown, anxious and often unable to complete his thoughts—and this from a former professor who loved to speak in fluid paragraphs. At one ceremony after the king's death, Pridi fainted. After his allies won elections in August 1946, Pridi, exhausted, took a temporary leave from formal roles in politics.[41] And to shut up his political opponents, he instituted temporary censorship laws, banning allegations about the king and arresting politicians who claimed Pridi had a role in the death—arrests that bitterly disappointed friends like Thompson who never thought they'd see the former Free Thai leader taking away freedoms.[42] "Everyone is pretty disgusted with the government, including myself," Thompson wrote in one classified cable.[43]

Worst of all, after being pardoned by the government on war crimes charges in early 1946, Pridi's old enemy Phibul was plotting a comeback and now had his ammunition. Phibul quietly gauged his support in the military, the palace, and the business community, and he poured money into newspapers to attack the government and call for a "savior" who could deliver Thailand from the unrest and corruption flourishing under Pridi.[44] The identity of that "savior" was no secret: soon after the articles, Phibul promised to return to politics in order to restore Thailand's glory, and he formed a new political party. Given the chaos of Pridi's messy young democracy, more and more Thais looked longingly back to Phibul's ordered authoritarianism.

7

In the early years after World War II, with Soviet and American forces scrambling for influence across the Continent, nearly the entire U.S. policy-making apparatus had focused on Europe. Asia remained left for second—thought of second and planned for second—just as it had been during the war.

General Douglas MacArthur, now comfortably ensconced as proconsul and virtual emperor in Tokyo's Dai Ichi building and uninterested in taking commands from Washington, enjoyed nearly total license to remake Japanese politics and society. He was treated by the American press—especially *Time*, which wrote of MacArthur in terms normally used by a lovesick fifteen-year-old—as an authority on all of Asia, despite the fact that the general had not stepped on the Asian mainland in decades.

With American ally Chiang Kai-shek's forces losing one battle after the next and often handing over their American-supplied weaponry to the advancing communist forces, the Truman administration seemed lost for a solution in China. Harry Truman sent a mission led by George Marshall, probably the most respected American public figure but also an aging man who really wanted to retire to a country estate. Marshall's attempts to unite Chiang and Mao into one China failed totally.[1]

Truman took less interest in Southeast Asia, but by the late 1940s the tectonic plates of policy making had begun to shift, and Southeast Asia would soon command Truman's attention—and the minds of his next four successors. At the State Department, the Pentagon, and the National Security Council, only the most committed—or delusional—of conservative hawks refused to see that Chiang was going to fall.

The Generalissimo himself had been making plans for his forces to evacuate men, money, and mistresses to Taiwan, and when Mao took over, the United States would be faced with not one communist power but two sizable enemies. In the early post–World War II days, Moscow and Washington had still cooperated tentatively, but any pretense of cooperation had vanished by 1947; the two superpowers, both unused to global responsibility and both almost scared of their strength, faced off.

In Europe, the lines between Moscow and Washington had already been drawn, with the Soviets dominating the East, and the western Allies, following the new mantra of "containing" an expansionist Soviet Union, controlling most of Western Europe. But in Asia nothing was settled, no firm lines had been drawn. And with the Republican Right hammering the Truman administration for not doing enough to save Chiang and for generally being soft on communism, the White House believed that Southeast Asia could be the place to make a definitive stand against Soviet and Chinese power.

By the late 1940s, the Truman administration had become convinced that Moscow was paying more attention to Southeast Asia, even though reports from operatives on the ground like Jim Thompson and his friend Alexander MacDonald noted that the Soviet presence in places like Thailand remained skeletal. (Contrary to rumors that Moscow had hundreds of agents in Thailand, the Soviet legation in Bangkok contained only six diplomats by the end of 1948).[2]

Truman's secretary of defense, Louis Johnson, who had been publicly contemptuous of his own administration for being soft on

Chinese communism, pushed the National Security Council, in a memo that would become known as NSC-48, to launch a broad plan to contain communism in Asia and support noncommunist forces in the region.[3] Perhaps feeling this pressure from above, Pentagon and State Department staffers, few of whom had lived in Asia, began noticing what they saw as Moscow's expansionary intentions.

In September 1947, one senior Kremlin official declared at a Communist Party conference in Poland that the world would be divided into "two camps": imperialists and people's democracies (that is, communist states). Some State Department Russia specialists saw this speech as a statement of Soviet plans to forcefully spread communism. State grew even more worried after a Southeast Asian communist conference, held in India shortly after the Poland meeting, endorsed the Kremlin's views of global division into these two camps. Charles Reed, the head of the Southeast Asia desk at the State Department, announced, "Moscow is turning more and more attention to the Far East, particularly in Southeast Asia."[4]

Not only Jim Thompson but also other American intelligence operatives tried to make the case to Washington that any struggle in Southeast Asia was more complex than it seemed, more nuanced, and that the United States should not alienate Vietnamese, Cambodian, or Indonesian fighters trying to push out the colonial powers.

"I have been in continuous touch with the Lao and Vietnamese delegates here [in Thailand]. They are still very friendly and give the attitude that they would prefer us to the Russians, but their patience is getting sorely tried," Thompson wrote.[5] "The communists [in Thailand] don't seem to give a whoop about liberation," he wrote in another cable. "They are just interested in their own petty squabbles."[6] In fact, there were virtually no organized communist groups in Thailand that could seriously challenge the Thai government.[7] In one intelligence report in 1948, the U.S. embassy in Bangkok concluded, "It was generally believed that the number of Siamese communists was insignificant."[8]

But Washington was not looking for nuance, and what mattered in this policy debate, in the end, was not an understanding of Asia's politics but an understanding of U.S. politics. Sour and destructive after more than fourteen years out of power, the Republicans had hit on an issue that could hurt Truman's party, and they were going to ride that issue as far as possible.

Republican charges of communist influence at the State Department led, in 1947 and 1948 and subsequent years, to investigations of virtually anyone who'd spent time in China or Vietnam and to purges of men and women who'd once advocated an American relationship with anticolonial fighters like Ho Chi Minh. The White House began requiring government officials to sign loyalty oaths, and State and Pentagon employees soon learned that you didn't advance your career by pushing friendships with any foreign leader who could even be considered a leftist.

Kenneth Landon, the most distinguished expert on Thailand in the U.S. government in the 1940s, was grilled by the FBI about his views toward Ho Chi Minh and had the files in his office and his basement at home ransacked numerous times, the papers left scattered and the cabinets overturned.[9] When China finally fell to Mao in 1949, and in 1950 unprepared and undermanned American forces scrambled onto the Korean Peninsula to prevent North Korea and China from overwhelming the South, the call for a total purge of communists from the U.S. government got louder and more dangerous, the demands to hold the line against communism in Southeast Asia grew fiercer, and the embarrassed Truman administration had no choice but to respond.

Also by the middle of 1950, America's first military aid for French forces had arrived in Saigon, and the shift to Southeast Asia as a center of U.S. foreign policy was complete. "The American containment policy in Southeast Asia arose from the ashes of its failed policy in China," concluded one comprehensive assessment of U.S. Southeast Asia strategy. "In a brief few months (in the late 1940s) this policy transformed an area [Southeast Asia] that most Americans barely knew existed into one deemed so vital its defense justified a major effort to keep it from falling into the Soviet orbit."[10]

The Thai parliament building, with its soaring domes and the wide, manicured boulevards of Bangkok's Dusit district outside, looked more like it belonged in some serene and stately European capital like Vienna than the crowded and cacophonous Thai city. But inside, the political battles fit right into noisy and chaotic Thailand.

After a temporary leave of absence, Pridi, haggard and withdrawn, had returned to help command the government, but still he struggled against the weight of the regicide rumors, the spiraling street violence, and his party's own corruption and incompetence.[11] Imposing censorship laws had cost Pridi some of his liberal allies as well, and assassination attempts on opposition politicians, even if they couldn't be linked back to Pridi, added to the sense that the country was becoming ungovernable.[12]

Pridi had little control of even his closest friends, who sensed their government would not last long and seemed determined to steal as much as possible before they left office. Government officials hoarded the best rice, the imported automobiles, the highest-quality fish, and the large stacks of bank notes supposed to have been taken out of circulation. Furious at being left with broken, dirty grains of rice, in a country once known as the rice bowl of the world, in late 1947 crowds of poor Thais marched to Parliament, demanding better food to eat.[13]

No one doubted that Pridi Banomyong was smart, but, as one acquaintance remembered, he was book smart, which didn't always translate to the real world, especially the world of gutter politics.[14] Phibul didn't have that problem. Despite Pridi's immense intelligence, it was the charming and suave Phibul, not Pridi, who saw how the world was changing and how he could take advantage of it—perhaps because Phibul also realized that old loyalties never mattered as much as you thought.

Throughout 1946 and early 1947, Phibul and his allies had been attacking Pridi's government, accusing it of complicity in regicide. The newspapers had been preparing the ground for the return of former Japanese collaborator Phibul, whose earthy charm and handsome, almost regal bearing—a crisply buttoned collar atop a starched military dress shirt—seemed unaffected by World War II and years in political exile.[15]

On the evening of November 7, 1947, the opposition struck, catching Pridi unaware. Rumors of a coup had circulated through Bangkok's diplomatic community for weeks, but Pridi usually dismissed the rumors, sure that even if he had angered the army by diminishing its prestige and cutting its budget, he still enjoyed enough support in the officer corps and in the navy, which was loyal to him, to prevent any rash actions.

But Pridi had pushed aside enough army men and made enough enemies that he could not be too confident in his safety. During World War II, some Thai officers had served in Shan State, a rugged, mountainous, and particularly harsh part of Burma, full of warlords and internecine feuds between ethnic groups, some of whom still allegedly cut off the heads of their enemies as totems. (In Shan State, the army officers also learned how easy it was to cultivate opium in northeastern Burma, knowledge they would soon put to use.)

Many of the Thai soldiers had suffered horribly in Shan State: they'd been sent to the war with minimal supplies of food and medicine, and during the rainy season in Burma, many died from malaria and other tropical diseases.[16] At the end of the war, withdrawing back to Bangkok, the soldiers had to walk thousands of miles home with little air transport, and bandits attacked the troops on roads and buses, stealing their money or killing them.[17]

When they returned to Bangkok for medical care, the soldiers found "with resentment that nobody in the capital seemed to know or care about the hardships they had suffered," according to one Thai historian.[18] This shared hardship and shared resentment built a bond among the survivors of the Shan State campaign.[19]

So on November 7, a small group of rebel army officers, many of whom had not only straggled back from Shan State together but also been sidelined by Pridi after World War II, and who had plotted an overthrow for months, rolled their tanks through the city streets, seizing arsenals and the radio station and marching troops to the Ministry of Defense. The next day, on the radio, one of the coup leaders, Phin Choonhaven, told Thais why the rebels had to act. The civilian government, he declared, had proved ineffective: rice prices were spiraling, average people had little to eat, and immoral politicians just spent their time arguing over nothing. As he spoke over the radio, Phin sobbed almost uncontrollably, as if overcome by the responsibility that he and the other rebels had taken on.[20]

Bangkok residents, many of them still struggling with the after-math of the bombing of the city and Japanese occupation during World War II, now found themselves again surrounded by thickets of machine-gun nests hastily set up along major streets. The rebel officers, including a colonel named Luang Kach, a man with an angry red complexion who waved a .38 pistol around his head as he spoke, knew to attack the nerve centers of the city.

The rebels arrested many top politicians, but the prime minister, Dhamrong Nawasat, managed to escape the dance he was attending by sneaking into a car as rebel soldiers stormed into the garden where the dance was hosted.[21] The rebel soldiers parked their tanks at the most important intersections throughout Bangkok.[22] The prime minister, the police chief, and other allies of Pridi drove maniacally around the city, trying to avoid the tanks and escape capture; the actual army commander, who was not close to the coup makers, tried to keep his men in the main barracks to prevent them from joining the rebel officers launching the coup.

But as more tanks rolled out onto the streets, and as the men Pridi had expected to come to his defense refused to intervene, the army commander could hardly keep the barracks locked up, and average soldiers who'd had no advance knowledge of the coup joined in. Within thirty-six hours, and with little bloodshed, the rebels had control of the city. Soon they would reveal a new, more regressive constitution—which they had written before the coup and kept hidden in a water jar—to the Thai people.[23]

Even as the coup makers took over more and more of Bangkok, they knew they could not completely succeed without capturing Pridi. Learning of the coup as he heard soldiers trade volleys of bullets with the police guard stationed outside his house, Pridi fled his home by the murky Chao Praya River, where half-naked children bathed while nearby, women dumped waste and feces right into the water. He said a rushed good-bye to his wife and jumped from a wall overlooking the river into a tiny sampan just as a tank swung around an intersection and crashed through the wooden gate outside his house.[24]

On the water, Pridi paddled away as soldiers rushed into his home and swarmed around his family.[25] From the other shore of the river,

Pridi spent the night driving on back roads around the city, avoiding the coup makers' roadblocks, but he would need foreign help to get out of the country. Phibul and the army were calling publicly for him to turn himself in. Dressed as a low-ranking Thai naval officer, Pridi snuck back into central Bangkok in an official royal marine car, which was unlikely to be stopped. If the coup makers did stop him, there were naval guards with submachine guns and bombs surrounding Pridi in the car, ready to fight.[26]

The car dropped Pridi at the private house of the British naval attaché, Stratford Dennis, an old World War II friend. Now harboring a fugitive, the attaché didn't know what to do, but he did mix Pridi a whiskey and soda. A prince close to the coup makers showed up at Dennis's door shortly after Pridi had arrived, and the attaché told the man that Pridi was probably heading north from Bangkok. Trying to avoid any more Thai spies, Dennis met with his ambassador and Edwin Stanton, the U.S. ambassador. They agreed that even though the political scene might be changing in Thailand, they could not just ignore their old ally, leaving him possibly to die in Bangkok. The army had already sent out search teams to hunt down Pridi, and soon they would send out boats to trawl the waters to stop any vessels from harboring the former leader.[27]

As quietly as possible, Dennis snuck Pridi out of the city. Near the mouth of the Chao Praya River, he bustled Pridi onto a pleasure boat flying the American flag and with the U.S. naval attaché aboard it. The Thai army's search vessel, hunting the water for Pridi, had turned back because of bad weather, and the Americans were able to slip Pridi onto an oil tanker heading for the safety of Singapore, a British colony.[28] Once there, Pridi immediately began planning his return to Thailand, but even though he didn't realize it at the time, his political life had all but ended.

Phibul refused an official position in the new government, preserving the fiction that he had no role in the putsch—though one colonel told Alexander MacDonald that during the coup, soldiers had carried Phibul to government headquarters on their shoulders.[29] The government granted itself wide-ranging emergency powers, claiming it was forced to launch a coup because Pridi had not only murdered the king but also plotted to kill his brother, Bhumibhol, and to create a communist republic.[30] And while Pridi had not enacted harsh revenge on Phibul and his allies after World War II but had allowed Phibul to be released from a war crimes tribunal, the coup government did not grant Pridi the same leniency.

The government locked up politicians with ties to Pridi. Army officers took over companies and banks owned by former supporters of Pridi, often helping themselves to the profits; Luang Kach would later be accused of looting millions from government funds.[31] Phibul oversaw the fabrication of charges in the king's death against several palace aides known to be close to Pridi; the men were charged, found guilty, and executed, with virtually no conclusive evidence ever presented against them.[32]

As he had done during World War II, Phibul demonized the Chinese in Thailand, announcing immigration quotas, banning Chinese associations, and claiming that Pridi, who like many Thais had some Chinese heritage, had been plotting a "Chinese invasion" of the country, ostensibly to convert Thailand to communism.[33] The government launched its own censorship laws, and censors left the newspaper run by Thompson's friend Alexander MacDonald covered in black splotches like some kind of Rorschach test.[34]

Some American intelligence operatives believed that the government considered tossing Jim Thompson out of the country because of his links to Pridi but that Thompson's remaining friends in the Thai army persuaded the coup makers to spare Jim, since such a deportation would have damaged relations with America.[35]

Most viciously, Phibul tried to wipe out any influential politician who'd ever had close links to Pridi, including most of Jim Thompson's friends. Some of the savvier Pridi men quit politics or left the country, but others were not so lucky. When the coup government held an election ninety days after the military takeover, it made sure to place Pridi loyalists under house arrest, limit the candidates allowed to run for office, and rig the ballot box, ensuring that the coup makers triumphed. In early 1948, Phibul became prime minister again, formally confirming his return to power.[36]

• • •

Few visitors to Thailand can help noticing that everyone in the country seems to be smiling at them, a sea of apparently hospitable faces. Thailand's tourism ministry has marketed the country as the Land of Smiles, and surely this seeming warmth is one reason that the kingdom today attracts over twelve million visitors per year, many more than neighbors like Cambodia or Vietnam do.

But few tourists realize that in Thailand, a smile often carries far different meanings than in the West. In a culture where visible displays of sadness, anger, or any perceptible emotion are frowned upon; where a *jai rawn*, a hot heart, is a curse; and where long-married couples greet each other at the airport with a chaste small bow, Thais smile to express a wide range of emotions, not just happiness. They smile when they are embarrassed, upset, or even furious at someone else—each type of grin conveying a slightly perceptible change in emotion and usually misunderstood by outsiders. Nearly every longtime resident in the country can recall when a Thai friend made an obvious mistake—got lost in traffic and ruined an appointment or simply didn't show up for an event—and responded with a half-smile, infuriating to a foreigner, rather than apologizing or at least looking upset.

The smile can also serve as a mask, concealing rage and intense brutality. Thai society disdains open confrontation, so emotions are usually repressed. Anger, ambition, lust, terror, even love—all these human feelings are normally, in Thailand, repressed behind the masks of smiles. But the price of this repression can be serious: occasionally, individuals, crowds, or even the whole country seems to explode into paroxysms of violence. One longtime foreign resident of Bangkok remembers watching Phibul and Pridi walking, arms linked, through a garden party in Bangkok only days before the coup and the military's attempt to arrest or even kill Pridi.[37]

Under Phibul's rule, one man above all—one powerful officer who would go down, in a famous phrase, as "the worst man in the whole history of modern Thailand"—managed to smile while indulging all his most destructive human qualities.[38] The ruthless and graspingly ambitious police deputy director, Phao Sriyanond, personally saw to it that Phibul's enemies were eliminated; he often attended their executions, where he'd smoke a cigarette as the firing squad machine-gunned them.[39]

Phao, a naturally skilled politician with swept-back hair above a high forehead and heavy and expressionless eyes, was a direct and straightforward leader in a country of misdirection and obfuscation. This straightforwardness would greatly endear Phao to foreigners and help him win American aid. He seemed set on a course for power from early in his life.[40] From early on, too, he showed almost no compunction about how he eliminated potential rivals. Phao married the daughter of Phin Choonhaven, a prominent general, solidifying his alliances within the Thai security forces, and, unlike Phibul, apparently genuinely decided that Thailand faced a mortal threat from communism.

Soon after assuming the deputy directorship of the police, Phao began casting around for new ways to make money and build up his power and control over more areas of the country; he eventually settled on the opium trade, which he would dominate, and the national gold market, from which he would steal a fortune, allegedly depositing it in Switzerland. At one point, when Phao already had established himself as one of the most powerful men in the country, a study of his wealth revealed that he sat on the board of directors of twenty-six leading Thai companies.[41]

Under Phibul's rule, Phao quickly established his reputation, which he seemed to relish, for not employing a cloak of civility (the normal Thai custom) to hide his willingness to use extreme measures. When Phao's police department grabbed four politicians known for their sympathy to Pridi, the men never made it out of police custody. When the police finally released the men's dead bodies, the corpses were riddled with bullet holes and replete with signs of torture, including swollen eyes and ears, burns that likely came from cigarette butts, and shattered legs. The police insisted that the men had been shot while trying to escape. No policemen were harmed in the incident.[42]

The police, led by Phao, eventually even tracked down Tiang Sirikhanth, one of Thompson's closest friends and a prominent pro-Pridi populist. When the bodies of Tiang and several of his friends were recovered in a forest, it was clear they had been strangled to death, then burned and mutilated almost beyond recognition, their faces pushed into the ground. This was a horrendous insult in a country where the top of the body is viewed as sacred, and under normal circumstances no Thai would ever even touch another's head.[43]

Jim Thompson had lived long enough in Thailand to have few illusions about the meaning of a Thai smile. "This has developed into the most tragic week I have ever spent in my life," Thompson wrote to his sister Elinor after the first four men, all of whom he knew well, were murdered. "At this point I feel completely listless, let down, and useless."[44]

Thompson's nephew Henry happened to be with him when he learned his friends had been killed. "I'd never seen Jim so shaken," Henry said. "It was like having your own brother killed."[45] Thompson, wrote his friend William Warren, saw politics through the lens of his personal relationships, and he never totally recovered from the coup. With his friends being tortured and killed, he began to despair for his adopted country's political future, and a grim fatalism slowly crept into him.[46]

"These were some of the men who had first taught him to love Asia . . . who had given him his first real glimpses of the life behind the Eastern façade," Warren wrote. "Thompson went to the Buddhist temple where the rites for the four officials were held, and the memory of it remained with him to the end of his days in Thailand: the formal photographs of the dead men beside their funeral urns, the terrified wives and children clustered around the crematorium, the ubiquitous policemen and plainclothesmen watching every arrival carefully in search of more suspects." The letters Thompson wrote at the time, Warren remembered, "were the letters of a man shaken to his depths and abruptly aware of the frailty of idealism."[47]

Phibul had his coup, but it would hardly matter, if no one recognized his government. American and British criticism of the coup—or worse, sanctions—could force the coup government to hand back power. Shortly after the coup, Jim Thompson and his allies, like the ambassador in Bangkok, Edwin Stanton, fought Phibul with the desperation of men who knew that if they lost, they might have no future in the country. Thompson, after all, had abandoned his whole life back in America, rarely speaking to his siblings, and he had started a clandestine affair with no obvious end. Thailand and his friends there were now almost all he had.

Immediately after Pridi's ouster and desperate flight, most American operatives in Bangkok took a hard line against the new regime. Stanton told his bosses back in Washington that his loyalty to Pridi was so great, dating to World War II, that he flatly refused to recognize Phibul's "highly distasteful" government.[48] Refusing to recognize the government, Stanton argued to Washington, would drive Phibul's "henchmen" out of power and return the United States to its role of defending democracy.[49]

Thompson hid several of Pridi's allies and then helped them to escape from the country, while also quietly meeting with Lao and Cambodian fighters to see whether they might make an alliance with Pridi's men.[50] The Thai police weren't stupid, especially on Phao's watch, and Thompson, a man who under Pridi had been treated almost like royalty in Thailand, now found himself under constant surveillance. Thompson told his sister Elinor that the police followed him everywhere, and he worried about even stopping at friends' houses for fear of casting suspicion on them, too.[51]

Thompson, Stanton, and other friends in the embassy were fighting a losing battle, though at first they did not recognize they'd already lost, that Phibul had effectively gauged the shifts in American foreign policy. Ken Landon, a man who realized that the United States might have much in common with anticolonial fighters like Ho Chi Minh, was now back in Washington, and he saw much better than Thompson or Stanton that U.S. policy had changed and that dissenters from the new policy of containing communism would be punished ever more harshly.

The anticommunist purges Landon feared in the late 1940s would only become much worse: in February 1950, at a speech in Wheeling, West Virginia, Wisconsin senator Joseph McCarthy pulled out of his pocket a list of alleged communists employed at the State Department, launching the United States into perhaps its most paranoid and hysterical period.

"Dear Ed," Landon wrote in a letter to the ambassador to Thailand, according to Landon's memory of it. "Times have changed. . . . It's a matter of recognizing who is in charge of the shop and who you have to do business with, and that's Phibul."[52] If the ambassador refused to go along with the new American policy, Landon made clear, the State Department would have no choice but to relieve him of his job.

By 1949, Landon, a man who'd once been a fierce advocate for Pridi and the Free Thai, had become one of the most ardent backers in Washington of Phibul, pushing the United States not only to recognize the Thai government but also to begin sending Bangkok military aid.[53] Perhaps Landon, under surveillance by the FBI, just wanted to keep his job. But in his seemingly thorough conversion, Landon echoed the shift of most of his Washington colleagues.

With communist guerrillas launching attacks in Burma, Malaya, and the Philippines, with Mao consolidating his victory in China, and with the French and their puppet emperor in Vietnam losing battle after battle, the West did seem to facing an existential crisis. In a time of crisis, there seemed to be little time to parse the nuanced differences between a Southeast Asian nationalist and a Southeast Asian communist.[54] "It began to seem like, no matter what we said, Washington wasn't interested, until we said exactly what they wanted to hear," remembered one political expert in the embassy in Bangkok.[55]

The United States, Landon told Ed Stanton, could not waste its breath on moralistic foreign policy, not at a time when China was falling to Mao and the Thai military could actually control the country, providing stability in a way that Pridi and his fractious democrats never could.[56] And unlike Pridi, who had wanted Thailand to continue its historical neutrality, the "bending in the wind" diplomacy that once had allowed the country to avoid being consumed by colonial powers, Phibul and the coup government seemed to understand the changing global situation and were willing to embrace the us-or-them mentality the Truman administration coveted.[57]

On a trip to the United States, Phibul declared, "The Third World War is inevitable between communism and the Free World," and the coup government promised London that Thai forces would cooperate in Britain's battle against the communist insurgents fighting in the British colony of Malaya.[58] Phibul and the coup government labeled a wide swath of opponents as communists, starting with Pridi and extending from populists from the poor Northeast to union leaders. Communist infiltration into Thailand, Phibul declared in 1949, had become "alarming," potentially threatening the country's stability, though he offered little evidence to support his claim and admitted to one reporter, in an unguarded moment, "I don't think there are any real Siamese Communists."[59]

At the same time, Phibul always made sure to gently warn Americans that if they didn't continue their support for him, he could always turn to the Soviets, who courted him as well.[60] One American official in Thailand, in a cable back to Washington, bought the whole story, concluding that "If such [U.S.] aid is not forthcoming the army will, along with the Field Marshal [Phibul], reorient its position toward communism."[61] This fear that Thailand—or any ally—could always turn to the Soviets soon became entrenched in American policy, which only allowed Asian autocrats to wield more power over Washington.

A lifelong diplomat, Edwin Stanton had gained respect in Bangkok for his straightforward manner, but he surely also understood that surviving and advancing in the Foreign Service meant bending to Washington's desires. Stanton himself had, in 1947, admitted that there were few communists active in Thailand—only one declared communist sat in Parliament before Phibul's return—but by 1949, as Landon made clear that ambassadors who acted on their own would not be tolerated any longer, Stanton too would advocate sending military aid to the Thais as a means of holding Bangkok in the American embrace.[62]

Stanton would praise Phibul's "pleasant friendliness," which "made it difficult to credit stories of his past dictatorial ambitions," even though at the time that Phibul—who was naturally charming—seemed so friendly, his ally Phao was arresting, mutilating, and

81

executing opponents of the government.[63] In 1949, Washington launched the Mutual Defense Assistance Act with Bangkok, opening a tap of military aid that allowed Phibul to use the assistance to reward his supporters. Within a few years, that American aid would mushroom, transforming Thailand's whole economy and political system, indebting Bangkok to America, and ensuring that the Thai military would dominate the country for decades to come.[64]

8

In the early morning, as the hazy sun rose over the rice fields of the Thai Northeast and wiry men with ropy muscles and Buddha amulets around their necks urged their water buffalo out onto the rutted roads, the silk-cultivation day began. For most silk-cultivating families, raising silkworms on local mulberry trees, along with rice farming, had provided their clan's livelihood for generations. The daily routine had not changed much over that time—maybe for millennia. Some textile experts believe that Thais have been cultivating silk for over three thousand years and that the craft came to the country along with immigrants from China. Excavations of Baan Chiang, an older prehistoric culture located in modern-day Thailand, have revealed a cluster of silk thread.[1]

Northeastern families might not trace their skills back to Baan Chiang, but for at least a hundred years the routine had varied little. The silk cultivators ate a breakfast of *khao tom*, rice soup maybe flavored with a few bits of pork.[2] Then the family would head out to the barn to check the sensitive worms, making sure the creatures had enough mulberry to eat and watching that the worms were kept fastidiously clean, since any disruption in the outside environment could throw off the worms' growth.[3] Once the worms made their cocoons, the family would boil them, killing the pupa and preserving the delicate and valuable thread that emerges from the fat cocoon.

Nearly every Northeastern family taught its girls to weave from a young age, and skilled weavers were traditionally valued as brides.[4] Taking the delicate thread, the girls would gather it onto spools. Eventually the girls would begin to weave, sitting at ancient wooden looms, the shuttle clacking back and forth as their fingers crafted intricate patterns with the threads. Finally, they would color the fabric with dyes made from indigo, betel nut, or turmeric.[5]

Raising worms and producing silk had never been a way to get rich. Most farming families in the Northeast slept in one room, often with the parents and the kids together on the floor or in a simple bed. If they were lucky, the worms would produce enough raw silk that the family could get a decent price from the middlemen who journeyed to the Northeast to buy.

For years, demand had been strong. During the era of the absolute monarchy, royals gave one another fine silks as gifts, and women in the royal family needed massive quantities of silk for their *phasin*, long skirts in which the fabric was folded and wrapped around the body rather than tailored, so that the *phasin* subtly suggested the woman's curves while leaving a suitor plenty of fodder for his imagination. The *phasin* was highly versatile: it could be incorporated into nearly any assemblage of garments, from a formal *chakri* outfit, in which the skirt was woven with heavy gold brocades, to a casual *ruan ton*, a simple striped *phasin* paired with a collarless blouse.[6]

But even when the market for silk in Bangkok was strong, the growers benefited little. The prices paid by the middlemen who came to the Northeast never went up much, since the buyers usually set the price with one another, and no farmer was rich enough to get to Bangkok to sell his silk himself. Once he took out the money paid to the policemen not to harass him, a silk grower could come home from market day with barely enough earnings to buy rice, cooking oil, and fermented fish, the major source of protein for most poor families. And after World War II, silk prices suffered even more. The Japanese had introduced many synthetic fabrics to Bangkok, and rich Thais now coveted rayon and other synthetics, which they saw as modern and worldly compared to silk.[7]

Since his first trips to the Northeast shortly after landing in Thailand, Jim Thompson, who'd been a designer, a painter, and an architect back in the United States, had been impressed with Thai silk, and he seemed to possess a natural eye for its quality and color. One of Thompson's OSS aides remembered him buying yards of silk on every trip up-country, and Thompson spent spare time in Bangkok strolling through silk shops on Sampeng Lane, a narrow alley in the heart of Chinatown packed with so many shoppers and hawkers and delivery-men rolling handcarts that the crowd pushed the pedestrians along, and they rode it like a wave.[8] Thompson would send silks printed with almost iridescent colors back to his sister Elinor or, later, quietly make the silk swatches into dresses that he could sneak to Irena Yost to wear.[9] "He was a natural; he could pick out the most beautiful silks, the most unusual, almost instantly, like he'd been doing it his whole life," remembered Jim's friend Jackie Ayer.[10]

Thompson couldn't help but notice, too, the almost feudal conditions of Thailand's Northeast, its social hierarchy as strict as any back at St. Paul's and Princeton, even if the clues to Thai class distinctions could be hidden to an outsider. While postwar Bangkok was beginning to develop economically, with new European fashions, new cars, and new high-rise buildings, rural Thailand looked basically the same as it had fifty years earlier. Throughout the Northeast, small villages clustered around a main street containing an open-air market selling fruits and vegetables and unrefrigerated meat, a *wat* where young novice monks tried to chant without breaking into fits of giggles, and perhaps a dusty bus stop where bicycle rickshaws gathered, waiting for fares from women who were leaving the market loaded down with bags of rice, bloody chicken pieces, and catfish that could be fried up and mixed into a salad with fish sauce and sour mangoes.

Thailand's hierarchy actually seemed much worse than America's: in Thailand, the pulling-yourself-up-by-the-bootstraps narrative didn't exist, and people born poor in the countryside expected to die poor in the countryside. Farmers, rural laborers, and virtually anyone from the poor Northeast, where people had darker skin and flatter faces than the Thais from Bangkok, were expected to take orders unquestioningly from the wealthy, from officials, from lighter-skinned Bangkokians, and from anyone connected to the royal family.

Many Northeasterners possessed little formal education. They wore ritual tattoos across their body, designed to protect them from evil spirits and bring them good fortune, or phallus-shaped charms under their pants to protect the body and attract lovers.[11] Even the physical nature of personal interaction was defined by social hierarchy: social subordinates tried to keep their heads below the heads of their superiors and used an entirely different, and deferential, vocabulary of words to signify their exact place in the social hierarchy. "One is judged by how faithfully one adheres to the requirements of hierarchical obligation," wrote William Klausner, an American anthropologist who lived in rural Thailand.[12]

Many poor Thais simply accepted their socioeconomic status as karma, a sign that in a previous life they must have committed terrible deeds in order to deserve their poverty now. The Buddhist clergy, who also sat atop the social hierarchy, did little to discourage this belief.[13] And when poor rural Thais dared to challenge their station, they could face extremely harsh consequences. People who did not respect local officials or who stole food from wealthy merchants would be attacked in the night or even killed.

From exile, Pridi Banomyong watched as his old rival, Phibul, consolidated control of Thailand, killed off Pridi's friends, and destroyed the projects and institutions Pridi had tried to build. Phibul courted the United States assiduously. He would embark on trips there and make a grand show of seeking out American assistance to build Thai democracy, improve public health, modernize the economy, and whatever else Washington wanted to hear.

Phibul's enforcer, Phao, was transforming the police department into a kind of tropical gestapo, relying on a massive network of informers woven throughout Thai society.[14] He even created a special elite police force of some one thousand men whom he could trust to unquestioningly carry out the most brutal attacks.[15] It was, wrote Frank Darling, a foreign academic focusing on Thailand, "One of the most ruthless and thorough suppressions of international opposition in recent history."[16]

Phao's power also stemmed from his access to seemingly limitless quantities of arms, much of them provided by Willis Bird. When the coup government had first deposed Pridi, Bird, like Thompson, had scorned Phibul and his allies, and in private he still clearly admired Pridi. Bird's son Willis Jr. remembered that at home, his father always called Pridi "a true American friend" and forbade anyone from saying negative things about the Free Thai leader.[17]

In a private letter that he sent to his old boss "Wild Bill" Donovan after Pridi fled, Bird seemed furious. "Let no one fool you that he [Phibul] intends to resign or leave the power to others. . . . This will be a dictatorship, pure and simple," Bird wrote. "Wish I had a few boys from S.O. [Special Operations]. Would take over the damn country myself the way I feel now."[18]

But Bill Bird seemed to get over any anger quite quickly. He had married a beautiful Thai woman named Chalermsri, the sister of Siddhi Savetsila, a powerful military officer who eventually rose to run the Foreign Ministry, and Bird's small private intelligence operation was blossoming into a major undertaking.[19] "If you were a foreigner living in Thailand, you had to have a well-placed Thai wife; it helped you immensely," said Bird's daughter.[20]

Without consulting U.S. embassy officials, few of whom enjoyed the type of connections to senior Thai military men that Bird now had, Bill Bird obtained and sold huge amounts of smuggled military equipment to Phao's police, which led other Thai generals to come to Bird for their own needs. Phibul himself sent an envoy to ask Bird to get the general smuggled machine guns, rifles, jeeps, and even tanks; other military leaders asked Bird to supply entire infantry divisions with arms.[21]

"Why is this man Bird allowed to deal with the police chief in such matters? Why was I not informed at once of what had happened?" wondered one bewildered U.S. embassy official after Bird had transferred American arms to the Thai police without any authorization from the embassy.[22]

And the arms were just a small part of Bird's game. Soon Bird would start arranging enormous loans to Thai politicians—he proposed that he could get a consortium of American businessmen to give Phao as much as eighty million dollars—and launching a massive paramilitary force that would play a major role in the Indochina wars.[23]

Living outside his homeland, cut off from much of his family, Pridi, who'd once been a meticulous planner, gave in to the rashness bred of desperation. Working with loyal allies in the navy, which had always been closer to Pridi than the army had been, he made plans to sneak back into the country and overthrow Phibul's regime by force. Some of Pridi's longtime aides warned him that he should hold off on his bold plan until the political atmosphere was more favorable to his return, until Phibul and Phao were weaker, until there were fewer informants in Bangkok ready to turn on him, but Pridi shrugged them off. "I have devoted my life to the country earnestly and honestly. . . . I want nothing more than justice," Pridi told them.[24]

Pridi took few precautions in case the plot failed; he spent precious little time mapping out the details of the plan, a failure that led to enormous bloodletting and the end of his political career. Accompanied by a loyal aide, Pridi contacted allies at the Thai naval base at Satahip and then snuck into Bangkok dressed as a naval officer and wearing a mustache as a disguise.

At Thammasat University, which he had founded more than a decade earlier, Pridi met with roughly two dozen of his loyalists, all heavily armed. Together they counted off the hours until the coup, going over last-minute details. Pridi, watched by his personal bodyguard, opened a set of wooden cases and handed out weapons, while others in the group tried to determine who, once they had started their rebellion, could be convinced to join their side.

If Pridi recognized the strangeness of his situation—waiting to launch an armed attack at the college he'd founded—he did not mention it. One writer noted, "He had no time to reflect on the irony of using this institution, which he had founded to promote the ideals of democracy, as the headquarters for an enterprise of desperate force."[25]

When the appointed time came, late in the evening on February 26, 1949, a column of Pridi's loyalists snuck toward the Grand Palace, less than one city block away. The rebels took the palace guards by total surprise at first, and another contingent of Pridi loyalists quickly seized one of the capital's major radio stations, from which they broadcast to the city that a provisional government had taken power in order to restore Thais' democratic rights. Messengers running to Pridi, staying near the palace, informed the former Free Thai leader that across the city, navy and marine officers seemed to be rising up to join the coup. Pridi loyalists commandeered cars and took over major intersections in Bangkok. Success for Pridi appeared near.[26]

Around Bangkok, diplomats began to hear bits of information about the rebellion. The wife of British ambassador Sir Geoffrey Thompson returned to their residence on the verge of tears after a Thai marine had stopped her car for thirty minutes; Sir Geoffrey poured her "a substantial whiskey soda," according to his memoirs, and then watched vivid flashes and tracers in the night sky, before ordering tea at dawn, as he considered the situation.[27]

Edwin Stanton, the U.S. ambassador, had been attending a party for Thai graduates of American universities when an aide whispered to him that a coup was in progress. He got in a few dances, even as scared partygoers quietly slipped away into the night; on the way home, Stanton found his car swerving past roadblocks suddenly set up across the city. When his car neared Witthayu Road, naval marines swarmed all over the street, setting up fortifications, and soon Stanton experienced his residence shaking violently from the machine-gun and artillery fire nearby. His embassy staff barely escaped exploding shells that landed in their gardens. "What's the trouble?" Stanton asked one Thai naval lieutenant. "Revolution," he replied.[28]

Despite their confidence, the rebels' success was not assured. At major intersections, the army fought back, while Phibul rallied his senior officers to ensure they did not turn against him. Within twelve hours of Pridi's initial attempt, the army began turning the battle of Bangkok: army and navy divisions now faced off against each other, firing artillery across the streets and leaving bodies in the roads, their heads blasted off.[29]

At the Makkasan railway station, a critical transportation hub, an all-out tank battle erupted between the two sides. Armed with bazookas, tommy guns, and grenades, Pridi's allies tried to wipe out an army tank regiment, but the intense tank fire mowed down the navy troops before they could toss grenades into the tank hatches or get off shots with their bazookas.[30] Around the station, bodies lay crumpled on the roads and inside their vehicles. Ultimately, Pridi's men failed to defeat the tank regiment or to take over the army's tank barracks, which would have given them command of the motorized cavalry, a powerful force.

The Makkasan battle was but one indicator of Pridi's desperation. Across the city, the army fought back tenaciously, and many senior officers who Pridi had assumed would join him once the coup was under way never came around to his side.[31] The rebels dug in inside the palace walls, which ringed the temples, throne halls, precious treasures from centuries of Thai history. From their positions, the rebels battered government forces gathered outside with machine-gun fire and grenades.

Phibul's men fought back with antiaircraft cannons while desperately trying not to destroy the treaures housed in the palace. As the artillery fire smashed into the royal residence, the government troops attempted to storm the palace gates, knocking down one entrance as bullets rained on them and forcing the rebel leaders to flee for their lives out the back of the palace.

Even though the government troops had seized the Grand Palace, the fighting continued for three days. But by the third day of the rebellion, having failed to seize the main arsenal and other centers of power, which would have allowed Pridi and his allies to quickly gain a position of control and win popular support, the rebels scattered and fled. Though previous coups, like in 1932 and 1947, had been accomplished almost bloodlessly, a point of pride in Thailand, this time hundreds of Thais lay dead or wounded on the streets of the city.

Pridi managed to escape and hide out with friends in Thailand for six more months, refusing Phibul's entreaties to surrender and moving from safe house to safe house under the nose of the army. Pridi eventually made his way to the People's Republic of China, where he would stay for decades.[32] Any hope he had of returning to power was gone. "Pridi himself had lost incalculably by the plot's failure," wrote Alexander MacDonald. "Premier Phibul could logically justify heavier expenditures for measures now 'to maintain peace' and could in various ways hold down the opposition."[33]

With Pridi's career in Thailand so obviously finished, Jim Thompson considered whether he should stay in the country. He had repeatedly asked Irena to marry him, but she always refused to leave her children, and her husband, increasingly powerful in the Foreign Service, could clearly make Thompson's life in Bangkok intolerable.[34] When Irena would get ready to leave for a trip to Europe, Thompson would beg her to stay with him, to upend her life as he had his, but she never did.[35] At times, Thompson wondered whether he would ever have a family of his own or whether he had given up any chance of that.[36]

Already frustrated with increasing constraints from Washington—in one cable Thompson complained, "I am getting more limited all the time and there is not much left for me to cover"[37]—Thompson had formally resigned from the U.S. intelligence service in 1947, though he continued working closely with the intelligence agency as a private citizen, arranging meetings with Indochinese fighters and providing regular intelligence briefings to embassy officials.[38]

Even the new American intelligence officers arriving in Bangkok—young, committed anticommunists—realized that whether or not they agreed with his politics, no one knew more about the region than Jim Thompson, and they should seek him out.[39] Still, many of Thompson's Thai friends had been killed, and his niece remembered that he could never again talk of the murdered Thais without tearing up.[40]

Thompson remained intensely bitter that his bosses in Washington had never taken him up on his plan to launch a massive network of agents throughout Thailand and Indochina who would have gathered intelligence and build links to fighters throughout the region. "There is so terribly much ground that could be covered here, and this part of the world appears in a worse and worse mess the more you find out,"

Thompson wrote in one cable. "It seems so damned important that America really understands and really knows what goes on out this way and I am afraid there is lots we are going to miss."[41]

Back in Washington, anticommunist hysteria, heightened by the Soviets' development of the atom bomb and the initial debacle and long stalemate of the Korean War, was leading to widespread purges throughout the federal government. After forcing the State Department to rid itself of anyone who could be accused of being a "loyalty risk," including many employees who had no ties to the Communist Party, Senator Joseph McCarthy moved on to the CIA, which he seemed to believe would bring him even greater publicity if he attacked it.[42]

To avoid a public investigation by the senator, CIA chief Allen Dulles agreed to conduct an internal investigation and to tighten recruiting standards. In effect, Dulles's promise meant the removal of many CIA employees simply for displaying liberal political views and the silencing of freethinking CIA staff, who often developed a knee-jerk anticommunist line in order to avoid any questioning of their political backgrounds.[43]

Americans Thompson once could trust no longer seemed like confidants. "Friendships which used to be so firm exist no longer. . . . I find myself almost on a road by myself as I seem to argue against all sides," Thompson wrote.[44] Alexander MacDonald was on his way out of Thailand, and most of Thompson's old friends at the embassy had moved on to other postings.[45]

"I don't think Jim ever considered, even after all his Thai friends were attacked and killed, that he could be hurt," said one close friend.[46] "He just considered himself untouchable, like no one would ever try to hurt someone who'd been as rich and powerful as him.

"Jim always had a temper, a darker side, he needed people around him all the time, to be social, but other times he could withdraw to the corner of a room and barely speak to anyone. For him, politics was all personal—and he took his friends' demise personally; he never fully trusted anyone again."[47]

But Thompson didn't give up entirely. He had stayed too long in Thailand already, cut too many ties in the United States to go back there, and he needed a plan to survive. Later, Thompson also told his friends that, with the Indochina war starting, he couldn't abandon his Lao, Cambodian, and Vietnamese friends—he needed to find some new way to help them survive.

From his trips to the Northeast, Thompson had realized his natural skill as a designer and had seen that he could combine his talent with a different way to help the locals than just his intelligence work. An acquaintance at the U.S. embassy, James Scott, who worked as the commercial attaché, had suggested that a smart businessman might be able to build an export business with Thai silk.[48]

"Jim didn't want to just give up on his ideals. . . . He thought starting a silk company, if he did it the right way, different than the traditional Thai businesses, could help the people in the Northeast, make them powerful in their own destiny," said one of Thompson's early colleagues.[49] So Jim Thompson decided not to leave Thailand. He would stay and try to make a business out of silk—a business that, ultimately, would only enhance his fame and power. No one was helping the poor, and Thompson could be their benefactor. He eventually let his silk weavers largely control his company, and he used the proceeds from silk to raise the living standards of thousands of Thais; these were strategies that most competing silk companies viewed as insane.[50]

So with around twenty-five thousand dollars in initial capital and a small group of investors, including old friends from the United States and one member of the royal family, Prince Sanidh Rangsit, Thompson launched his company.[51] "Everyone thought Jim owned the silk company, but even in the early days, he only owned something like 25 percent, and then [over time] Jim gave away much of those shares, too," his nephew Henry said.[52]

Thompson found a few weavers—most of whom doubted that a foreigner knew anything about silk—gave them swaths of raw silk and dyes, and began producing small samples of patterned, almost fluorescent-bright cloths.[53] Experienced weavers who had worked in the industry for years warned Thompson not to try, arguing that almost no one had been successful exporting Thai silk.[54] "It would appear that the idea of starting a silk industry had very little to recommend it to a man past his fortieth birthday, who had never worked in the textile business and knew nothing whatever of its production end," wrote Thompson's friend William Warren.[55]

Even as the U.S. government began pouring money and eventually troops into Thailand, the U.S. business community in Bangkok remained relatively small—small enough that most foreign businesspeople knew each other personally. Every morning, foreign businessmen would gather for coffee at a hotel or at one of the few Western restaurants. Bird, Thompson, and MacDonald; the correspondent Jorges Orgibet; and Harold Palmer, who had served in the OSS in Bangkok and now shuttled back and forth from Washington as a lawyer working for the Thai government—they ordered up Western-style coffee, not the sickly sweet Thai iced coffee loaded with condensed milk and sugar.

At night, most of the same crowd would get together again, at one of the new cabarets like the Silver Palm, where you could get a decent steak or a gimlet, all the Mekong whiskey and soda you could drink, and a Thai "girlfriend" at any hour.[56] Willis Bird didn't consider many Americans his close friends, but he rarely skipped a coffee, partly because he didn't want to miss any gossip that could help his business and intelligence operation.[57] "He didn't have a close circle of friends, because he was always on guard. He didn't let many people get close to him," said one intelligence operative who worked with Bird.[58]

Willis Bird's frequent attendance at the coffee shops didn't make him any more loved among the Americans.[59] Bird frequently appeared at the side of General Phao, Phibul's enforcer, a dangerous man reviled by most of the Americans who'd been in Thailand since the war. Bird's shape-shifting infuriated men like Thompson, especially as Bird grew closer and closer to the most powerful and venal Thai generals. When Phao traveled to Switzerland, presumably to stash money in some of his bank accounts, Bird traveled with the general; when Bird hosted other foreigners at his house, Phao invariably made an appearance, though Bird was careful to maintain cordial relations with the other senior military men as well, just in case Phao ever lost power.[60]

When people criticized Phao for his alleged ties to drug dealers or for his foreign slush funds, Bird defended the general with a stony face, insisting that Phao donated his money to charity and that the head policeman would never get into drugs.[61] Bird had even gotten in with the royal family—very difficult for foreigners, who were normally kept out of the incestuous and bewildering royal inner circles. Bird had quietly begun supporting members of the royal family living in exile, paying for the rent on their house in New York and for their other needs.[62]

By 1949, Bill Bird had realized, too, that the intelligence game, the wild politics of Thailand, compelled him far more than any business deal he could make, though he wasn't going to give up his company. "He was very interested in the excitement of Thai politics, of the coups," remembered Bird's daughter.[63] At least, Bird was interested while he was in the center of the action. By the late 1940s, the Thai army, navy, and police generals all competed for the attention of Bird, their key arms supplier and liaison to America's conservative national security establishment; they lavished him with presents and medals, took him on overseas trips, and unlocked the inner circles of elite Thai society for the American.[64] Bird not only had the contacts and the effective secrecy to make an intelligence operation work, he also was extremely skilled with logistics, and he took great pride in overseeing a complex operation like an airlift or an arms deal.

By the early 1950s, Bird had become perhaps the most trusted foreign counselor and mentor to the Thai leadership. Thais "had become almost reverent of Bill Bird . . . of his ability to solve almost any political crisis," said one longtime CIA operative in Thailand.[65]

In late 1949, Bird made his position as the key foreign aide to Thai leaders official, establishing a group called the Narasuan Committee, which included generals like Phao and Sarit Thanarat, a powerful, vain army man with a face powdered white and thick black hair that he tamed with massive amounts of oil, so that every strand could be combed exactly right.

The Narasuan Committee, theoretically formed to develop ways to combat communism, would turn into a kind of shadow government, a place where the most powerful Thais could quietly meet American intelligence operatives and could manage Thailand's—and Southeast Asia's—nasty, messy politics without the scrutiny of the press or voters.[66] Soon the Narasuan Committee would expand, and Bill Bird would not only be managing Thai politics but also helping to plan an entire secret war in Indochina, when the CIA needed a private, plausibly deniable Bangkok intelligence organization to broaden the looming battle.[67]

Jim Thompson and Willis Bird had never been close, but they had respected each other's knowledge, and from the time they arrived in Bangkok, they had shared coffee many mornings and often sought each other out for intelligence and advice. But as Bird drew closer to the ruling junta and Thompson grew increasingly alienated in his adopted land, their interactions became terser, stilted, and more formal. In private, to a few close friends, Jim Thompson admitted that he couldn't understand how Bird could have changed so quickly—though in reality, Bird hadn't really changed who he was at all.

"The pragmatic Bird adapted readily to, and profited from, the new situation [America's support for the military regime]," wrote one analyst of postwar U.S.-Thai relations. Meanwhile, Thompson "proved incapable of blithely casting aside friendships in the changed political currents."[68]

Bill Bird also seemed far more willing to change his views on Thailand's political system. Like Thompson, Bird had been a social democrat in the OSS, but his son, Willis Jr., remembered that his dad "always said democracy was best, but democracy in Thailand could be so open to corruption, it might not work to let everyone in Thailand vote, because you'd just have their votes all bought." Instead, Bird thought it better to have predictability, even if that meant generals who dealt out a mix of predictable economic growth and predictable brutality.[69]

Though he could be a political romantic, Jim Thompson could see where American policy might lead. "I think Jim realized that if we continued pouring in aid to the Thais, building up our presence there, going down this line, eventually we'd be in the war in Vietnam, too," said Denis Horgan, the young aide to General Ed Black who came to know Thompson well in the 1960s.[70]

Bird saw much the same. One intelligence operative who worked closely with Bird for years remembered that he had constantly criticized the prosecution of the Vietnam War and predicted it would ultimately end in defeat. "But Bird would say that as long as we're having this war, he should be involved."[71]

In private, Thompson began to disdain Bill Bird, calling him a traitor to old OSS friends, even a murderer for helping the Thai generals track down Pridi's old allies. Thompson vowed never to help Bird out again, and he warned his friends not to get involved with any of Bird's arms deals.

9

In 1949, Senator Joseph McCarthy shocked the State Department and the CIA into massive internal purges, starting an anticommunist fervor that spread throughout the federal government and into realms of everyday American life. Hollywood stars, artists, low-level political aides, and anyone else could be called to Congress to prove their loyalty or could have the FBI poring through their whole lives. Congressional hawks called on the Truman and then the Eisenhower administration to take any action, to do anything, to prevent another defeat to communism like the loss of China.

American fear made it easy to justify increased spending in Asia, especially after the communist government in Beijing, high on its new power, created the Thai Autonomous People's Government, a communist-supported Thai exile regime in southwestern China, a move viewed by Washington as a Chinese decision to establish a potential base for guerrilla operations in Southeast Asia.[1] In 1949, Secretary of State Dean Acheson called on the House of Representatives to authorize an open-ended new disbursement for fighting communism in Asia, starting at seventy-five million dollars annually and forming part of a much larger fund of aid, worth over a billion dollars, to be earmarked for the Cold War in Asia.[2]

Faced with the lesser of two evils, the United States, as it often would, picked conservative autocrats over communists. As America's financial commitments in Asia grew in the early 1950s, the Thai generals were only too happy to play along with Washington.[3]

Even in the late 1940s, after Phibul returned to power, Bangkok had retained relations, formal or informal, with communist countries like China, but now, with Eisenhower in office, the Thai leadership joined the United States in declaring Beijing an outright enemy. Thailand sent troops to fight with the multinational forces arrayed against China in the Korean War, and in 1954 the Thais joined the first formal anticommunist arrangement devised in Asia, the Southeast Asia Treaty Organization, or SEATO, which joined the United States, Thailand, the Philippines, Australia, and other countries in a regional alliance, committing the United States to come to Thailand's defense if the kingdom was attacked. American military assistance to Thailand mushroomed, from four and a half million dollars in 1951 to fifty-six million dollars in 1953, and with this aid the first large contingents of American military advisers began to arrive, setting the stage for a buildup that eventually would make much of northeastern Thailand a de facto U.S. military base.[4]

The CIA's presence in Thailand was increasing as well, with as many as two hundred covert operatives arriving. American economic aid flowed into the country, too, to build new roads, schools, agricultural projects, ports, and airstrips and to pay for thousands of Thai students, teachers, and businesspeople to come to the United States for university or short training courses. Thai businesspeople looked for American partners for their companies, convinced that American expertise and products were superior to the British and European products that had been popular in Thailand before the Second World War.

In the scramble for U.S. aid, police general Phao usually won out. "Despite Phao's repellent political activities, the Americans, like the British, developed a deep respect for him and the police," wrote Daniel Fineman in a comprehensive study of post–World War II

U.S.-Thai relations. "[American] military advisers considered the [Thai] police the most competent force in the country. . . . Phao's leadership was forceful and his drive undeniable."[5] One longtime CIA contractor in Bangkok put it more bluntly. "Phao," he said, "could get shit done."[6]

Phao's rivals within the Thai government, General Sarit Thanarat and Phibul, were far less comfortable dealing with Americans. Sarit in particular seemed to loathe the United States and the CIA, which had built Phao's police into a potent force equal to his army.[7] Even without direct American assistance, Phao could manipulate events to ensure that his Thai rivals suffered. And Washington's actions, if not designed to favor him, wound up doing so, since the U.S. decision to supply the Thai police with as much weaponry and money as the army—a highly unusual decision, given that the army normally does most of the fighting—suggested that Phao enjoyed strong backing from the White House.

Like the old absolute monarchs, the generals took whatever they wanted from Thailand, considering it the prerogative of their rule. They got a cut from all big business in the kingdom. Gem mining, logging, construction, ports—every large Thai business owner knew that he had to deliver some percentage of the profits to the army and to make sure that if a top military man wanted to get his friends or relatives into that industry, the owner found him a seat on the board or an easy job. Generals commandeered Thai women, wrote two historians, "as kings once had, with a special interest in beauty queens."[8] Phao, Jim Thompson told his friends, was constantly roaming Bangkok in a rage, with anyone who doubted him turned into a police suspect.

Phao himself took personal control of the highly lucrative opium industry, which flourished in the lawless area of Laos, Thailand, and Burma known as the Golden Triangle, where small bands of former Chinese Nationalist soldiers fled after Mao's communists had won the civil war. After fleeing China, the Nationalists maintained their contacts with intelligence operatives in the United States and with the Thai military and police, and from their base in the Golden Triangle the Nationalists settled into a comfortable life as drug barons.

With close links to the Nationalists, links facilitated by his friend Willis Bird, Phao could use bands of police—who, after all, could easily avoid police surveillance—to smuggle opium down from the Triangle to police-controlled warehouses in the northern Thai city of Chiang Mai. From there, the police would stack the opium on private police airplanes to fly it to Bangkok, where it could be loaded onto ships bound for Hong Kong or made into heroin.[9] Within a few years, Phao's police gangs had established themselves as the most powerful opium syndicate in the country.

Jim Thompson never warmed to Thailand's autocrats as his official counterparts had, and he had kept his close personal links to old resistance fighters in Vietnam, Laos, and Cambodia—men who, by the late 1940s and the early 1950s, were considered sworn enemies of the United States. To build up their forces for the fight against the Dutch and the French, the Lao, Cambodian, Indonesian, and Vietnamese rebels needed modern weapons, and more of them; they had the numbers and the morale to overwhelm the French and the Dutch (and later, for the Vietnamese, the Americans), but they lacked real firepower.

Firepower, in fact, was almost all that was keeping French and Dutch hopes in the region alive; when the Vietnamese finally smuggled heavy guns into an area surrounding the French fortress at Dien Bien Phu, they destroyed the beleaguered French garrison there.

Bangkok had for years been these insurgents' arms depot. The Japanese had left behind vast stocks of guns, ammunition, and even artillery after their defeat, and during World War II, the OSS had smuggled plenty of modern, American-made weaponry into Thailand as well, enough to equip at least a hundred thousand men.[10] Some of those arms had been seized by the Thai military and police, but other caches of weapons lay untouched in safe houses, swamps, and offices that the Japanese and the OSS had used during the war. One study estimated that a number of secret supply missions by the Allies during World War II dropped several hundred tons of weapons into Thailand, some of which were the most modern models of infantry weapons available at the time. After the war, the Thai generals were happy, for the right price, to sell surplus submachine guns, grenades, howitzers, and ammunition even to communists they had formally sided against.

Rampant corruption and the generally lax Thai police force made gunrunning out of Thailand even easier. "Buying arms in Thailand was as easy as buying beer," said one Vietnamese militant who operated in Thailand, in an interview with a Vietnam scholar.[11] Indeed, Bangkok, with its modern banking system and excellent transport links, became the arms and financing hub not just for the Vietnamese but also for Lao, Cambodian, and Indonesian fighters, who could open up local propaganda offices in the Thai capital as long as they cultivated the right police and army generals in Bangkok.

Still, the resistance fighters couldn't just rely on their Thai contacts—politics in Thailand shifted too easily, and friendly police and generals could easily be gone the next day. Eventually, as the United States and local conservative Thai leaders became more powerful, even the venal Thai generals would close down the local offices of groups like Ho Chi Minh's Viet Minh.

So, according to several sources, some of the Southeast Asian fighters depended on Jim Thompson. Thompson, with his knowledge of arms stocks and his contacts among the Thai leadership, could arrange arms deals for insurgents more easily than any Thai broker. Because of his old OSS ties, Thompson knew where the United States had left arms caches in Southeast Asia after World War II, and he and other former OSS men, who enjoyed the immunity of working for the new world power, supposedly could get these weapons without having to wade through a thicket of Thai police and other officials asking for bribes.[12]

Thompson had already suggested, several times, to his bosses in the OSS that he should create a new U.S. intelligence office in Bangkok, headed up by Thompson and presumably more sympathetic to Southeast Asian nationalists than the men Thompson now saw coming in to Bangkok from the State Department and the army.[13] His superiors clearly did not warm to the idea, and instead Thompson spent much of his later time in the OSS dealing with bureaucratic cables.

But if he could not convince Washington to make him the local intelligence chief, he could wield power in other ways. When one prominent Lao resistance leader, Thao Oun Saninikone, came to Bangkok, he'd meet repeatedly with Thompson, according to Thao Oun's personal journal, and Thompson would introduce Thao Oun to sympathetic Western journalists and diplomats and several French and Thai intelligence agents. Thompson himself clearly and openly sympathized with Thao Oun: he stayed with Thao Oun when he traveled outside Bangkok and carefully reviewed Thao Oun's plans for his movement. When some of Thao Oun's allies were jailed in Thailand and threatened with deportation, Thompson was furious and tried to use his connections to free them.

Thompson even told Thao Oun that American officials in Thailand were trying to convince Washington to support the Indochinese resistance fighters. At one point, Thompson seems to have convinced Thao Oun—and perhaps himself—that the U.S. ambassador in Thailand was pushing Washington to intervene in Indochina on the side of the nationalist movements. This was a major exaggeration, if not an outright falsehood, since relatively soon after World War II, rebels like Thao Oun were being shunned by senior American officials.

But Thompson was not being deceptive; he seemed to honestly believe that Washington would ultimately ally itself with these nationalists, these men like Thao Oun, whom he saw as indigenous democrats. (Later, when Thao Oun and other rebels had been forced on the run by the French and rightist local forces, many would find jobs as weavers and growers for Thompson's silk company.) "They [the French] are desperate at this point in Indochina as they know they can't possibly hold on," Thompson wrote to his sister Elinor.[14] He was right, but he did not imagine that once the French left, the United States would essentially take its place fighting the Vietnamese nationalists.

As Washington increasingly allied itself with the French forces in Southeast Asia, hoping to stop any communist advance, the U.S. government became so concerned about rebel weapon stockpiles that as early as 1950 it launched a secret investigation, spearheaded by the embassies in Bangkok and Saigon and working with French diplomats, into the alleged arms smuggling of Thompson and several other former OSS men. The joint investigation found Thompson, as well as two American colleagues in Bangkok, suspected of being involved in trafficking that could have included a wide range of smuggling to the Viet Minh forces, as well as arms trafficking to Indonesian republicans battling the Dutch, who like the French were trying to reclaim their pre–World War II colonies in Asia.[15] (Later, in the 1950s, after Indonesia had thrown out the Dutch, the CIA would arm Indonesian separatists trying to overthrow the left-leaning government in Jakarta.)

Thompson "abetted the release and concealment of parachute-delivered American weapons (a stockpile for his future trafficking) instead of gathering them for allied forces' use [at the end of World War II], or to hand over to the Thai government," the investigation stated. Thompson was in constant contact with a range of different guerrilla fighters, whom he met just after World War II, and he had "close and mutually beneficial relationships with the leaders of the Viet Minh, Khmer Issara, and Lao Issara," the main Southeast Asian fighters, the investigation concluded.[16]

U.S. intelligence had been watching Thompson since the end of World War II, in fact. Shortly after the peace with Japan, the OSS launched its own secret internal investigation into allegations that Thompson had been freelancing wildly, developing plans to mount an intelligence operation to support the Vietnamese fighters, without gaining Washington's approval.[17] Thompson had given a colleague "his plan for Annamese [Vietnamese] operations," the investigation believed; he was making his own intelligence plans and then allegedly leaking the information about ultrasecret operation plans to friends, another prohibited activity.[18] If this is true, wrote Thompson's bosses, "when he reaches Washington, consider that he should be regarded as insecure"—a security risk.[19]

Thompson was put on leave while the OSS investigated his behavior, and even though the organization ultimately officially cleared him, it also concluded that it had not been able to get enough information about the Thompson affair to make a very informed decision. Many in the OSS remained suspicious that he was pursuing his own policies, especially when it came to helping the Vietnamese.

Indeed, another study of the Vietnamese fighters and their contacts in Bangkok revealed that Thompson had been the primary conduit in Thailand for information flowing to and from the Vietnamese nationalists, and that when one of the Indonesian leaders traveled to Bangkok in the late 1940s, he set up a clandestine arms-buying operation there and met with Thompson and another well-known American agent operating in the Thai capital.

One of Thompson's former OSS colleagues, a man named John Wester, who also allegedly had been involved in this arms trafficking, would be arrested by authorities in Singapore for weapons smuggling; the investigation had concluded that Wester was "in charge of a large-scale black market weapons operation."[20] Another investigation found that two other Americans were running an arms-trafficking syndicate, moving arms from the Philippines into Thailand and other parts of mainland Southeast Asia. But the U.S. and French governments took no direct action against Thompson at the time, in part perhaps because he still also served as a valuable resource to American intelligence.

While Jim Thompson was suspected of helping to traffic arms to independence fighters throughout the region, Willis Bird was not under suspicion; he openly admitted to friends and associates that he was helping to move arms throughout Southeast Asia. The difference was, Bird was aiding the new allies of the U.S. government—and, of course, making plenty of money off the deals himself.

In 1951, Bird had taken over as general agent for the Sea (for Southeast Asia) Supply Company, a Bangkok-based front organization for the CIA. Sea Supply was theoretically incorporated in Florida but actually operated primarily out of an office in the center of the Thai capital, at the Bangkok Sports Club, the main social hangout for foreigners. Its location was hardly a secret, and nearly everyone seemed to know who worked for Sea Supply.[21]

"Bird thought rules and theories were just bureaucracy—I think he believed democracy was a good idea for Thailand, in theory, but for now, he needed to get the job done, and it was easiest to avoid the rules and deal directly with the generals," said one of Bird's old colleagues.[22] Though Phao supposedly managed the police, Sea Supply equipped his men with tanks, speedboats, bazookas, planes, and mechanized artillery, which hardly seemed necessary for policing; the average Thai beat cop got almost nothing.[23]

By the early 1950s, Sea Supply began arranging for American advisers to train Thailand's border police, a paramilitary group also under Phao's command, who could patrol the frontier with Laos and still allow the Thai government to claim that it had not deployed troops to the border, since these men were still technically police. Yet the border police learned about guerrilla warfare, airborne landings, and other tactics of war; in reality, they became like another army unit. Through Sea Supply, the CIA gave the border police thirty-five million dollars and eventually built an even more powerful force, an elite group of border police that would later be inserted directly into the secret war in Laos.[24] Some Thai historians claimed that Sea Supply had helped Phao sneak gold bullion into the country and then divvy it up and distribute it to Phao's favored police officers, whom he called his *asawin*, or knights.

Of course, as Sea Supply delivered on its contracts, Bird, its general agent, made a profit off of each deal.

Bird's old friend from his OSS days in China, General Claire Chennault, had more ambitious plans. A ferocious, perpetually scowling aviator from rural Louisiana with a pug nose, leathery skin, a jutting jaw, and half-deaf ears from years of sitting near plane engines, Chennault had been one of the first U.S. Army leaders to understand the importance of air power, well before the Second World War.[25] Chennault had fought with Chiang Kai-shek in China during World War II, leading the Flying Tigers, a motley group of volunteer U.S. Army pilots whose planes, decorated with the leering, bloody faces of tiger sharks, had supported and often rescued Chiang's beleaguered forces. Chennault's men had proven a decisive force: they'd destroyed over two thousand Japanese aircraft.

The Flying Tigers' general had also decisively proved himself an acquired taste. During the war, Chennault had squabbled incessantly with the American commander in China, "Vinegar" Joe Stilwell, another man with strong ideas about how to conduct a war and with precious few social skills. A traditional infantry commander, suspicious of the utility of air power, Stilwell had grown so angry with Chennault and his airmen that after Stilwell and his ground forces were badly defeated by the Japanese in Burma, Stilwell refused to be airlifted out to safety, instead hacking through the Burmese jungle for weeks until he reached the safety of India, exhausted, frail, and ill.[26]

After the war, Chennault, an ardent anticommunist, naturally wanted to use his aviation experience and contacts in China while also doing anything he could to stop the communist advance in a country he now knew well.[27] His army depleted from fighting the Japanese, Chiang quickly lost ground to Mao after the end of World War II, and in 1946, Chennault's political and business ambitions came together. Chennault and his business partner, Whiting Willauer, had bought several airplanes to set up a private airline, Civil Air Transport (CAT). Given Chennault's contacts, it was soon getting work ferrying supplies to Chiang's forces and setting up nascent commercial aviation in China, sometimes carrying pigs and goats alongside people in the passenger compartment.[28] While launching CAT, Chennault played the Washington game. He pushed the Truman administration, which was quietly concluding that Chiang's corrupt regime was a lost cause, to increase its commitment to China—a commitment that, of course, would benefit CAT's business. Chennault toured the United States, warning that any loss to communism would trigger a run of "dominoes"—countries falling one by one to communist forces—and touting a plan in which Washington would pour aid into the Nationalist forces, allowing them to retreat to the rough desert regions of central and western China, where the Chinese communist forces could not reach them and Chiang could regroup for a battle to retake the country. The State Department dismissed the Chennault plan, but its core idea of resisting a string of dominoes falling to communism gained a ready audience in the CIA, which would prove critical to the airline's survival.

The domino theory would ultimately become a central motif of the U.S. war in Indochina. By 1954, Eisenhower himself had embraced the domino concept, saying in a news conference that year, "You have a row of dominoes set up, you knock over the first one, and what will happen to the last one is the certainty that it will go over very quickly." Eisenhower continued to emphasize the domino theory to justify American intervention in Indochina, and the Kennedy administration picked up the thread, with the president again arguing that Washington had to support South Vietnam because if its government fell, other nations in Southeast Asia would topple to communism.[29]

Even without the approval of the U.S. government, CAT began not only ferrying nonmilitary supplies to Chiang's forces but also, increasingly, bringing them ammunition, making CAT a player in the Chinese civil war—and leading the State Department to threaten to seize the passports of CAT's pilots.[30] But by 1949, Chiang was fleeing for Taiwan, the communists were overrunning China, and Chennault's business plan suddenly seemed less promising.

By early 1950, with debts mounting, Chennault's airline faced bankruptcy and appeared close to shutting down altogether; some weeks, the airline could not even pay its employees.[31] CAT did help to supply the new national airline of Taiwan, and it approached South Korean leader Syngman Rhee, another staunch anticommunist, to offer its services for airlifting arms to his forces.[32] But these contracts could not keep Chennault's venture alive: it needed a larger, stable pool of revenue if it was going to survive.

In Southeast Asia, Chennault saw far greater opportunity— wars that were winding up, not down, few established local competitors, and a rapidly growing CIA budget dedicated to the region. Chennault, at least, still harbored ambitions of using CAT to roll back communism across Asia and eventually to retake China from Mao's forces by invading the People's Republic from Korea and Burma.

Bird, remembered his son Willis Bird Jr., had less grand plans. "He [Bird] didn't support the communists, but he was realistic," said his son. "He'd known Mao, he understood Mao's power, he didn't think they were going to retake China. . . . But he figured, this region was as good a place as any to have a war, so why not be involved?"[33]

Still, by the early 1950s, Chennault had recruited Bird, who considered the general one of his greatest heroes—Bird, who normally showed little emotion, would tell friends he "loved" Chennault—and together CAT and Sea Supply would dominate clandestine aviation in

Southeast Asia. In 1950, Chennault had convinced the CIA to purchase CAT, ending any financial risks for him and his partners; with the CIA backing, Bird saw that clandestine air transport in a region where war was coming could bring enormous profit. "My father always calculated every business opportunity," said Bird's son, "and this [aviation in Southeast Asia] was another one, the best one."[34]

In 1951, CAT pilots, working with Sea Supply in Bangkok, began delivering arms to Chennault's old allies, the Nationalist troops of Chiang Kai-shek. Only this group of Nationalists wasn't in China anymore: instead of fleeing to Taiwan after the communists won in 1949, they had marched into northeastern Burma, where they had set themselves up as local warlords, living in a series of fortified complexes.[35] To entice the CIA, the Nationalists in Burma would tout their anticommunist credentials and occasionally plan an ambitious, and unlikely, attack on China itself—theoretically to help oust the communists, though in reality these Nationalist fighters, like Chiang on Taiwan, had no interest in waging real war again.

When some Nationalist soldiers did attempt to invade southwestern China in 1951, they were quickly turned back by the communist forces after only sixty miles, and their attack alienated the Burmese government, which was furious that Washington would support an army operating on Burmese territory. The CIA, with Thai support, had backed the plan for the Nationalists to invade China, and observers in Burma had seen Western advisers arriving to assist the Nationalist forces, run by a general named Li Mi.[36] Still, after the invasion proved a failure, the agency denied involvement, blaming it solely on private American citizens like Bird.[37]

The Burma airlifts would prove a model for CAT's operations in the future. Using a theoretically private airline provided the CIA with deniability if operations went wrong or intruded onto supposedly neutral territory, but the pilots, agents, and soldiers provided by Bird and Chennault were as good as, if not better than, the CIA's own men, and Bird and Chennault boasted stronger connections among Asian leaders than most CIA operatives had.

"CAT and Sea Supply would be like the perfect operations for my father," said Willis Bird Jr. "He worked with the CIA, but he'd never have joined the CIA. He had total disdain for them, thought they were a bunch of amateurs in the way they handled their operations. This way he could just take their funds and do the job himself, and he could get the job done right."[38]

Bird had become known for his covert work, so he necessarily relied on the agency for jobs. "Bird might not have been a professional CIA person, but everyone [in Bangkok] identified him with CIA, with covert operations, even if CIA would deny it," said William vanden Heuvel, who served in the Bangkok embassy in the early 1950s.[39] Bird never tried to draw attention to himself—he didn't have the innate charisma of someone like Jim Thompson—but, remembered an old friend, Bird's quiet style was in a way more effective when he disagreed with the agency or his Thai contacts. "Bird was quiet but definitive— he'd say this is the right way and this is the wrong way—this is the way it should be done, and this is the way it's not done," the friend recalled. "That lack of self-doubt can be powerful."[40]

CAT would prove extraordinarily influential, able to find a role in—and make some money from—nearly every crisis in Asia during the height of the Cold War. To make Southeast Asia the major front in the Cold War, the CIA would need this kind of private airline, a shuttle service that could be trusted, quiet, and skillful, that could operate on short notice, and that could fly into war zones or areas with minimal U.S. government presence. With men drawn from Chennault and Bird's roster of old wartime buddies, CAT could provide just those types of pilots.

CAT would, in many ways, provide a template for the future of CIA operations. With the fear of Soviet power rising—in the wake of the Sputnik launch, the Soviet test of an atomic bomb, and the Soviet domination of Eastern Europe—Washington advisers who advocated caution in fighting back against Moscow, men like George Kennan who did not see the Soviets as trying to remake the world, were being silenced or simply pushed out of their jobs.

And with the type of latitude from Washington that would be impossible today, in an era of instant news and aggressive partisan congressional investigations, the agency—and, especially, its station chiefs on the ground in key cities—could operate its own little fiefdoms in many of the hot zones of the Cold War. Aggressive American covert intervention throughout the Third World was becoming the norm, on a scale unthinkable before the Second World War, when the United States had virtually no foreign intelligence capacity.

The CIA's expansion and global reach would be pushed even harder by Allen Dulles, who served as CIA director under Eisenhower. American agents would help to change regimes in Guatemala, Iran, Chile, and Congo; they would finance and support regional rebellions against the left-leaning Indonesian president Sukarno and against Chairman Mao; they would meddle in elections everywhere from Vietnam to Italy and Greece.

But even if the agency under Dulles could operate largely unexamined by the public and the press, and its new covert action wing had nearly limitless resources being poured in, its station chiefs did not necessarily want to commit themselves, long-term, to some of these leaders they'd created or sometimes plucked from nearly total obscurity. If the agency could help to make these leaders, who knew how long someone like Phao or his rivals would last in power? They certainly did not rule by democratic elections and the popular will, so if their tenuous grip on power—kept through their guns and the agency's money—slipped even a bit, men like Phao did not have much net below them.

So, working through front operations was a must, but too often, in the early days of the OSS and the CIA, these front groups, formed under a new covert action wing in 1948, had been amateurish and unprofessional, a loose combination of CIA men and random freelance "assets," who often turned out not to be assets at all. Even though the agency would, in later years, acquire a reputation for omnipotence and power, earlier on it more often became known for bungling jobs: operations in the European theater of war ate up resources and left the OSS men holding files of useless information, or local officials bought up in southern Europe simply vanished with the American money. Even by the early 1950s, with the agency full of more experienced men and women, operations failed far too often for Dulles's comfort.

• • •

Though the army had defeated Pridi's attempted coup in 1949, the navy still harbored enormous resentment toward the army generals, and in June 1951 they struck. A group of navy and marine officers attempted again to oust the generals in charge of Thailand: Phibul, Sarit, and Phao. As American officials handed over a ship named the *Manhattan* to Phibul as a gift from the United States, watched by monks in yellow robes and diplomats dressed in tuxedos and long gowns, a band of Thai marines boarded the gangplank of the boat, which was docked near the Grand Palace.[41]

Phibul had been standing alongside the U.S. ambassador, who'd been about to formally present him with the ship. The rebels seized Phibul at gunpoint while apologizing to the diplomat guests for ruining their party.[42] Grabbing the Thai leader by the arm, the marines hustled Phibul onto a waiting and heavily armed navy battleship, the *Sri Ayutthaya*, while shooting across the decks of the *Manhattan*, forcing women in high heels and men in white tuxedos to dive for the decks and hustle into the ship's hold as machine-gun fire thudded into the ship's masts.

Inside the *Sri Ayutthaya*, the rebels locked Phibul inside a cabin. Meanwhile, in other parts of the city, groups of junior naval officers launched coordinated attacks. One contingent of navy and marine officers seized a prominent radio station, while another group of junior officers took over the navy's fleet headquarters, potentially putting a sizable array of warcraft at their disposal. Other navy men attacked fuel depots, power stations, and other critical infrastructure, throwing the city into a terrified darkness as Bangkok residents, who'd grown blasé about coup rumors, now boarded up their stores and retreated into locked compounds, with some businessmen patrolling their neighborhoods with their own weapons. Attacks on fuel depots sparked explosions that boomed overnight and fires that spread through slum areas, where there were few fire departments and many houses made of cheap, easily flammable materials.

The navy lost again. The junior officers who launched the coup had counted on the help of the navy's senior leaders (who had not been in on the coup planning) and on overwhelming the army and police forces in Bangkok before they had time to respond. But it was a mistaken assumption by a group of men who'd planned too quickly and haphazardly for an attempt to overthrow a government. The rebels had failed to arrest most of the senior Thai army and police generals other than Phibul. The navy's most senior officers, probably realizing that the *Manhattan* rebellion was destined to fail, did not join the coup, and rather than ceding ground to the rebels, the army and police, who had sizable forces stationed in the capital for just such a possibility, fought back fiercely.

Along with the army, Phao's police played a critical role in suppressing the *Manhattan* rebellion. Police units deployed alongside the army on street corners and major intersections and stormed into naval bases across Bangkok, launching intense block-by-block fighting, with some areas changing hands four or five times the first evening of the rebellion. The policemen and army soldiers had license to act ruthlessly, and they took that license eagerly. They made little effort to distinguish between civilians and combatants, firing wildly into buildings and homes where naval officers supposedly were hiding out, and often massacring innocent bystanders in the process.

Adding to the government's no-holds-barred counterattack, the generals authorized the air force to essentially carpet bomb parts of the city. Air force bombers dropped payloads on navy ships docked near Bangkok and even bombed the ship holding Phibul, the *Sri Ayutthaya*, a gamble that worked. As the navy vessel listed and burned, Phibul escaped his cabin and his captors, jumped overboard, and swam to shore, into the hands of loyal forces, as the battleship sank in the river. The bombing shot flames above the temples and monasteries of the city skyline and added to fires burning out of control.

With the Thai air force controlling the skies over Bangkok, by the second day of the rebellion the government had regained control and taken the offensive against the navy rebels, and many of the coup plotters had begun planning their escapes from Thailand. A brutal mopping up began. Army and police troops charged up Ploenchit Road and other arteries, bayonets fixed, to shoot and stab groups of navy soldiers—and many civilians—to death. In other parts of the city, the army and police rolled out mobile artillery and took turns shelling and gutting office buildings, military encampments, and even schools in an attempt to totally shatter the navy.

Within two days, the police had forced most of the navy men to surrender. As police and army troops hunted them across Bangkok, some naval officers hastily changed out of their uniforms to avoid being shot on sight by roving policemen. By the end of the third day, the rebellion had fizzled out altogether, and police and army troops hastily gathered bodies from the streets and burned some of them before a real death count could be established. Still, historians later estimated that as many as twelve hundred Thais had died in the fighting, most of them civilians, and another eighteen hundred or so had been wounded.

Phibul had survived the *Manhattan* rebellion, just as he had survived previous coups and alleged attempts to poison him, but the rebellion had strengthened Phao and weakened Phibul, who, locked in the ship cabin, had played little role in suppressing the navy and would now find himself almost powerless on the Thai political scene. After the failed coup, most Thais realized Phao had become the most powerful man in the country. Phao received a promotion, giving him even more power, and with Phao's backing, Thailand started creating institutions that mirrored America's: an anticommunist law like the U.S. loyalty oath, and red-hunting teams just like the ones at the FBI.

Under Phao, Thailand's leadership became even more brutal, even further from the ideals of men like Pridi whom Jim Thompson had idealized. Phao's police widened their targets beyond the opposition politicians they'd once attacked, arresting writers, peace activists who protested America's nuclear weapons arsenal, newspaper editors, even bookstore owners, all marked as communists. The police allegedly specialized in particularly brutal slayings designed to instill fear in other dissidents: in 1954, a member of parliament opposed to the government was strangled, his body dumped in the Chao Praya River; in 1953, a left-leaning journalist was gunned down on his honeymoon. As Thai historians Chris Baker and Pasuk Phongpaichit had noted, the police developed a motto that encapsulated Phao's approach to dissent and his willingness to take any measure he deemed necessary: "There is nothing under the sun the Thai police cannot do."[43]

10

When Willis Bird's old mentor from the OSS, "Wild Bill" Donovan, took over as U.S. ambassador to Thailand in 1953, Donovan quickly made clear that he had no interest in working through official embassy channels. Instead, Donovan would report directly to President Eisenhower. In the region, he would rely on his own contacts, setting the foundation for an entire American policy-making apparatus in Southeast Asia that existed separately from the embassies.

Donovan pushed the Thai government to create a psychological warfare organization designed to oversee an anticommunist, pro-America propaganda campaign in Thai newspapers, universities, and cultural organizations—a campaign that then could be expanded into other parts of Asia.

"Donovan came in with his own men and he clearly was relying more on the CIA station than on the State Department itself," said Kempton Jenkins, who served in the U.S. embassy in Bangkok. "Donovan was running his own operation, all over Southeast Asia, setting up his own meetings with leaders, bringing the news right back directly to Eisenhower."[1]

Indeed, rather than making requests through normal diplomatic channels, Donovan traveled from Bangkok through Southeast Asia to assess the state of American intelligence in the region, the same way he had journeyed through Europe and Africa before World War II and used that trip as the foundation for his wartime intelligence operation. This time, he used his time in Saigon, Bangkok, Singapore, and other capitals to make the case that the United States needed in Southeast Asia the kind of comprehensive and aggressive intelligence operation it was building in Western Europe, which had previously been a much higher priority.

This enlarged, separate intelligence operation would initially rely on Donovan's allies. "Bird already had a history of [covert] operations and Donovan trusted him," said William vanden Heuvel, Donovan's aide. "Bird and General Phao were the first people who met us at the airport and it was clear from the beginning that Donovan's close relationship was going to be with them."[2]

By the mid-1950s, Bird and his Thai allies could see clearly that Laos would prove to be an opportunity on all fronts: political, military, and business. Civil Air Transport had already obtained a few jobs in Laos; it ferried military supplies to French forces in the early 1950s before they pulled out from Indochina upon their disastrous defeat at the northwestern Vietnamese outpost of Dien Bien Phu in 1954. At Dien Bien Phu, Chennault's pilots had flown through heavy Vietnamese antiaircraft fire, which shredded their fuselages and wings and killed one of Chennault's top captains, to drop artillery pieces, guns, and ammunition to the surrounded French garrison.[3] But facing an overwhelming Vietnamese force, the French ultimately had to surrender.[4]

Tiny Laos had the unfortunate distinction of offering strategic benefits to all of its neighbors. For the Thai leaders, Laos was a vital buffer state, a piece of land separating Thailand from the Vietnamese communists. For the North Vietnamese, Laos would become a vital backyard, a land where they could smuggle supplies along what would become known as the Ho Chi Minh Trail, send raw troops to gain experience, and hone their revolutionary rhetoric. Even for Washington, Laos served as a buffer, and for the CIA it was a kind of testing ground, a place where the agency could learn to run a kind of proxy war that it would use in the future in many other countries, including Afghanistan in the 1980s and again in the early 2000s.

Even as he recognized the value of Laos, Bill Bird also understood the need to make himself critical to the expanding CIA mission there, despite his antipathy for CIA operatives. Bird initially had tied his power in Thailand to Phao, who had played upon his CIA backing to solidify his own position among the Thai generals. But by the mid-1950s, just as Phao seemed to have consolidated his control of the Thai junta, the police general, normally possessed of the near-perfect political instincts necessary to survive in Thailand's ruthless military culture, made a series of mistakes that cost him.

All the top generals were corrupt, but Phao had too publicly flaunted his wealth, grabbing control of industries ranging from opium to gold, taking seats on the boards of most major Thai companies, and allegedly shuttling the profits to private banks in Switzerland. Phao had tied himself so closely to his American backers that as anti-American sentiment grew among Thai intellectuals and officials furious that a country that had never been colonized suddenly seemed to be turning into a puppet, his rivals were able to use those U.S. ties against Phao. Newspapers heaped on anti-American vitriol, and the State Department, which had never preferred Phao as the CIA had, quietly moved to strengthen his rivals.[5] In the summer of 1955, Phao approached the U.S. embassy to suggest that the Americans tacitly allow him to eliminate his rivals; the ambassador, worried about more fighting in the streets of Bangkok, refused.[6]

In the summer of 1957, a mob, probably whipped up by Sarit himself, marched to Sarit's house and demanded he get rid of Phao. To cheers, he promised to do so; soon Sarit's army units rolled out into the capital, and Phao fled to Switzerland. Eager to finish off Phao's allies, a crowd of Thais then marched to the Bangkok office of Sea Supply, its location an open secret. Inside and on the roof of the building, CIA agents were frantically burning documents, and when the mob arrived at the offices, the CIA station chief, a man named John Hart, stood, virtually alone, in its path. The crowd backed down; Thailand's soldiers, some of whom had accompanied the protesters to the CIA station, still badly needed the agency.[7]

Despite Phao's reputation for simple, single-minded ruthlessness—one historian said that "everything he [Phao] deemed communist he detested and everything he detested was labeled communist"[8]—Sarit, who had used his support for "democracy" as a weapon against Phao, didn't prove any more tolerant. After taking sole control of the government, Sarit banned all political parties, set aside the constitution, and authorized mass arrests and even summary executions of writers, editors, and other activists suspected of communist sympathies.

Overall, in the late 1950s and early 1960s, Sarit presided over what was probably the most repressive regime in Thai history, a contested title given Phibul's pseudofascist World War II government and then the harsh suppression of opposition politics in the late 1940s and early 1950s. Still, even Sarit's excesses did not dissuade U.S. support for the Thai government: Secretary of State John Foster Dulles sent Sarit a secret cable thanking him for his continued support for the United States and the West and making no mention of Sarit's vicious actions against opponents.

Yet as Phao's rise suddenly halted, Willis Bird, his closest and most fervent American supporter, remained untouched, still living and operating in Thailand. "When Phao fled, most of his allies fled too, or some were tracked down and killed," said one longtime associate of Bird's. "But nothing happened to Bird. . . . He might not have been as close to Sarit, but after Phao was gone, Sarit and Bird still worked together. Bird advised Sarit."[9]

The other Thai generals weren't stupid. Through Willis Bird, Phao had gained a close connection to the CIA and a lifeline of money and weapons—Phao had secretly traveled to New York, home of the CIA's purchasing operations, and in 1954 had made a public visit to the United States, where he was praised lavishly in Congress—and with Phao gone, Sarit wanted the same access to the Americans.[10] Sarit knew, too, that unlike Phao, whose bluntness and charm had pleased his American backers, Sarit's stern manner and alcoholism—he'd routinely appear drunk at diplomatic events—made him an unloved man among most American officials.

Unlike Jim Thompson, who had increasingly become a nuisance if not an outright danger to the Thais and their American allies, Bill Bird had proved himself invaluable, even invulnerable, despite some U.S. embassy officials' hopes to get rid of him and his seemingly uncontrollable operations. While Bird had built up the Narasuan Committee in Bangkok, a group of his friends in Washington, including the former ambassador to Thailand, "Wild Bill" Donovan, had been creating a Thailand lobby in the American capital, modeled on the powerful China lobby that backed Chiang Kai-shek. Through public editorializing and private arm-twisting on Capitol Hill, Donovan, who was paid roughly a hundred thousand dollars annually by the Thai government for his lobbying services, made sure that senators and representatives knew Thailand, came to Thailand, and realized that Thailand now was central to U.S. foreign policy.[11]

Donovan also made sure to calm American politicians' nagging concerns about Thailand. There was corruption in Thailand, Donovan admitted in one article, but it was the legacy of the World War II Japanese occupation, and the Thai government was "taking firm measures to stamp it out." Thailand wasn't a democracy, but its leaders allowed open criticism in the press, and the country "is not a police state."[12] Both of these claims were blatantly untrue—the government of Phao and the other generals was looting the state as rapidly as it could get away with, and under Phao the police routinely arrested, tortured, and sometimes executed dissidents—but to an audience in Washington that knew far less about Thailand than, say, China or Japan, Donovan's words were comforting.

In Bangkok, Thais and Americans both knew Bill Bird was the link to that lobby back in Washington. "Everyone [among Thai leaders] needed Bird's ties, his knowledge," said one longtime intelligence operative in Thailand. "They couldn't get rid of him even if they wanted to."[13]

• • •

While Bird's knowledge and his access to arms had made him integral to the American operation in Thailand, Thompson's idealistic ways, his refusal to go along with changing policy, and his withdrawal into his silk company were winning him few friends among U.S. policy makers. By the mid-1950s, the CIA had issued a warning to all employees in Bangkok not to trust Thompson and to avoid soliciting him for briefings—a warning, one CIA source said, that was one of the strictest he'd ever seen in the agency. The U.S. ambassadors in Thailand and Laos, too, privately warned Thompson to stop meeting with resistance fighters, who now were turning their guns on both the French and the Americans.

Some embassy officials and CIA officers still met with Thompson, realizing that he knew more about Thai and regional politics than virtually anyone else, only to find that after they met with him, Thompson told everyone he knew about the meeting and exactly what they had discussed—a decision by Thompson that only infuriated agency headquarters more.[14] "Thompson had so much influence in Bangkok, he was so visible, he'd known so many people, that he represented America much more than any CIA officer," said one agency source. "So it frustrated the agency enormously that he wouldn't play along with them."[15]

In person, Thompson could still be charming. When CIA station chiefs from Bangkok or Saigon came to Thompson's house, he would serve them bowls of green *keng kiao wan* curry and crunchy rice puffs that tasted like salty air while he quietly listened to their theories about how the United States had to make a stand in Southeast Asia or communism would come to dominate the world. When they left, he would turn to the other guests and tear apart the agency's main arguments.[16]

The FBI's hunt for communists now extended to Thailand, eight thousand miles from Washington. In 1953, the bureau launched an investigation, personally approved by director J. Edgar Hoover, into James Harrison Wilson Thompson of Bangkok, suspected of un-American activities—though what exactly those activities consisted of was not outlined by Hoover.[17] Jim Thompson wasn't a communist; he reportedly kept cyanide pills in his bedroom to swallow in case communists actually ever overran Thailand.[18]

But Thompson was hardly surprised when he found out about the FBI investigation. As America waded into war in Indochina, a man who once had equated the U.S. government with the American values he cherished no longer made such a link. By the 1950s, he'd begun suggesting to friends that real patriots kept their ideals, no matter what their leaders did. Thompson could now unleash tirades about Washington or the Thai generals in the middle of an otherwise boring dinner party, and some U.S. embassy officials knew that he remained in contact with old resistance fighters from Laos, Cambodia, and Vietnam.

"The U.S. embassy in Laos was extremely pissed off to find Thompson continuing his contacts with these resistance fighters, which was totally against U.S. policy," said one former official with access to classified cables regarding Thompson.[19]

"Jim didn't seem to care anymore what happened to him if he criticized the U.S. or the Thais," remembered one frequent guest at his dinner parties in Bangkok. "He could have a volcanic temper, and it would just explode, since he was so sure he was right."[20]

The FBI took at least two years to thoroughly investigate Jim Thompson. The bureau quizzed old friends from St. Paul's, Princeton, and Delaware, tracked down roommates from his time in New York, found associates from his architectural work, and went through the embassy and police files on Thompson in Bangkok. (His old prep school friends, many of whom had not seen him in three decades, declared they had "a high regard for Thompson's personal integrity [and] considered him a loyal American of good character.")[21] The bureau looked for any documents it could dig up on Thompson in Washington government agencies, old landlords, or creditors in America. It pored through congressional records on un-American activities to see if Thompson's name had ever come up. (It hadn't.) The FBI secretly interrogated his business partners in Thailand, his bankers, and his closest friends before ultimately concluding that Thompson was not guilty of "un-American" behavior.[22]

The Thai police, possibly working with the bureau, tailed Thompson constantly as well. He often saw cars following close behind him on the streets of Bangkok, and he noticed men picking through his trash or lurking in the alleys overnight outside his home.[23] When he made phone calls, Thompson sometimes heard clicking sounds, like a tap. He sometimes blotted out critical comments in his letters to his sister, sure they'd be opened and read.

"He'd become even more of a secretive man, never telling anyone where he was going or even sometimes what he was thinking," said one old friend.[24] Thompson warned his nephew Henry that he should be prepared to take over the silk company if Thompson should vanish, and he told other old friends that he could be murdered, just like his old Free Thai associates.[25] "Life is quite different and sad now," Thompson wrote to his sister Elinor. "Everyone is suspicious of everyone else."[26]

Even after the FBI had concluded its investigation, the embassy and the CIA station in Bangkok watched Thompson carefully. Thompson himself admitted, to a few select friends, that he might be innocent of J. Edgar Hoover's claims but that he'd hardly qualify as innocent if that meant just following the embassy line. Despite fearing that his letters to the United States would be opened, Thompson still could be acidly critical. "With all the fine high principles that our country was founded on, it is ghastly to think that we should support such a foul, filthy, corrupt, tottering regime as we have in French Indochina," Thompson wrote in 1951.[27]

He hadn't totally given up: he still tried to convince the diplomats he knew that American policy was alienating potential friends in Asia, and when Bill Donovan was the ambassador to Thailand in 1953 and 1954, Thompson met frequently with his old boss from the OSS. Donovan's aide, William vanden Heuvel, remembered that Thompson would almost plead with Wild Bill, who did have close personal ties with President Eisenhower but could hardly decide U.S. policy by himself, to stop the escalation in Southeast Asia and reconsider backing men like Pridi even if they had to return from exile, a virtual impossibility.[28]

It wasn't just that the CIA, the embassy in Bangkok, the State Department, or the FBI wanted to find out exactly what Jim

Thompson was doing; some of Thompson's Thai friends warned him that he shouldn't try to build up his silk company, either. Rich and powerful Thais resented an American telling them how to run the country's most famous traditional industry, even if they had let that industry fall into disrepair.

"Thompson was doing something Thais should have done, and they considered that an insult," said Philippe Baude, a French diplomat who was close to Thompson. "It was a loss of face for the Thais, and face is so important in Thailand."[29]

Thai business owners certainly didn't like an American running the silk industry who wouldn't adhere to Thai companies' tough, often brutal management of their employees—a man who would instead try to make his silk growers and weavers part of the company's management.[30] The middlemen who had colluded for years, forcing growers in the Northeast to sell them raw silk almost at a loss, feared a man who was trying to break their power by paying higher prices for the Northeast silk.[31]

Thompson didn't pay much attention to any warnings. The silk company would give the Thais skills and income the state could not, and who would harm such a benefactor? "The silk farmers, when we first went to see them, they had little cash and huge amounts of debt to the middlemen before they met Jim Thompson," said one of Thompson's longest-serving Thai employees. "They had beautiful fabrics, but they lived with no electricity, no water, like it was a century ago."[32]

"One of the wonderful things about this business is that it has created employment for many people . . . silk cocoons have become an important factor in boosting the economy of the Northeast," Jim Thompson told one reporter.[33] He boasted to friends that he'd created employment without relying on American aid, or even trying to Americanize Thais at all—he was helping them relearn their own industry, not selling them Coca-Cola, he would often say.[34] Or, as Thompson frequently told friends, he was "like a missionary but with better visual results."[35]

Though he might not have said as much in public, in his mind, friends thought, Thompson saw the silk company as a kind of template, a template for how America could have helped Thailand, if it listened more, if it tried to help the Thais do what they did best, rather than convincing them to make transistors for Japanese companies or open up local bottling plants for Coca-Cola. "I don't think Jim would have known what the word *microenterprise* meant; that wasn't something people said back then," said William Booth, who took over managing the silk company after Thompson vanished. "But it was in his mind. He wanted to keep the silk company small so that the workers learned, understood their craft. . . . He hated when big American companies or foundations would come in and try to bankroll the silk industry in Thailand."[36]

To Thompson, the silk company was, in many ways, an extension of his personal beliefs: as much as he could, he was letting the Thais determine their own fate, develop their own company, and make their own future. He would provide guidance and his talent for design, but he was not going to bring in a system and impose it on them, and above all the company had to remain definitively, publicly, *Thai*.

"Jim always said it was a Thai company, even though he was the face of it, and he meant it that way," said Thompson's nephew Henry. "That's why he never tried to gain control of the shares of the company, or bring in many other Americans, or raise a lot of money in America. It was as democratic a company as possible—profitable, too. . . . Could he have applied this model to all of Thailand? I don't know—most of the big Thai companies were controlled by a couple families and I don't think they really cared about democracy. But he was trying to bring what he'd brought to politics to business."[37]

Jim Thompson had started the silk company with little real business experience and had relied on an investor in the United States, George Barrie, for much of the initial capital, but like Willis Bird, Thompson had proven a natural salesman. When the cruise ships that now stopped in Bangkok pulled into port, Thompson would casually stroll the docks, a swatch of delicate Thai silk over his shoulder, until some of the tourists noticed the intricately patterned fabric and asked where they could buy it. He would pull the same trick in the lobby of the Oriental, the first luxury hotel built in Bangkok back in the late nineteenth century, with its almost comically obsequious staff and its view right across the Chao Praya River. In the Oriental's lobby, Thompson would sit with silks draped over his shoulder until guests noticed the bright colors and shimmering textures.[38]

And when he got the visitors into his tiny first shop, a cramped warren of a space with most of the middle taken up by a central table that was really an antique bed of former King Chulalongkorn, the real show began. Dressed in his usual white pants and long-sleeved silk shirt, his hair brushed back over his tanned high forehead, Thompson would drape silks over female customers' shoulders and backs, naturally matching one swatch with the next. As he moved, Thompson revealed the beauty of fabrics and shades the women had never seen before—how it matched their face or eyes, how it blended with their long strands of pearls. Inevitably, he would convince, almost hypnotize, the customers that they must, must go home with a whole armful of his silk.[39] "He was like an actor—he could just enthuse about how marvelous the silk made a customer look, while staring at me across the room and making faces behind the customer's back," said one friend who worked in Thompson's shop.[40]

Despite the challenges of starting a company in a foreign country, having little real business experience, and entering an industry Thais viewed as their own, Jim Thompson did enjoy several advantages. The postwar rise in American household incomes, as well as the focus on Asia by *Time* and *Life* and other magazines owned by Asiaphile Henry Luce, had sparked a new American interest in the Far East; the United States, a country that before the Second World War had mostly ignored the rest of the world, suddenly gave itself a crash course in internationalism. Shorter jet flights to Asia, more comfortable cruise ships, and new around-the-world travel packages launched a tourism boom to the Far East, allowing American tourists to take in Thailand, Japan, and Hong Kong in one go.

A new generation of American travel writers, wrote Christina Klein, an academic who studies tourism history, created "an impression of Asia as suddenly wide open to Americans and available for their visual and economic consumption," of a continent welcoming to mass travel, and particularly welcoming to victors of the Second World War who came carrying dollars, a currency coveted by nearly every nation. In

1947, Klein found, only two hundred thousand Americans held valid passports; by 1959, seven million Americans would travel abroad.[41]

To capitalize on this new U.S. interest in the Far East, Thompson took a small sample of his silks to New York City, where through the introduction of an old New York society friend, he got an appointment with Edna Woolman Chase, editor of *Vogue*, the fashion-industry tastemaker. Thompson spread his silks on Chase's desk, eager to make the most of his short time with her. Chase, like many of Thompson's first customers in Bangkok, had never seen such lush colors and patterns in a material; she immediately told her staff that they could not leave the office that day without looking at this Thai silk. Soon after, Chase featured Thompson's creations in the magazine, introducing the fabric to every designer and highbrow fashion icon in America.[42] Jim Thompson's Thai Silk Company, it seemed, would survive.

After the debut in *Vogue*, Thompson's fame grew rapidly and exponentially. Older members of the Thai royal family, who remembered the era before synthetics, found Thompson's tiny shop and recommended his silks to other royals; wealthy Thais, who had shunned silk for the seemingly more modern synthetic fabrics, rediscovered their own tradition, and elegant silk gowns came into fashion again in the Thai capital.[43]

The producers of *The King and I*, the Broadway musical based on a book about an English governess in nineteenth-century Siam, decided to use Thompson's silks for the costumes in the production: robes brocaded with gold silk thread and jewels. The musical would be a smash, bringing even more publicity to Thompson's tiny company, and Thompson got an avalanche of new orders for stoles, brocades, and simple swaths of silk, some sewn with so much gold thread that if you took out the gold, you could melt it down and make a functional object with it.[44]

In many of the early years of the company, exports nearly doubled from the previous year, and at times Thompson faced a shortage of raw silk because of the vast demand.[45] In 1953, the United Nations appointed Thompson to travel to Burma and attempt to revive its silk industry, but he soon concluded that Burma's economy and government were too hopeless for him to make much impact there.[46] Soon, newspaper and magazine writers had learned about the spy–turned–silk king, a natural for a color profile. *Reader's Digest, Christian Science Monitor, Time, Atlantic Monthly*, and nearly every other major publication would send a reporter to the tiny silk shop.[47]

Other Broadway and Hollywood producers called on Thompson, and his fabrics appeared in *Ben-Hur* and other films and shows. By the mid-1950s, the company's foreign arm had showrooms in New York, Boston, Chicago, and many other cities across the United States.[48] By then, designers were incorporating Thai silk into gowns, scarves, blouses, and other pieces in their collections, and Thompson began traveling regularly to Milan, Paris, and London to show his silk at fashion shows.

As Thompson's company expanded, the lives of the silk growers and silk weavers improved, too, and an industry that had been dying was clearly revived—exactly the kind of social transformation that Thompson had, in his own way, hoped the company would bring. The renewed demand for silk gave the weavers year-round jobs instead of the three- or four-month jobs they'd had before. By the late 1950s, Thompson's silk business employed more than two thousand Thais in growing, dyeing, and weaving the fabric, and any year the company made sizable profits, Thompson demanded that the money be not only given to shareholders as a dividend but also returned to his weavers and other employees as large bonuses—some years, a bonus equaled a full year's salary. This kind of reward was not totally unknown in American or European companies at that time, but in Thai firms, where a small rich group of owners usually dominated the company and nearly everyone else made low wages, the bonuses were relatively alien.

"Jim had an ideal of fairness, of how to treat everyone, and that came through in the company clearly," said his nephew Henry.[49] Bangkok weavers who once lived in old metal shacks overlooking a stinking canal now bought themselves new homes. Hearing about the opportunities with the company, whole families of silk weavers migrated from the Northeast to Bangkok, where they'd show up at Thompson's house, sometimes in the middle of his dinner parties.[50]

"Weaving children who might, at best, have looked forward to a sixth-grade education suddenly found themselves on planes headed for England, France, and the United States, and families that had been principally concerned with making ends meet on a monthly budget of around twenty-five dollars found themselves wondering where they could park a new automobile and what kind of television set they should buy," wrote Thompson's friend William Warren.[51] "I think the Thai employees looked at Jim like a god," Warren said.[52]

11

Perched at the top of the stairs to his house, smoking a long cigarette, Jim Thompson waved down to the crowd of guests who'd
arrived at his home on Soi Kasem San for dinner. Usually that meant
six or eight invited guests, enough to fit around the antique gaming
tables he used to eat off of in his dining room, with many of the invi-
tees clutching letters of introduction to Jim Thompson like they were
priceless documents.

Frequent visitors to the house recognized the usual mix of people
at dinner: local friends, shoppers from his store, and, of course, many
of the world's most glamorous, rich, or powerful people. Kennedys,
Eisenhowers, Barbara Hutton, Truman Capote, Somerset Maugham,
Benny Goodman, nearly every prominent royal or heiress in Europe—
they all just had to eat at Jim Thompson's house when they came
through Bangkok, since you couldn't come to Thailand without sitting
at the table of this most famous man.

Thompson would escort his dinner guests up around his balcony,
past a stone figure of the god Vishnu, and then out to the veranda
overlooking the murky Klong Saen Saep, where canal boat conductors

blew their whistles and riders hopped off the still-moving boats onto rickety docks. Underneath their feet, the guests could see the antique teak planks of Thompson's floor, polished to a high sheen by the frequent movement of stockinged feet. From a side door, the houseboy Yee would emerge, bearing tumblers of imported scotch and cubes of ice. Thompson would lead a short tour, taking several guests through the front hall, into the dining room, downstairs into the garden of frangipani and palms and jasmine plants, and then under the house, built on stilts in the old-fashioned Thai way, though most Thais in Bangkok now preferred Western-style homes.

Thompson's home actually was a collection of traditional teakwood Thai houses, joined together and painted a soft red, with some of the original dwellings dating to the early nineteenth century. To get the houses to Bangkok from rural Thailand, Thompson had floated them down to the capital on a massive barge.[1] At a time when most wealthy Thais were abandoning traditional dwellings, Thompson's decision to preserve—and live in—traditional homes shocked some of his friends, but soon living in older teakwood homes became the rage of Bangkok. Other rich men and women competed to build their own Thompson-style traditional palaces.

Unused to the enervating Bangkok heat, and dressed in suits and long gowns, some of the visitors would slip into Thompson's study, where a weathered sixth-century Buddha image overlooked the only air conditioner in the home.[2] The rest of the crowd would follow through hallways where stone Buddha images sat in niches carved into the walls like impassive sentries, and descend the stairs under the house, where Thompson had amassed perhaps the finest private collection of Southeast Asian art in the world. Few other collectors seemed interested at the time, but his art would spark a revival of demand for Southeast Asian painting and sculpture. At markets, monasteries, and temple fairs, Thompson often had his pick of carvings, wall hangings, Buddha heads, and other ancient items.

Some Thais were jealous of this foreigner buying up antiques, but Thompson always told his friends that without his patronage, many of these classic objects just would have been lost or destroyed. Thailand's Fine Arts Department was not exactly working hard to save them, and many looters were pillaging the country's older temples. Still, some friends worried, amassing so much of the country's history in his house could lead to trouble.

These traditional Thai houses that Thompson combined were not exactly comfortable places to live, even though fitted with modern plumbing and electricity. Thompson's home could be brutally hot inside, despite allowing breezes in; it had few comfortable places to sit or read, and the priceless antiques Thompson arrayed around his house made guests and even himself so careful they often could not relax. But comfort and relaxation was not the point. Thompson, wrote his friend William Warren, created his home like a theater, with every item situated for the greatest theatrical effect, as the finest backdrop for Thompson's dinners and his stories, the best to enhance his legend.[3]

At 6:30 p.m., in the Thai Muslim silk village of Baan Krua across the canal, Thompson's weavers were still at work, the men dipping thin skeins of silk into pots of dye before washing off the excess into the canal, the women frying hunks of chicken underneath jacaranda trees. While the sun set abruptly just after 6:30, going down in what seemed like seconds, as it always did in the tropics, Thompson would take two or three of his female dinner guests into a longtail canal boat and across the water, cameras around their necks, to see the silk village. Like a play whose performers, long rehearsed in their parts, knew exactly what to do, the weaving families—men with white skullcaps like fezzes and pencil mustaches, women with long skirts and worn plastic sandals—would bow slightly to Thompson as he ran his hands through their latest pieces of thick, heavy silk and studied the brightly colored bobbins for each weave.[4]

To add to the drama, Thompson would sometimes suggest—falsely—to his guests or visiting reporters that he traveled to work and his house every day solely by longtail canal boat, like some kind of ancient Venetian, though in reality he used a car and driver. "Nai Jim, Nai Jim," the weavers would call out as he smiled slightly and put his hands to his chin in a bow of his own. Around Thompson, the foreign women he had brought over would snap pictures or occasionally buy the silk right off of the weavers, the Thais playing along, smiling and bowing to each foreign guest.[5] Thompson's smile seemed genuine,

133

though; his friends knew he never much enjoyed spending time in the office, and he appeared happiest among the weavers or the growers up in the Northeast.

By 9 p.m., back at home with his dinner guests, who were tired of snacking on puffed rice cakes and crispy spring rolls, Thompson, in a crisp shirt and tie, would usher them into his candlelit dining room, where Yee would bring out crab salad with green mangoes, Chinese melon soup, or Panang curry—simple dishes often bought on the street, but unique enough that guests often remembered, decades later, exactly what they'd eaten at Jim Thompson's house.[6]

Around the dining room table, the guests would move from course to course as Thompson narrated one story about Thailand after the next: how he'd found this Buddha or that wall carving in some obscure temple, hidden behind an old screen; how he'd wandered into a country fair out in the Northeast and been forced to dance the *ramwong*, the slow twisting Thai folk circle dance, until all the village headmen had laughed or bought him drinks or both.[7] Yee would patter in, in his bare feet, to refill drink glasses or offer plates of fruit for dessert. Chewing on guava and papaya, the guests pressed Thompson for more: more stories of how he'd reinvented his life in Thailand, just as they could dream about doing for themselves; more gossip about generals, politicians, and spies. Thompson almost never said no, and when he listened to his visitors, he could make each one seem like he was focused only on that individual.

"Jim would go on endlessly, trying to ignore the fatigue with which these almost nightly dinner parties were gradually undermining him," wrote one old friend, Rene Burrow. When anyone would get up to leave, Burrow remembered, Thompson would counter with "Oh, don't go yet. It isn't late. Let's all have a nightcap."[8] Yee would pour another round, and the evening would continue, even as across the canal, Baan Krua went quiet for the night.

Nearly every day, winter or summer, monsoon season or the heat of April, Jim Thompson hosted these dinner parties, brought his guests across the river, and told his stories, sometimes filling his home with 120 people or more. Thompson, said his friend William Warren, was his own greatest invention: if people came to Bangkok expecting to see a silk king with a lavish house, impeccable manners, and a court of admirers like a monarch, then Jim Thompson would play that role, even if it exhausted him.[9] And if at first he was uncomfortable playing a king, if in the early years in Thailand he could still be shy with other foreigners, he clearly grew into the role.

"Every night, no matter what else was going on, Jim would have people over for dinner so that he could entertain them, so he could tell them the same stories of his life, show them his weavers, give them that bit of exoticism, of fantasy they'd always wanted," said one friend. "Maybe he got tired of telling the same stories, maybe he'd complain about the strain of constantly hosting, but he still did it."[10]

By the late 1950s, in fact, that strain had become clear: Thompson routinely checked into Bangkok hospitals with bouts of flu, dysentery, pneumonia, gallstones, or what he described as various "amoebas" running through his system; at one point in the early 1960s his doctors had him gulping down over forty different pills per day. "I have really been snowed under by visitors," Thompson wrote to his sister in one of numerous letters in which he complained about maintaining his lifestyle. "When you have to do it all yourself and show everyone the house, it is exhausting."[11]

Of course, holding dinner parties didn't hurt business—late at night, long after the weavers had finished for the day across the canal, and after glasses of scotch and bellies of curry, wealthy guests would ask Thompson to open up the shop just for them, and they'd go home with thousands of dollars worth of silk. But for a man who had never remarried, who had found his proposals to Irena spurned time and again, who could not convince most of his siblings to come visit even though he begged his sister Elinor to visit, the dinner parties also served as a kind of substitute family.

"Jim seemed like this bon vivant, but sometimes you'd look at him, and he'd be quiet, in the corner of the room, watching everyone, and you'd realize that this was really a lonely man," said his nephew Henry. "After his Thai friends were killed or people like [old OSS colleague] Alex MacDonald left the country, he didn't trust people, and he might have seemed to have a lot of friends because of all these parties, but his close circle of friends got smaller and smaller."[12]

"I often wonder if it [Thailand] isn't just a way to make the years pass faster," Jim wrote to his sister, adding, "I have no wife and children to work for and be responsible for."[13] Increasingly, by the late 1950s, Thompson would disappear from Bangkok for days at a time, to hunt for art and antiques in the countryside or just to vanish for a walk somewhere in Thailand, leaving little notice of his whereabouts.[14] But when he was in Bangkok, Thompson desperately made sure he never ate dinner alone. "Jim always had to be surrounded by people," said his friend Jackie Ayer. "At the end of the [work] day, if no one was there, he'd invite people over from the shop just to have people over."[15]

After Irena, Thompson tried one more time to have a real love life other than furtive affairs. For years, he had quietly coveted Amelia "Meli" Rangsit, the part Swiss and part Italian wife of his friend Prince Sanidh Rangsit, and a woman whose old-fashioned bobbed black hair and full, intense lips could make her seem sultry and reserved at the same time. While Meli was married, Thompson kept his feelings to himself, maintaining a close friendship with her but often reminding her that Sanidh was cheating on her, and he would bring her lavish presents whenever he came to visit the prince.[16]

After Meli separated from her husband because of her inability to bear children, Thompson took a chance. When he traveled to Europe, he would visit Switzerland, where she now lived, sometimes surprising her and, nearly every time, asking her to marry him. She refused. Still, during one of Meli's trips back to Thailand, where she stayed in Thompson's house as a guest, he upped the stakes. "Allow me to ask you for your hand one last time," Thompson told her at his house, according to a family member who later discussed the incident with Meli.[17] He handed Meli a gift wrapped in silk; inside, surrounded by a pure white camellia flower, was a giant diamond ring he had bought, the stone fitted inside an antique setting. Touched, Meli still refused his love, refused his entreaties to come to his room that night and accept his proposal.

After Meli, Thompson still chased women—he'd become famous in the city for bedding the wives of French, British, and American diplomats. But the women had to be married—that was the rule, since he couldn't get too involved with a married woman who would be moving on to a new diplomatic post soon. He might boast of these diplomat wives jousting over his hand—in letters to Elinor, he'd complain of beautiful women who all wanted him, and one who threatened to commit suicide if she could not have him—but these women would eventually leave Bangkok, along with their husbands and children.[18] They were no risk to his psyche, since there was no chance of real and lasting love.

By the end of the 1950s, even the silk company, which at first had seemed to bring Thompson nothing but joy, only made him lonelier. "All my weavers and staff are fighting, mud-slinging, and behaving like perfect bastards—all, I suppose, because they are just not used to making so much money," he wrote to his sister. "Maybe I am ruining them instead of helping them."[19]

Weavers asking for higher pay, flaunting their new cars, or walking out the back of the shop with yards of fabric was one thing, but one of Thompson's closest friends in the company, Thao Pheng, brother of the Lao militant Thao Oun, who'd known Thompson well, tried to steal Thompson's designs and open his own silk shop nearby.[20] Thompson hired a lawyer and ultimately reached a settlement with Thao Pheng in the mid-1950s, allowing his former partner to open his own store near Thompson's, but Thompson did not recover from the shock, even after his company had long survived Thao Pheng's. "I am afraid I won't get away from here [Thailand] for years myself as there is no one I can trust or that the rest of the company will trust," Thompson wrote to his sister in 1955.[21]

If his narrowing circle of trusted friends and associates made Jim Thompson lonelier, the rapid changes in his adopted country drove him into even greater personal isolation. The Thailand of 1945, when Jim Thompson had arrived, had some elements of a modern, Westernized country—phone lines, automobiles, an international airport—but even those conveniences often did not work, and much of the time so little had changed that it was easy for an expatriate to imagine himself still living in a nineteenth-century kingdom.

Jim had been fleeing the pressure and modernization of New York, so Thailand in 1945 was, in many ways, exactly how he wanted it, the type of exotic place where he could be someone who stood out, which he'd always desperately desired. He might not welcome the poverty or the feudalism of rural Thailand, but he enjoyed the simplicity that came with Thai society then, the uniqueness of being a rare foreigner in Bangkok, and a life of barges and canal boats instead of highways. "I am afraid I like backward places that need to be developed better than all the high-powered superhighways, motels, and gigantic cities," Thompson wrote to his brother.[22]

"He had a kind of idealized image of Thailand, of himself as the protector of the 'real' Thailand, and he didn't like giving that image up," said one old friend.[23]

Thailand in 1960 no longer seemed so unique, and a foreigner in Bangkok, even one as famous and connected as Jim Thompson, hardly seemed so unique, either. Along with American military assistance, the U.S. government was pumping in economic aid, which helped to build new highways, airstrips, port facilities, power plants, and other infrastructure. Under the Thai generals, the government controlled political discourse tightly, and the top generals took a stake in every major business, but the regime still encouraged free enterprise and international trade.

Managed by a cadre of Western-educated bureaucrats in the Bank of Thailand and the Ministry of Finance, Thailand began to modernize its economy, using government-directed loans and grants and Japanese and American capital to build industry, set up manufacturing centers for foreign companies, and mechanize agriculture in rural areas. The economy began to take off, and by the early 1960s, Thailand was one of the fastest-growing nations in the world, its development strategies studied and copied by many other countries. In the 1950s, Thailand's economy grew by over 5 percent annually, and in the 1960s, the economy boomed even faster, growing by 8.4 percent annually.[24]

Taking advantage of Thailand's natural assets, including its pristine beaches and baroque, ornate temples, the government also built one of the most successful tourism industries in the region; even though fewer than fifty thousand foreign visitors came to Thailand annually in the mid-1950s, by the end of the 1960s, the country was attracting more than half a million each year, and flashy new hotels sprang up across Bangkok to cater to the tourism influx.[25]

Filling the new factory jobs in Bangkok, building the new high-rises, driving the new taxis that replaced trishaws and ferried Thai businessmen in sleek suits—all this new work required manpower. In the rural Northeast, where many Thais still lived, even the mechanization and modernization of agriculture could not make life much easier: crops still fell prey to droughts and uncertain monsoon seasons. So by the end of the 1950s, many Northeastern families had migrated to the capital, which swelled from a medium-size city into a modern megacity, its new suburbs eating up rice paddies as developments spread from the old city center.

In the 1960s, according to Thailand historians Chris Baker and Pasuk Phongpaichit, the population of Bangkok expanded from 1.8 million to 3 million people, and that figure was most likely an underestimate, since official censuses often missed many migrants to the city.[26] Entire neighborhoods of Northeastern Thais grew up in the outskirts of Bangkok. Bars opened in Bangkok serving the whiskey of the Northeast and playing *mor lam*, a Northeastern style of music whose wailing guitars and yodeling-type vocals called to mind an Asian Hank Williams or Johnny Cash.

The migration and modernization had an unmistakable visual impact on Bangkok and even on the smallest villages in Thailand. To widen roads and make room for more cars, the government began filling in most of the canals along wide roads like Rama IV Avenue that had once earned Bangkok the sobriquet the Venice of the East; the new tarmac, which destroyed waterways and many trees, made an already hot city even hotter, nearly baking areas of pavement in the summer. Traffic, hardly a worry back in 1945, when the trishaws and occasional cars had wide boulevards in the city's Dusit district to themselves, began to darken the city skies with smog and choke its residents; soon Bangkok would become known as one of the most polluted cities in the world.[27]

Jumbles of square office blocks that wouldn't have looked out of place in Stalinist Eastern Europe and mansions for the wealthy that competed for opulence, mimicking the Palace of Versailles or other European castles, sprang up along main streets and side roads with little advance planning, dwarfing the temples that once centered communities. Other middle-class Thais tore down traditional teakwood houses like the ones Thompson preserved to buy into new Western-style apartment blocks. Thais in many traditional industries abandoned their businesses for office jobs or construction work. New paved roads snaked into even the most isolated parts of the capital and the rural areas of Thailand, opening up commerce but also allowing developers to slash down jungle, create arid wastelands, and displace elephants and other revered Thai fauna.

Of course, that same development was also allowing average, middle-class Thais to buy the consumer goods that Americans had been accustomed to, to put air-conditioning into their sweltering homes, to enjoy vaccinations and other medical care that would drastically cut infant mortality, and to send their children to secondary school and college for the first time. Modernization also expanded the ranks of the middle class and began to break down the traditional hierarchies, prompting more Thais to question the almost feudal social structure, to throw out old ideals of nonconfrontation.[28]

This modernization was, for the most part, Americanization. Though Britain traditionally had educated Thailand's elite and Japanese investments helped drive the boom, it was American advisers, American loans, and American schools that truly changed Thailand. Thousands of Thais now studied at the American-run English-language program in Bangkok, watched films sponsored by the U.S. embassy, or traveled to the United States to attend a university. To many middle-class Thais in Bangkok, anything American was better. Students at Chulalongkorn and Thammasat universities scorned Thai movies, with their cheap production values, for the Hollywood films now coming to Bangkok; their parents joined the Rotary Club to hear American speakers coming through the city; Thai cabinet officials fought to get into newspaper photos with visiting American politicians or to shake the hand of some minor dignitary from Washington.[29]

The Americanization of Thailand also meant more Americans arriving. Many more—and not just the upper-class intelligence officers and occasional businessmen who had come in the mid-1940s, men and women whom Jim Thompson was naturally comfortable around. The whole spectrum of American society arrived in Thailand now, widening social circles dramatically in Bangkok. Army grunts from the South and the rural West came to help oversee the new roads and airports being built up, to train the Thai military and police, or just for a quick visit to the brothels springing up on Petchaburi Road.

In the 1950s, Washington and Bangkok had been careful to camouflage the American buildup in Thailand: U.S. soldiers usually entered the kingdom as tourists and kept a low profile, rarely dressing in uniform. By the 1960s, that changed dramatically. So many U.S. troops came in every day—by the late 1960s, there were nearly fifty thousand of them in Thailand—that it became impossible to hide them or pretend they were arriving just for a bit of relaxation. American generals and other senior officers landed in Bangkok seemingly every day, and now in their official dress uniforms.[30]

Along with the GIs and higher-ranking U.S. military advisers, other segments of American society were coming to Thailand: middle American tourists on a round-the-world trip; recent college graduates who'd heard about the cheap lifestyle and business opportunities in the Far East; salesmen from Xerox and General Electric and every other big American company that had established branches in Bangkok, bringing with them their entire American lifestyle. Enough American-style restaurants, supermarkets, private schools, and clothing shops had opened up in Bangkok by the 1960s that a foreigner could re-create a decent facsimile of home.

Not everyone in Thailand was thrilled by the Americanization. Some middle-class Thais, who remembered the post–World War II period and now saw how the United States was backing generals like Phao and Sarit, lashed out at America, fearful that Thailand was becoming just a client state. Even during the most intense periods of repression in Thailand in the 1950s, when the military dictatorship approached the totalitarianism of China or, later, Cambodia, the United States did not reconsider its assistance but repeatedly increased economic aid no matter what the generals did.

Some students and Bangkok intellectuals also worried that Americanization would destroy Thailand's traditions and culture; by the 1960s, less fearful of military rule, they would take to the streets of Bangkok to demonstrate against America and their own rulers. In the rural Northeast, where the U.S. military presence was growing the fastest, many locals appreciated the cash coming into the economy, but they resented the brothels and cheap beer bars being set up just outside the bases as well as the half Thai, half American boys and girls being born, often to fathers they'd never see again. Even as early as the late 1950s, several of the more outspoken Thai newspapers regularly filled their pages with anti-American vitriol; they played up incidents like a brawl between U.S. soldiers and local Thais in the fall of 1956, highlighting the fight in splashy headlines.[31]

Jim Thompson wasn't going to protest the change in the Bangkok streets or join the salons of Thai intellectuals who exchanged anti-American articles and poems, but the changes in Thailand only added to his increasing feelings of isolation. "Jim liked it when he was the American in Thailand, since there weren't many others—he didn't want America reproduced in Thailand," said his nephew Henry.[32]

From the Chom Si temple overlooking the town of Luang Prabang, Laos, the historical seat of the country's royal family, the scene in late 1959 looked little different than it might have decades earlier. On the narrow peninsula jutting out in the Mekong and Nam Khan rivers, home to most of Luang Prabang's shops and markets, women in long wraparound *phasin* dresses and chewing wads of betel nut sold fresh baguettes each morning.

At dusk, makeshift stalls opened in the same market area, offering spicy raw papaya salad, fried Mekong River catfish, and glutinous sticky rice served in miniature wicker baskets and eaten with *pa dae*, a dip of chilies and sun-dried fish that had been pounded into a paste. From the monasteries along the main streets, now lined with pastel-colored colonial-era houses and bistros that looked like they'd been imported whole from the south of France, young novice monks, their shaved heads and long robes unable to conceal the fact that they were still just boys, chattered and kicked make-shift soccer balls.

The French had built avenues of homes in Luang Prabang, but most of the colonists had left by 1959, and the city seemed again like an extension of a Lao village, with water buffalo grazing not far from the peninsula and, nearby, fishermen tossing their long conical nets into the Mekong. France had never invested much in Laos; Paris viewed Vietnam as the prize of Indochina, and Laos as a backwater, if charmingly languid.

A few Frenchmen had stayed on after Laos gained formal independence in 1954—they had married local women or just could never imagine returning to cold, frazzled post–World War II Paris—and ran simple cafés on the Luang Prabang peninsula, where waiters with fake berets set up blackboards written in French and served espresso and finger cakes in addition to Lao coffee filtered with condensed milk. In the royal palace, set back from the three-wheeled taxis and bicycles of Luang Prabang's main streets, the king of Laos, Savang Vatthana, still theoretically ruled the country as head of state, as the monarchy had done since the eighteenth century. In reality, a coalition of politicians based in the newer capital of Vientiane ran Laos, but the king, though a clumsy politician known for weeping in public and driving around in a convertible, still carried weight. Average people still worshiped the royal family: like their peers in Thailand, many Lao citizens kept photographs of the king in their homes, and when the monarch appeared in public in Luang Prabang, men and women would prostrate themselves on the ground before him.

But by the late 1950s, this idyllic little kingdom had become one of the hottest firefights of the Cold War. Strange as it would seem to a visitor to the sleepy, tiny country today, in the late 1950s and early 1960s, Laos, as much as anywhere in the world, was where Washington would set the future of its foreign policy. And as the fighting in Laos built from a small sideshow to the conflict in Vietnam to a secret war in which the United States created the largest covert operation to that time, Laos also would definitively end any hopes Jim Thompson had that his views of Asia would ever prevail. It would be

Willis Bird's approach, instead, that would dominate in Laos—and, for many decades, everywhere else.

By the late 1950s and early 1960s, battles erupted not far from the sleepy Luang Prabang bistros selling fresh baguettes and homemade pâté; soon the war would come to Vientiane, which had been almost as tranquil—once sleepy enough that wives of foreign diplomats could water-ski there on the Mekong and Western reporters could just wander up to government officials in the street and talk with them.[33]

With communists gaining ground in Vietnam, the Eisenhower administration saw the tiny landlocked country as a bulwark against communism spreading farther west, into Thailand, Burma, and even India. So tiny Laos became a critical domino, one that many in the Eisenhower administration thought could not fall—or at least they convinced themselves of the kingdom's enormous importance. If the United States did not take a stand in Laos, "we will have demonstrated to the world that we cannot or will not stand when challenged," warned Admiral Arleigh Burke, chief of naval operations, to the Joint Chiefs of Staff. "The effect will quickly show up in Asia, Africa, and Latin America."[34]

Was that contention accurate? Would a more left-leaning government in Laos have meant political change throughout Asia or as far away as Latin America? Few people in Washington would have publicly challenged Burke, for to do so risked being labeled a communist sympathizer. Like Jim Thompson, many State Department officials, and quite a few journalists who visited the tiny kingdom, still considered Laos peripheral to any real conflict against communism. But at a National Security Council meeting, Eisenhower himself warned his administration, "We cannot let Laos fall to the communists, even if we have to fight, with our allies, or without them."[35] With the president having come down so strongly, taking an opposite view, seeing Laos as anything other than a domino in the anticommunist struggle, became ever harder.

Departing office, Eisenhower told his successor, John F. Kennedy, that Laos would be the most important foreign policy crisis he faced and that Kennedy might well have to send American troops to war there.[36] By 1961, Laos's three-way civil war—among rightist forces backed by the CIA, a more neutral and moderate group, and left-wing guerrillas who enjoyed the support of North Vietnam and the Soviet Union—had seriously damaged the country's traditionally consensual politics.

In the late 1950s, the country had pieced together a fragile coalition government containing politicians from both the Left and the Right, but a Lao officer named Kong Le staged a coup in 1960, spraying howitzer and bazooka fire across Vientiane, the shells landing in temples, houses, and farms all over the city. Fighting intensified, with assassinations in Vientiane picking off prominent politicians, shelling setting fire to the simple thatched-roof Lao houses, and, at one point, shells hitting the U.S. embassy, according to a comprehensive account of the fighting by historian Roger Warner.

Eisenhower proved correct: the Lao crisis took up much of the Kennedy administration's first months in office, though Kennedy had originally seen other places, like Cuba, as far more important. Just as critical, under Eisenhower and Kennedy, the United States would decisively opt for a covert battle in Laos and would make the tiny country a major battleground, one of the least-known big fights of the entire Cold War. By the end of the fighting in Laos, American planes had dropped more tonnage on the country than on all of Europe during World War II, and the CIA and its Thai allies had built a vast proxy army in Laos.

Kennedy wasted little time trying to educate Americans about the importance of the tiny kingdom, which most people in the United States had probably never heard of before. Shortly after taking office, with communist guerrillas gaining territory in Laos and nearing the capital, Kennedy went on national television to declare that a communist overthrow of the Lao government "quite obviously affects the security of the US."[37] (He deliberately mispronounced the country's name as "LAY-os," rather than the correct "louse" or "laaw," fearing that average Americans would not take seriously a nation whose name sounded like a small bug.)

American journalists and policy analysts scrambled to learn about the tiny kingdom, and while once Vientiane had been covered by occasional wire service reporters, now journalists from the *New York*

Times and other heavyweights parachuted into the city to scope out the new Cold War battle. The U.S. embassy in Laos began to expand from a tiny shell into what would become, along with Laos operations based in Thailand, a vast complex of intelligence operations. And back in the United States, at its recruiting grounds at Ivy League schools, army officer academies, and white-shoe Manhattan firms, the CIA began looking for a few smart, fearless young men who'd be willing to work as case officers in Laos, living in the rural Lao highlands along with the agency's proxy fighters.

Still, Kennedy also wanted to at least temporarily resolve the Laos crisis in order to focus on Cuba and other challenges. By the next year, Laos was officially no longer at war: the Geneva accords of 1962, signed by fourteen nations, would establish the country as neutral territory, prohibiting "the introduction of foreign regular and irregular troops, foreign paramilitary formations and foreign military personnel into Laos."[38] But almost as soon as the Geneva documents were inked, Washington and Hanoi were breaking their promises, building Laos into a major battle. Vietnamese aid continued to flow to the communist Lao guerrillas, and soon the North Vietnamese would use supply routes through Laos to equip the Viet Cong in South Vietnam.

In August 1962, Kennedy authorized a new secret U.S. military aid program for Laos, hiding its existence inside the much larger aid program to Thailand.[39] That covert American program in Laos, which would include launching a massive air offensive against the Lao communists and their Vietnamese allies, and building an entire U.S.-backed proxy army in Laos, would become the largest paramilitary operation ever undertaken by the CIA at that time.[40]

In terms of its physical and human toll on one country, the twilight war in Laos would rival the war in Vietnam itself. And the secret Laos war would prove a natural fit for Willis Bird, a man with extensive links among Thai leaders, a penchant for secrecy, and a preference for fighting proxy wars against communism.[41] It would also finally destroy any last hopes that Jim Thompson had for his vision of the U.S. role in Asia: an America that used its power to build democracy in the region, that could distinguish between local grievances and global communism, and that inspired Asians as a liberator, not as a new colonizer. For Jim Thompson—who loved Laos, in many ways, more than Thailand—the Laos war would prove crushing.

As the North Vietnamese gained support and military strength, driving out the French, their regional ambitions expanded. An expeditionary force of Vietnamese communists had launched a rapid raid into Laos in 1953, drawing within a few miles of Luang Prabang and terrifying the conservative Thai generals, who feared the battle-tested Vietnamese forces. In response, Thai leaders in the late 1950s and early 1960s drastically expanded their relationship with the United States. The American military presence in Thailand had grown throughout the early 1950s, but Bangkok had been careful to maintain at least a semblance of independence, not least because of rising resentment among Thai intellectuals about the relationship with the United States.

But by the early 1960s, the Thai generals abandoned even that pretense. In 1962, Secretary of State Dean Rusk made a commitment to Thailand's foreign minister that the United States would unilaterally come to Thailand's defense if the kingdom was attacked by communists. Seemingly permanent U.S. bases were being constructed in Ubon Ratchathani, Udon Thani, and other cities on Thailand's eastern border, along with new American intelligence and communications facilities in the Northeast.[42]

Thailand's military would soon commit its own forces to the battle in Laos and would begin allowing American forces to launch reconnaissance flights over Laos from bases in the Thai Northeast, flights that ultimately would morph into bombing runs to North Vietnam and Laos. CIA advisers trained Thai hilltribes, ethnic minority groups living in the mountains of the north, to fight a guerrilla war, with the possible objective of sending them to battle in Vietnam. American military officers privately began calling Thailand "our unsinkable aircraft carrier," though they were careful not to use that term in front of their Thai counterparts.[43]

Even after the French withdrawal from Indochina, Bird and Chennault had maintained business in Laos, and now the growing American involvement would help them enormously. Bird had continued to help deliver U.S. foreign aid to Laos and to support

American military advisers operating in the tiny kingdom. In 1959, as intense fighting broke out again in Laos between conservative and leftist forces, the Civil Air Transport, which by the late 1950s boasted a fleet of over thirty planes, launched new airlifts into Laos to supply the agency's favored fighters, and the United States sent a team of Special Forces into Laos to train pro-U.S. Lao soldiers.[44] Within three years, though, this training would expand into a massive proxy war, and Bird's connections would make him central to that battle.

For Jim Thompson, the barely secret violation of tiny Laos, most of whose people still lived existences of rural subsistence and had no interest in the global political struggle that had landed on them, proved even more wrenching than the militarization and Americanization of Thailand. By the late 1950s and early 1960s, Thompson's health already appeared to be faltering, and he shuttled in and out of fancy Bangkok hospitals.[45]

The war coming to Laos seemed to drain his mental state and hasten his physical deterioration. Thompson's first job in Thailand had involved working with exiled Lao leaders; many of his first weavers came from exiled Lao families; Thompson still traveled frequently to Laos to visit top politicians; and despite the war, Laos remained a far more traditional Asian society than Bangkok and thus more appealing to Thompson. "Laos makes me feel sick," Thompson wrote to his sister in late 1960, as he convalesced yet again in the hospital after coming down with pneumonia. "I am afraid this is the beginning of a long struggle for that poor little country."[46]

12

If in 1960 the fighting in Laos had made Jim Thompson sick, he had hidden it, but by the mid-1960s most of his friends were worried about his physical and mental health. A man who had tried, ever since coming to Thailand in 1945, to work hard enough to make up for what he seemed to consider forty wasted years in America could not slow his pace as he aged into his sixties, and he seemed unable to restrain his disgust and sadness at the war in Vietnam, Laos, and Thailand.

Thompson checked in and out of the Bangkok Nursing Home, one of the city's premier hospitals; he took antibiotics and tinctures of opium to numb pain and sleep better; he submitted to the probing of his colon and the drawing of his blood every half hour to clear his body of dysentery and various tropical bugs.[1] He warned his sister, "I often wonder how long I will last at my present pace."[2]

"His mind was in turmoil, he was not well and he was sleeping badly," wrote his old friend, Rene Burrow. "He became more irritable and rather recklessly outspoken [about U.S. policy]. . . . For a long time he toyed with the idea of abandoning everything but he could not bring himself to make the final break [from Thailand.]"[3] Burrow believed that Thompson seemed increasingly resigned and fatalistic; Burrow's wife, Andree, arrived at Thompson's house one evening to find him so sick he couldn't get out of bed, but he refused to call a doctor; at work, Thompson, who'd always had an explosive, but rare, temper, would storm out of the shop or the weavers' village after screaming at employees, a cardinal sin in nonconfrontational, smile-even-when-murderously-angry Thailand.

Thompson considered simply taking six months off, admitting he had grown "stale and ill-tempered," then worried that the company would collapse without him; he refused to spend any evening alone, dragging people home from his shop to eat with him. At other times, he tried to recover his energy by going hiking in northern Thailand or the Cameron Highlands of Malaysia, which he'd come to know well.[4]

"More often than most of his friends knew, [Thompson] suffered periods of depression," Burrow wrote. "As it was in his nature to wish to present to the world the façade of an active, indefatigable being unaffected by age, he tried to hide any signs of fatigue."[5]

Thompson's silk company had remained profitable into the 1960s—it grossed some $1.5 million in 1965 and employed over three thousand people—but as it profited, it had attracted numerous and dangerous competitors.[6] The media had nicknamed Thompson the silk king, and the moniker stuck, but the press attention had also attracted other businesspeople to the industry. While the Thai silk industry had been all but dead in the late 1940s—some of Thompson's first weavers back then had been working part-time as plumbers, since they couldn't find weaving jobs—by the mid-1960s, at least 150 other silk companies had opened up in Bangkok, and one of the companies, Star of Siam, built a hundred-loom weaving factory in northeastern Thailand, Thompson's home base.[7]

By the mid-1960s, Thai growers were producing over five hundred thousand pounds of silkworms per year. Large American organizations like the Rockefeller Foundation had gotten into the game, funding weaving and silk-growing operations in Thailand.[8] On the corner of Rama IV Avenue and Suriwong Road, just north of the streets developing into the center of Thailand's banking industry, Thompson would put his silk company's spacious new showroom; on the opening day in 1967, Brahman priests chanted and blessed the shop and offered fish, fruit, candies, and a whole pig's head to the miniature spirit house installed outside the store.[9] The shop was a major step up from the cramped tiny old showroom, but Suriwong and the surrounding streets already boasted many other wholesale silk dealers and tailors offering ready-to-wear silk garments, so cheap tourists didn't even bother to bargain over the prices, the normal custom in Thailand.

Other companies raided Thompson's silk firm for weavers and office staff, paid taxi drivers to steer tourists to their stores, or contacted Thompson's printing plant to steal his designs; too often, some of Thompson's own employees left to start silk companies, bringing with them Thompson's designs.[10] When they produced knockoffs of Thompson's most famous patterned silks, competitors could easily sell them at the floating markets outside the city, where women in straw hats would call out their wares in singsongy Thai and paddle up next to one another to buy and sell fruit, vegetables, clothing, and other items.

The floating markets, perhaps the most famous postcard scene of Thailand, were being rendered useless by the modern supermarkets springing up in Bangkok, but they still attracted tourists with cameras, and so the old women kept paddling their dugout-style canoe boats, but they started selling carvings, weavings, and other souvenirs for travelers. "You could get copies of the latest designs we'd made, a few weeks later at the floating markets," said one of Thompson's employees.[11]

Thompson always publicly seemed unconcerned about competitors, convinced that his bonuses and fair treatment would earn staff loyalty, that his fashion sense and knowledge of the industry would allow him to triumph over any competitor, and that his refusal to mix rayon with his silk or to forgo his daily inspections of his weavers would ensure quality a customer would notice.[12] "Thompson's company was known among all the businesses in Thailand for taking care of its staff—I'd worked for many companies in Thailand before, and here there was no boss-worker dynamic," said one of Thompson's longtime employees.[13]

151

Thompson disdained the large American foundations suddenly trying to invest in the silk industry; they wanted to turn silk into big business, the antithesis of Thompson's old-fashioned, almost cottage-industry style.[14] And his artistic knowledge and style was clearly ahead of his competitors: Thompson would take photographs of items in Thai museums and then ask his printing plant to reproduce the designs on silk, or he would bring back sculptures and temple wall paintings from the Thai countryside and attempt to develop silks based on their ancient patterns.[15]

"Jim saw weaving as an art and the weavers as skilled producers, not like a factory industry," said one of the company's longest-serving Thai employees.[16] Later, Thompson's skill would matter—while nearly all his competitors eventually failed, his company would survive, up until the present day—but back in the 1960s, that survival hardly seemed assured.

Thompson didn't take the precautions common to other companies operating in Thailand, where the laws and the courts were mostly a fiction and real influence stemmed from personal ties. A more skilled, sharper-edged businessman like Willis Bird would have known how to operate: Bird spent much of his time cultivating prominent politicians who could protect his business if it was threatened or delivering a regular flow of gifts and probably cash to powerful policemen who worked in his area.

Through Thompson's connections in the international fashion industry and his network of sales offices around the world, the Thai Silk Company remained by far the largest exporter of silk in the country, but within Thailand the company was more vulnerable.[17] "He still thought he was doing Thailand such a service that no one would ever really harm him," said his friend Philippe Baude.[18]

Still, Thompson seemed to have inspired enormous personal jealousy among Thai businesspeople. "They resented him dominating the silk industry, the idea of a silk king, they resented him buying up their art and antiques, they resented him presenting himself as the expert on their country," said Baude. "You could realize how reluctant the Thais were to come to [Thompson's] house."[19]

Up in the Northeast, where Thompson's company had provided a source of income to many villagers, his initiatives now sometimes competed directly with Thai government-run development programs designed to increase income in the Northeast, where the government was worried poor farmers might turn to communism. The government development programs, an easy source of cash, often degenerated into windfalls for local officials, who were not happy to see any competitors threaten their money pits.[20]

The Thai generals, who rarely missed a business opportunity, had also begun to take an interest in silk. The wife of army chief Sarit, backed with government money and government connections, opened her own silk business, building a large plant on the Bangkok outskirts filled with over 150 looms and some of the most modern silk equipment she could buy, and she tried to poach many of Thompson's weavers.[21] "She was a vile woman, just as ruthless as her husband," said Thompson's friend Ethan Emery. "She would take any chance she had to crush Thompson's business, but Jim always just said he wasn't worried."[22]

Many of Thompson's acquaintances believed Sarit's wife was behind an episode that, more than anything else, soured a man who'd once been almost a naive idealist.[23] Over two decades, Thompson had amassed one of the finest private collections of Asian art and antiques in the world, keeping most of the sculptures, pottery, paintings, temple hangings, and other items in his now-famous house. He had found many of the items at crumbling temples or other monuments, purchased them from antiques dealers, or found them in abandoned caves across Thailand. Thompson was not an art salesman and had always planned to leave his objects to Thailand; in his mind, if he had not bought these antiques, they would have been destroyed or just fallen apart.

But as with his silk business, Thompson was so sure of his integrity that he didn't bother to cultivate Thai government art and antiquities officials or pay police inspectors, as many of the disreputable antiques dealers in Bangkok normally did.[24] "One reason I bought [objects] was to keep them in the country," Thompson told one reporter in 1962. "So many Thai art objects are being smuggled out."[25]

In his mind, Thompson seemed to have amassed a lifetime of duty to Thailand. After all, in early 1962 the king of Thailand had awarded Thompson the "exalted order of the white elephant"—Thai monarchs traditionally kept white elephants, either albinos or animals with pale skin, as symbols of their power—for his work in restoring the silk industry, and Thompson donated the money made from tours of his house to a Thai school for blind children.[26] His company had helped to empower Thai women, since it had given many female weavers jobs in a highly conservative society. He had publicly tried to defend traditional Thai culture—or, at least, his perception of it—by decrying the buildup of American troops in the kingdom and the Americanization of Thai society, manners, and arts.

But to many Thais, including perhaps influential people like the senior generals and their spouses, Thompson appeared to have used his Thai art collection, like his silk business, to make it seem like he knew more about Thailand than Thai people themselves. Some Thais simply resented Thompson's success. "If you're a foreigner, you'll never truly be accepted by the Thai people," said one former member of the Thai royal family. "They'll be your friend, but you'll never be accepted" in what is still a relatively insular society. "Jim thought he was accepted by the Thais. That was a mistake."[27]

But Thompson also didn't court powerful Thais the way he might have. Thompson wasn't openly boastful—that wasn't the old money style he'd grown up with—but he didn't exactly stop talk that he was "more Thai than the Thais"—that he, not they, was the expert on their art, their culture, their traditional industries, their politics.

Unlike Thompson, Willis Bird came from working-class roots, seemed uncomfortable in fancy social venues, and could be cold and harsh in his business dealings, but he understood that when dealing with powerful Thais, he had to play the role of supplicant, to massage their egos, to accept that he was the *nong*, the lower man in the Thai hierarchy, to a *phi*, a man of higher status in Thailand, like Sarit or Phao.

Jim Thompson, for all his charm and high-class manners, never seemed to understand this basic survival skill. Instead, he gladly accepted these accolades, a mistake in Thailand. For instance, one friend of Thompson's told a reporter, "Nobody ever heard of Thailand until Jim Thompson invented Thai silk."[28] Thompson, of course, hadn't invented silk—he had revived the industry—but that kind of statement infuriated powerful Thais.

Thompson himself, while claiming to preserve Thai culture, often expressed his frustrations at the limitations he faced in what was, even after twenty years, a foreign country to him. In letters, he'd call Thais "backward" and lazy compared to neighbors like the Vietnamese, and to friends he'd complain about the challenges in finding effective office managers, of trying to restrain his anger to fit in with the local culture. Often, particularly after years of emulation as the silk king, he simply wouldn't play the role of *nong*.

In 1962, Jim Thompson finally realized the limits of Thai acceptance. In the summer of 1960, and then the following year, Thompson had purchased five carved Buddha heads made from white limestone; he had paid twenty-five hundred dollars for them, and he'd learned that the heads, believed to be a thousand years old, had come from a cave in northern Thailand.[29]

He had told officials from the Thai Department of Fine Arts about the find, and they had sent several officials up to northern Thailand. At the caves, local villagers, Thompson believed, were embarrassed that they had sold off the priceless sculptures to dealers, so they claimed that foreigners had come to their caves and simply stolen the limestone heads.[30] In the Fine Arts Department, and in other parts of the government where Jim Thompson had not won many friends, the villagers' story might have been exactly the opportunity necessary to humiliate Thompson.

In September 1962, the government sent two menacing men to Thompson's office to subtly imply that he might have stolen the heads and that he should consider giving them to the Fine Arts Department.[31] They implied—though of course they didn't say—that if Thompson didn't offer the sculptures as a gift, there could be consequences.

In early October, friends warned Thompson that the police might raid his house looking for the heads or possibly other items the Fine Arts Department wanted to seize, but Thompson mostly ignored the warnings. He did write a letter to the head of Fine Arts, explaining that he'd made Thailand his permanent home, that he was dedicated to its culture, and that his house, even more than collections by wealthy Thais, had preserved Thai art and culture.[32]

The Fine Arts Department did not respond, at least not in a letter. On October 10, after a police colonel arrived at Thompson's office, the American rushed home only to find that crowds of police had invaded his house, bringing with them a pack of local news reporters and photographers. The Thai police demanded the five limestone heads, making a great show of writing Thompson a lengthy receipt for them, but he knew that paperwork meant nothing in Thailand. To protect the items, Thompson himself packed them into a car and brought them in to the authorities, then he went home to plan how to dispose of the rest of his collection.

Despite the lengthy receipt, no one from the government offered Thompson any reimbursement for his expensive sculptures.[33] "The government can take what they want, but I don't know why they had to bring the police in, and make me look like an old criminal," Thompson wrote one friend several days after the police raided his home. "But I guess that's why this is still considered a backward country."[34]

Thompson attempted to use his connections to save the collection—and his reputation. He pleaded with acquaintances in the Fine Arts Department to return the heads, but at a lunch with the head of the department, Thompson and the man barely spoke, and the conversation went nowhere.[35] Thompson went to the U.S. embassy to ask it to intervene, but after years of denigrating American policy, he'd lost most of his allies at the embassy.[36] American officials did argue Thompson's case to senior government officials and even to the royal palace, but the Thais refused to do anything.[37]

Thompson's supposed high-society Thai friends, who'd eaten at his house, laughed at his stories, and joined him on trips up-country to hunt for antiques, didn't help, either.[38] "What probably hurt most was the silence of the Siam Society," a Bangkok organization dedicated to Thai art, culture, and history, wrote Thompson's friend Rene Burrow.[39] "They made no effort to go to his aid."

After the invasion of his home, Jim Thompson seemed, to friends, like a vastly different man. For years, he'd lectured friends who'd felt wronged in business about how they were living in a foreign country, how they had to adapt their behavior to Thailand and accept Thai mores, but when he found himself the alien, the outsider in a Thai society where he thought he'd been accepted and loved, he couldn't control himself.

The seizure didn't, in Burrow's words, force Thompson to "admit that he was himself responsible to a large extent for the envy and hostility which had developed in a number of Thai circles."[40] Instead, the incident curdled his feelings toward Thailand. Thompson had long ago grown bitter at U.S. policy, disdainful of American officials, and sick of the U.S. buildup in the region, but now, a convert scorned, he was utterly furious at his adopted country.

"When I returned to Bangkok in 1964 for a visit and 1965 to live again, I was struck by the fact that Jim's attitude [toward Thais] . . . had suddenly become rather hostile," said Murray Fromson, a CBS correspondent who'd known Thompson well.[41] Fromson had met Thompson before the house invasion but had left Thailand for several years.

Thompson changed his will to leave his house to a foundation rather than to the Thai nation, he stopped buying Thai art, and he all but stopped interacting with Thai government officials and many of the members of the extended royal family he'd once known well.[42] He quickly disposed of the rest of his Thai Buddhist art collection, selling it or giving it away to museums before the Thai government could take even more of it—a move that only further alienated many Thais, since it seemed to confirm that Thompson had something to hide.[43]

Thompson had once ignored the police tails on his car or the occasional strange clicks on his telephone line, but now he told friends, like CIA operative Campbell James, that he suspected the Thai authorities watched him constantly. At dinner parties and other public events and in his letters to friends and relatives, Thompson kept up a constant rhetorical attack on the Thai Fine Arts Department, other Thai collectors, and Thais in general. Convinced that the Thai government was monitoring him, Thompson would call the authorities "dirty little Thais" in conversations with friends and relatives.[44]

In private, Thompson's depression worsened, and though he still tried to swim every day at the Bangkok Sports Club, his small potbelly grew, his face became fuller and more rounded, and his smoking seemed more desperate.

"He [Thompson] neither intended to sell his collections nor to remove them from Thailand, since the house was to remain a museum of Thai art and a testimony to Jim Thompson's affection for the country," wrote his friend Rene Burrow. "That his generous purpose had been repaid with such ingratitude was more than he could accept or understand." Ultimately, believed Burrow, "He never recovered from the disgust this attack on his integrity aroused in him."[45]

The feelings appeared to be mutual: in a country where displaying public anger, even when you are wronged, is the ultimate cultural faux pas, after Thompson reacted so strongly to the seizures, many of his Thai acquaintances cut him off completely.

"I'd speak with people in the [royal] palace, and I was shocked by how negative their views were about Thompson," said Sanidh Rangsit's former wife. When Sanidh, a prince and an old friend of Thompson's, dined with other royals, they'd say to him, "How can you be friendly with that traitor?" his ex-wife remembered. On other occasions, she recalled, members of the royal family refused to even speak with Sanidh or sit near him at receptions because of his links to Thompson. "They saw Sanidh as a traitor, too, just for who he knew," she said.[46]

When Thompson returned to America for his annual visits in the years after the home invasion, he began to more seriously consider moving back to the United States. His sisters and his brother now had their own grown children, some of whom he adored: he went hiking in the Himalayas with his niece Martha and invited his nephew Henry, who visited Thailand and seemed to possess innate financial sense, to come work for his silk company. (Henry declined; the pay was too low.)[47]

To these younger members of the family, Jim Thompson seemed impossibly glamorous, so different from their starchy society parents who poured the same cocktails and organized the same dinner parties seemingly every night. "I remember he was ultimately cool. He was the cool uncle. He was erudite, he was glamorous," remembered Thompson's niece Robin Graves.[48]

But these younger relatives' admiration was not necessarily enough reason to move. As long as Jim Thompson remained in Thailand, he would always have to play the character he'd created for himself, to be the garrulous silk king—he could never disown the role, since tourists and even many of his friends expected it. But on trips back to America, thinking about whether to move, Jim Thompson realized that virtually no one could even picture his life in Thailand, that he had few common reference points with old friends or with even his siblings, caught up in the politics of the Kennedy administration, the new culture of television, or the gossip of Delaware and New York divorces and affairs. He'd walk alone in the morning while on his trips to the United States, and sometimes he talked about the future of his company to his relatives. None of his family members volunteered to take over. "I don't know anyone [in the family] even thought that much about Jim being successful, because people in the family didn't necessarily view what Jim was doing [the silk company] as a success," said Henry Reath, his nephew. "It was sort of thought of as an avocation, quirky."[49]

Returning from vacations in America, Thompson now often seemed, to his friends, even more depressed. "He found out what every expatriate who lives somewhere like Thailand for a long time finds out," said Harold Stephens, a longtime journalist in Thailand who knew Thompson. "At the end, these foreigners realize they have no home."[50]

Even with some of his closest friends, Thompson still claimed that none of these stresses bothered him, and in public he remained the same generous host, dashing silk salesman, and shrewd political analyst. "Don't worry about anything. It's all OK," Thompson wrote in a letter in 1966 to the family of Dean Frasche; Dean was perhaps his closest friend in Thailand, a man who ate dinner at Thompson's house nearly every night.[51] But in so many ways, it wasn't okay.

13

Robert "Red" Jantzen might have been the CIA station chief in Bangkok, but he didn't exactly try to hide himself. A bearish, six-foot-four man with bright red hair and meaty hands, Jantzen matched his overwhelming physical presence with a bluff, overwhelming social style. He often spoke as if talking into a megaphone, and he relished the chance to outdrink Thai generals, who always socialized with alcohol in their hands.

Jantzen reportedly planted a secret miniature tape recorder on his body so he could tape conversations he had while getting ragged drunk with Thai officials, which he did so often that he became one of the most regular drinking buddies of army chief Sarit, an outright alcoholic. Jantzen would smack and punch friends on the back and arms, and he regaled his acquaintances with stories of how, after drinking, he'd once wrestled Praphat Charusathien, one of the senior Thai generals.[1] Jantzen and his wife entertained nearly every night of the week in Bangkok, in their palatial home with its six-car garage, and Mrs. Jantzen had become a pillar of the foreign women's social community in the city.[2]

But Jantzen wasn't just bluff and backslapping. In his previous posting as head of the CIA station in Singapore, he'd managed a coup attempt in Indonesia and built up the agency's paramilitary operations across Southeast Asia.[3] In Bangkok, he'd developed an intimate knowledge of Thai politics and used his macho manner to gain the confidence of the most important generals, men like Sarit and, later, Praphat. Other American officials often complained that they couldn't get access to Praphat because he was always with Jantzen.[4]

"Jantzen wasn't an analyst type. He wasn't necessarily so good at putting together information; he didn't have a good memory," said one longtime CIA operative in Southeast Asia. "He needed good deputies to do that. But he was skilled at the kind of personal interaction that is critical in Thailand, where personal trust is everything."[5]

Jantzen, who ran the station in the late 1950s and early 1960s, surely knew that CIA headquarters had issued a notice to agents in the field to avoid Jim Thompson, but Jantzen wasn't about to listen to Langley. Like several other expatriate women, Jantzen's wife volunteered as a kind of docent at Thompson's house, showing off its traditional style and interior antiques to tour groups several times a week.

Jantzen himself frequently dined at Thompson's house, when he wasn't entertaining at his own home; he knew that Langley was terrified of relying on information from anyone who could be accused of being a communist sympathizer, but he was convinced that Thompson could still prove to be a valuable asset. Plus, Jantzen liked Jim Thompson personally—he liked Thompson's easy, convivial style, even if it was partly an act.

Jantzen had reason to feel secure in his job. His bosses valued him: one superior at the agency called him "the greatest single asset the United States has in Southeast Asia."[6] After all, they'd trusted him with one of the most coveted jobs in the agency, and his access to Sarit and other generals gave him even more power. When, in 1959, Sarit had decided to invade neighboring Cambodia, Jantzen had privately persuaded the Thai leader to abandon his plan, which would have been catastrophic for regional relations.[7]

And since an agency station chief had access to far more sources of easily available funds than an ambassador, who couldn't just hand out cash, the agency men were courted intensely by the most powerful leaders in their host countries. When army chief Sarit traveled to the Northeast on one occasion, along with members of the royal family and many foreign diplomats, he noticed Jantzen sitting amid a crowd during a ceremony marking U.S.-Thai cooperation. Halting the ceremony, the army chief called for Jantzen and then invited him to a party with senior Thai leaders that night. And, Sarit asked Jantzen, could the station chief prevent the U.S. ambassador from coming to the party?[8]

Plus, Jantzen was not station chief anywhere, but in Bangkok. "Everyone wanted to go to Thailand at that time," remembered CIA operative Joseph Lazarsky, who served in several posts in Southeast Asia. "We knew in the agency that this [Indochina] was a place where you could make an impact, you knew Washington was watching, there was a lot riding on it, and you had operational freedom you'd never have today." Also, Lazarsky remembered, "It was Bangkok. It wasn't Kinshasa or someplace like that. People loved Bangkok."[9]

If in the 1950s the Americanization of Thailand and the explosion of what would euphemistically be called the "nightlife" industry in Bangkok had appalled many Thai conservatives, at least these changes had remained mostly off the world's radar. But by the 1960s, that was no longer possible: Bangkok's reputation for sex and sin, a reputation that actually did not reflect the intensely conservative mores of most upper-class Thais, had gone global. To attract more visitors, Thailand's tourism promoters, including the national airline, would feature advertisements picturing alluring and seductive young women; one ad for the airline proclaimed, "Some say it's our beautiful wide-bodied DC-10s that cause so many heads to turn at airports throughout the world. We think our beautiful slim-bodied hostesses have something to do with it."[10]

By the 1960s, the U.S. Army, which was paying for most of Thailand's defense budget and building a complex in the Gulf of Thailand that would become the biggest military construction job in Asia, would formally establish Bangkok as a "rest and relaxation" destination for GIs.[11] American soldiers would be granted a certain number of days, usually five, in the Thai capital after serving time in

Vietnam or other postings.[12] At the height of the R & R program, American soldiers were spending over twenty million dollars per year in Thailand just on means of "relaxation."[13]

Thai men had always visited prostitutes, and taking a *mia noi*, a minor wife, was common among wealthier Thai men, but just as Thai politicians had traditionally operated through nonconfrontational, backroom strategies, the sex trade for Thai men had flourished quietly, hidden in barbershops, massage parlors, and pharmacies that actually provided sex to Thai men. Now the red-light districts of Bangkok expanded and the brothels became public and far flashier, and the prostitutes became more aggressive and grabby, anticipating the desires of Western men who cared little for the behind-closed-doors traditions of Thai prostitution. Rather than hiding upstairs in a "barbershop," the prostitutes now sat on plastic chairs outside the bars along Petchaburi Road, hooting to soldiers walking by, asking them to buy the girls a drink, the first step in a well-choreographed dance that led to a nearby short-time hotel.

Bernard Trink, an enterprising American writer then working for the *Bangkok World*, one of the English dailies, would write a weekly column called "Nite Owl" on the most exciting brothels in the city. Trink's columns, which became some of the most popular in the paper, often appeared flanked by photographs of scantily clad Thai women wrapped around dancing poles or splayed in come-hither positions. Some estimates put the number of prostitutes in Thailand at three hundred thousand.[14]

Even smaller provincial cities, if they were home to one of the seven U.S. air bases in Thailand, developed copies of the Bangkok nightlife scene. In Udon Thani, where the air base, only forty miles from Laos, housed a squad of American bombers and fighters, GIs could ramble from the Silhouette restaurant, eating cheeseburgers, to the new bowling alley to a nightcap at the Playboy and Mona Lisa bars, which teemed with upcountry Thai women copying the short skirts, heels, and wildly painted makeup they had seen on trips to the capital.[15]

• • •

Most CIA station chiefs in the late 1950s and early 1960s had cash hoards that an ambassador couldn't match, but with the agency's operations in Southeast Asia expanding rapidly, Jantzen and his successors controlled an operation more like an army than a traditional small group of spies and their local contacts. In 1959, Willis Bird's airline, Civil Air Transport, had resumed significant airlifts to Laos, but even before that, the agency, and even the State Department and the U.S. Agency for International Development, had relied on Bird to quietly deliver assistance into Laos. According to an internal cable in 1958, the State Department and the U.S. embassy in Laos relied on Bird to approve proposed aid deals and vouch for the contractors operating in Laos.[16]

Unlike Jim Thompson, Bill Bird knew how to make business deals function smoothly in Southeast Asia. Bird had a sense of which powerful officials needed courting in order to protect his operations, and he probably wasn't above handing cash payments to people who could help his firm snag deals. In 1959, a U.S. House of Representatives investigative committee on aid to Laos found that Bird, who had a contract worth six hundred thousand dollars for construction in Laos, had been giving gifts worth twenty-five thousand dollars to one powerful U.S. aid official there to win deals.[17]

From his office in Bangkok, Bird denied the charge, but four years later that American aid official, Edward T. McNamara, would plead guilty to defrauding the U.S. government by accepting gifts including cash, among other crimes. Bird had been indicted alongside McNamara, but he did not return to the United States to face charges.[18]

The House investigation and hearings led to a lengthy report examining widespread bribery and graft in U.S. aid programs in Laos and concluding that Bird's company had obtained its contracts in Laos without any competing bids.[19] The allegations of corruption against Bird became so well known that when William Lederer and Eugene Burdick penned their thinly veiled satirical novel *The Ugly American*, about the growing U.S. involvement in Southeast Asia, they created venal American characters said to be loosely based on Willis Bird.[20]

After the aid scandal, Bird, who still considered himself a patriotic American, never returned to the United States. He took a less public role in agency operations in Laos and sold one of the planes he owned to another contractor, who would use it for Indochina airlifts; still, Bird continued to closely advise agency operatives handling Laos, including his brother-in-law, Bill Lair, who became a central figure in the buildup.

And if the charges in America dampened his political views, Bird did not let that change in mind-set show. "My father still socialized with Americans, thought of himself as an American—he never could understand the anti–Vietnam War protest because he couldn't see why someone would protest against the U.S.," said Bird's son. "But he was worried about what would happen to him [with the charges] if he went back to the U.S., so he never did."[21]

As the 1962 Geneva accords establishing the neutrality of Laos quickly collapsed, all sides rushed money and arms to their favored forces in the tiny kingdom. For the Vietnamese, this meant the communist Pathet Lao, mediocre fighters but, with the assistance of the hardened North Vietnamese army, capable enough to take territory and to put pressure on the government in Vientiane. The American-backed royalist Lao army often ran from firefights, and despite some three hundred million dollars in U.S. aid to Laos by 1960, the royalist troops seemed incapable of mastering the increasingly heavy weaponry handed to them or of even defending their own territory.[22] "Dollar for dollar, it's about as bad a bargain as international aid money has yet bought," one American official told a reporter about U.S. assistance to Laos.[23]

Disdainful of the royalist forces, the CIA found a different type of fighter. In the mountains of northern and central Laos, the Hmong hilltribe, a rugged ethnic minority group long discriminated against by the lowland Lao, feared that a communist takeover would only further destroy the Hmong traditional culture and livelihood. Most Hmong had little interaction with, or knowledge of, the technological and commercial revolutions changing Southeast Asian cities like Bangkok. Many Hmong could barely even conceive of an entity called Laos—no Lao government official visited their clan, they spoke no Lao, and they felt no loyalty to state or nation, any entity larger than their immediate families and clans.

By the late 1950s, the CIA had already identified the vehemently independent Hmong as potential anticommunist allies, but the agency needed local leaders to work with, since the Hmong were so atomized into clans and subclans, many of which had vicious grievances against one another. Very few Hmong spoke Western languages or had obtained any formal education. But there was one prominent Hmong leader, a squat man named Vang Pao, who spoke a sometimes bewildering mix of French, English, Lao, and Hmong.

The agency built modern airstrips for Vang Pao, and the CIA shipped the Hmong leader and his hilltribe army assault rifles, rocket launchers, howitzers, and food; as Vang Pao's fame and stock of weapons grew, other hilltribes from across northern Laos marched to his bases to join him. The agency's private airline, whose name had been changed from Civil Air Transport to Air America, handled most of the flights, though it would farm out some of the duties to other contractors as well. By the end of the 1960s, Air America, which had more than three hundred pilots and copilots, was flying some thirty helicopters and two dozen planes just to Laos and dropping millions of pounds of food, ammunition, and weapons to the Hmong fighters each month.[24]

By the early 1970s, the Udon air base in northeastern Thailand, one of the main bases for flights into Laos, employed over twenty-three hundred people.[25] The airline would recruit its pilots from the ranks of air force flyboys, offering them contracts worth over five thousand dollars per month, a sizable amount at that time; the pilots would theoretically leave the air force and enter civilian life, but their personnel files would still secretly remain among air force intelligence documents, and many pilots never really understood the extent of CIA involvement in the airline.[26]

But the pilots soon found out they would earn their money. As one historian of CIA aviation wrote, the Laos airdrops actually proved more difficult than flying in Vietnam. The airstrips in Laos tended to be rudimentary pieces of mud surrounded by mountains and low-lying fog, and antiaircraft fire from the communists' Chinese-made heavy machine guns could be merciless; some of the pilots who'd served in World War II found the Laos flying more treacherous than any combat they had witnessed.[27]

Still, by being based in relatively comfortable Thailand, the CIA airline offered a kind of dream job for adrenaline-craving pilots. "It was the sort of war where a man could leave home in the morning, risk his neck numerous times during the day, and return to the comfort of his house in the evening, enjoy a dry martini with his wife, and be served a good dinner by his servants," wrote aviation historian Christopher Robbins.[28]

By the late 1950s and early 1960s, Washington was spending about a hundred million dollars annually just to support the Thai Special Forces helping Vang Pao in Laos, and multiples of that amount to equip the Hmong fighters. Vang Pao developed an effective guerrilla battle strategy. When the Lao communists and their Vietnamese allies hiked through Laos during the heavy monsoon season, which made their vehicles get stuck in the mud and bogged them down, Vang Pao and his men would kill or wound a few of the enemy and then retreat into the hills, which was their home territory, after all.[29]

Vang Pao understood the Lao and Vietnamese tactics better than almost any American commander, and his men inflicted serious casualties, leading one U.S. ambassador to Laos to call him a "military genius."[30] Still, at times the Hmong took huge casualties themselves, particularly when the communist forces targeted the Hmong bases with heavy artillery. Though precise figures were impossible to obtain, some American journalists estimated that 50 percent of Hmong were killed in some battles.[31]

While publicly maintaining their commitment to Laos's neutrality, the Kennedy and Johnson administrations not only armed Vang Pao but also increasingly used American bombers based in northeastern Thailand to attack Lao and Vietnamese forces in Laos, a major escalation of the war. The American bombers were dropping enormous tonnage: in 1965, U.S. planes, which had only launched about twenty air strikes in Laos the previous year, launched over forty-five hundred strikes.[32] Eventually, the Thai bases would form the foundation of the Rolling Thunder bombing campaign against North Vietnam, too;

75 percent of sorties against the North would be launched from the Thai bases.[33]

This bombing was hardly secret: American journalists and aid workers in Thailand and Laos could watch the heavy bombers taking off for Laos and could interview Lao peasants streaming into Vientiane with stories of enormous bombs eviscerating their villages. But the White House consistently denied that it had upped what became known as the "twilight war" in Laos and even still refused to acknowledge its enormous air bases in Thailand. War critic Senator William Fulbright noted in one interview that American officials denied the Thai bases even as government contractors placed advertisements in newspapers looking for employees to work on the B-52 bases in Thailand.[34]

The Laos buildup appealed immensely to Willis Bird—it pleased him as much as it infuriated and disgusted Jim Thompson, who told his sister that America's only decent option was to back the Lao monarch, a neutralist who supported neither the Lao communists nor the conservative, U.S.-backed Lao generals.[35] Despite his involvement in the agency's Indochina airlifts, Bird had always privately been skeptical that France or the United States could actually win a ground war in Vietnam or Laos, and if Washington had to fight in those countries' rugged mountains and swampy and brutally hot lowlands, he preferred that the fighting not be done by Americans but by locals who understood how to fight there.

"My father believed in proxy wars," said Willis Bird Jr. "He wanted the fighters to be locals, so it was their war, not America's war, a war they understood—and, if there were losses, it'd be their losses, not American losses."[36]

A proxy war also appealed to Bird's natural love of secrecy, his belief that the most effective intelligence work in Asia was conducted outside normal government channels anyway. Bird's brother-in-law, Bill Lair, who managed the agency's Vang Pao operation from Thailand and was worshipped almost like a god by his Thai and Hmong charges, shared Bird's sentiments; Lair feared that as the agency increasingly took over and Americanized the fighting in Laos, Vang Pao and his men would lose whatever local legitimacy they enjoyed.[37]

Bird also didn't worry about the American buildup in Thailand being used for bombing Vietnam and Laos. The high-intensity bombing appealed to his desire to win, no matter what the endeavor. Bird was a naturally quiet man, but he never avoided a fight, and unlike Thompson, who mostly tried to ignore other silk companies, Bird seemed most content in business when his competitors were crushed and humiliated.

"My father thought that they shouldn't have any areas in Laos or Vietnam that were off-limits to fighting," said Willis Bird Jr. "If you're going to fight, fight—so you should really bomb them."[38]

14

Denis Horgan, the young aide to Ed Black, the commander of the U.S. forces in Thailand, didn't know what to expect from his tour in Thailand. He had learned virtually nothing about the country before the Vietnam War, and he wasn't even sure what the United States was doing in the Southeast Asian kingdom. When Horgan arrived in Thailand, he spent much of his time at the expanding American bases in northeastern Thailand, the ones that officials back in Washington denied even existed or claimed were purely Thai operations.

Horgan quickly learned an enormous amount about the country; he was naturally inquisitive and was a journalist in his civilian life. But Horgan never felt totally comfortable at a place like the air base in Nakhon Phanom, a Thai town that had been transformed into some combination of a bazaar and a sprawling military camp, with go-go bars and rock nightclubs outside the base and a bombing command center plotting routes to North Vietnam inside.[1]

Horgan had been enormously relieved, of course, to be sent to Thailand rather than to Vietnam. The greatest danger he faced in the

Thai Northeast, traveling around with General Ed Black, was probably contracting *tong sia*, a badly upset stomach, from the raw meat in the local dish called *laap*, a kind of mince made with lime, onions, chilies, and cilantro.

Still, Horgan opposed nearly every aspect of the U.S. buildup in Southeast Asia, and though he was no culture aficionado, he felt a sense of discomfort with the rapid Americanization of the Thai Northeast. But on the bases in Thailand, Horgan restrained his opinions. The antiwar movement in the United States had yet to gain real steam, and most American elites, as well as the soldiers out in Indochina, still supported the buildup in Southeast Asia.

Though Ed Black had little in common with his young aide—a lifelong military man, Black had learned to just follow army orders, not debate them, and he considered any antiwar protests unpatriotic—Horgan felt respected by the general and liked having him around. "He'd sort of boast about me when we'd travel around—I think he was kind of pleased that this war skeptic civilian kid, journalist, was working for him," Horgan said.[2]

When Black met with Thai leaders—like Red Jantzen, Black seemed to command more respect from the Thai generals than the U.S. ambassador did—he'd bring Horgan with him, treating the young assistant almost like an equal. At an audience with Thanat Khoman, the erudite and acerbic Thai foreign minister who was no fan of the United States, despite his military bosses' close alliance with Washington, Horgan sat right with General Black as the Thai foreign minister complained about all the bad local publicity the government was amassing from allowing so many GIs into the country.

General Black had come from a similar belief system as Jim Thompson's: a kind of old-fashioned patriotism, convinced that if the U.S. government made a decision, it was probably be the right one. Unlike Jim Thompson, though, Black had spent the decades since World War II in the military, in Washington and Hawaii and Vietnam, and he'd had little chance to question that belief system.

"Jim Thompson and the general [Black] were still close friends, but the way they'd look at the world had changed so much since they knew each other in the 1940s," said Horgan. "The general didn't really have another way to look at it than from the military view."[3]

Black often didn't even understand his old friend and his cynicism and fatalism, though he was clearly delighted to have been sent to Thailand, where he could see Thompson regularly. "Sometimes, I got the sense that the general was just all around puzzled at Jim, even though he saw how generous Jim was with him and with his time and his house—just puzzled with how Jim could have become so critical of U.S. policy, because I don't think these ideas really would have crossed the general's mind," Horgan said. "The general was a crisp, straightforward man. . . . He had a certain amount of exasperation" with Thompson.[4]

Thompson seemed to feel the same frustration with his old friend. Over scotch in the evenings, when Horgan and Black stayed at Thompson's house in Bangkok, the silk king would warn the general and his aide that America's views of Southeast Asia had become too stark, too black and white in a region that dealt in grays, where "you're either with us or against us" didn't make much sense to many Asian leaders, where many of the countries had histories with one another far older than the United States itself. Thompson had once believed that Americans could understand Asia, with its history and deep-seated animosities and confusion, but by now he had simply decided that it couldn't, and perhaps Americans should admit that.

Thompson's arguments didn't have much effect; the general had a different frame of reference for his life. Black had not lived in Southeast Asia during the period after World War II, had not really known men like Pridi, and had not personally witnessed that immediate post–World War II era in which average men and women in former colonies truly believed that the United States would be a different type of power.

Black also had little intimate knowledge of the effect of the war on local populations in Laos and Thailand, the very people whom Thompson had sought out as weavers and friends. The general met mostly a controlled sample of Thais, village leaders or government officials or wealthier Thais who'd benefited from American largesse and were happy to keep it coming. He rarely met the poorest Thai farmers, other than by driving by them on the roads of the Northeast or seeing them beg near bars outside the U.S. bases. But this small circle of Americanized Thai elites was not the whole story, and Black, like most American officials, knew only a slice of Thailand. Despite strong growth rates and vast American aid, large parts of the Thai Northeast remained impoverished and resentful of how U.S. assistance had bypassed them and American policy had entrenched military dictators.

There really had not been much of a communist movement in Thailand in the late 1940s and early 1950s, when police general Phao, with U.S. backing, had targeted and hunted suspected leftists, but by the late 1960s—with Thailand dependent on the United States but American aid not filtering down to the village level, with U.S. bombing in Laos audible to Northeastern Thais, who shared a language and culture with people in Laos, and with Thai government repression chilling political discourse— the Communist Party of Thailand *did* begin to emerge. Winning recruits among the poor in the Northeast, and eventually even some leftist students from the elite universities in Bangkok who fled to the jungles from government crackdowns in the capital, the Communist Party of Thailand built up local cells across the Northeast and in Thailand's deep South, where a Muslim minority already harbored deep resentments against the Buddhist-dominated central government. The Thai communists launched a series of hit-and-run attacks on Thai military and police throughout the Northeast; eventually, the party's armed wing would number at least ten thousand fighters.[5]

"They are spending thousands of baht [the Thai currency] building fancy buildings for Bangkok's district offices up here [in the Northeast] but nothing is being done for the people," one Thai communist told journalist Louis E. Lomax, who traveled through the Thai Northeast reporting on the impact of the American presence.[6] The Communist Party of Thailand eventually won considerable support from intellectuals in Bangkok who were furious at the effect of the war and of U.S. money.

Thompson did not sympathize with the Communist Party of Thailand, but he had traveled enough through the Northeast, without having spectacles staged for him as Black did, to see the roots of the popular anger that the party drew upon. As Horgan watched the two men, he realized that Thompson also saw, in his old friend General Black, an obliviousness to the corrosive effects of the American presence in the region, to the ways in which U.S. assistance was permanently transforming Asia, and often not for the better.

By 1967, Thompson had realized, the United States had all but cemented authoritarian rule in Thailand. Thailand had not been destined to become a military dictatorship, but the Americans' critical decisions in the late 1940s and early 1950s had all but ensured that it would become one. Now Washington could hardly change course, since only the generals could ensure continued support for the U.S. war effort in the region, which was unpopular among many average Thais.

The general did not take such a wide, historical view. He worked in a command center that would mark points on Indochina maps and send out bombers to attack them, but the officers in Thailand never had to see the consequences of their bombing raids—consequences Thompson always wondered about. "I never saw a soul on the beach, but every twenty minutes a giant tanker plane for refueling the fighter planes would take off from U-Tapao," Thompson wrote after accompanying Black to one base in Thailand near the coast where jets took off to attack Laos and North Vietnam. "It all seemed so peaceful except when you thought of what those big planes had to do and where they were going."[7]

When Thompson gently bantered with Black about the costs of a war in Vietnam, the two men's conversation, always polite and even jocular, would turn sour. Unlike Thompson, Black had seen a lot of death; he'd served far longer in the field than Thompson in World War II and, remaining in the military for decades, had attended many funerals. "The general might not see the results of the bombing up close," said Horgan, "but if Jim crossed the line, talked about the consequences of the war, the general sort of shut up, which he almost never did, and I think Jim realized not to say more."[8]

To Thompson, too, the U.S. military and the CIA were transforming traditional Thai culture in critical ways that Black probably did not even notice. In Burma and Thailand in the 1940s and early 1950s, the agency's backing for Phao had allowed the police general to consolidate his hold over the narcotics business. So too, in Laos, the agency's influence helped to transform the opium trade. The opium trade in Laos had previously been a small business catering to local needs—the Hmong traditionally cultivated opium, though Vang Pao prohibited his own fighters from smoking it—but in the 1960s it developed into a massive industry tied to global markets and eventually catered to the half a million American soldiers stationed in Southeast Asia, many of whom dabbled in opium to escape the war around them.[9]

According to the most comprehensive study of the drug trade in Southeast Asia, Vang Pao realized that opium, which could be smoked or processed into heroin, could become a bigger cash crop and possibly provide him and his people with a measure of financial security, even if the war turned against them. Though some CIA operatives on the ground in Laos were uneasy with the opium business, just as some had been uncomfortable abetting the opium trade in Burma, the alliance with the Hmong overrode any concerns.

Vang Pao and his allies used the agency-built airstrips and bases to ship cargoes of opium out of the country on planes owned by Corsican drug traffickers.[10] And when the Corsicans were forced out of the country—Lao leaders wanted a larger share of the drug business—CIA pilots, to accommodate Vang Pao, flew the opium themselves out of the Hmong regions to markets in the Lao capital and other cities.[11] The drugs did provide Vang Pao with cash, at least for a time, but they also had a corrosive long-term effect. Along with the CIA airdrops of rice to the Hmong, the growing opium business reduced Hmong villages' self-sufficiency and ultimately made many of them totally dependent on handouts to survive.

Political differences didn't keep Thompson and Black from spending time together, however, and Thompson was careful not to directly criticize his old friend or ever raise his voice at him. Thompson often flew up to the Northeast to hike with Black, whose wife wasn't going to be joining him in Thailand until later in his tour, and the general dutifully followed his old friend from one temple to the next, looking at wall paintings and sculptures. Black had absolutely no interest in Thai art, though—when Thompson would show him some artifact, Black would nod his head and mutter, "Huh, great," and later tell Horgan that Thompson had "gone too native."[12]

On some weekends, Black and Horgan would fly down from the Northeast to Bangkok and stay at Thompson's elegant house. The general didn't exactly fit in with Jim's dinner crowd, which often included designers, artists, and wealthy foreign socialites. But despite his long army background and jockish, straight-ahead demeanor, Ed Black did have a weakness for opening his mouth. Other military men warned him to stop chatting so freely with reporters, and over dinner at Thompson's house Black would regale tourists and Thompson's wealthy Bangkok friends with stories of life at the bases in the Northeast, even though the army wanted as little said publicly about these outposts as possible.[13]

"Ed Black was kind of a showboat, and later that wouldn't win him a lot of friends in the army," said one longtime Bangkok resident.[14]

When Black moved to Thailand, he was shocked not only by Thompson's views of U.S. policy but also by how his old friend seemed to be spent physically and mentally. Thompson and Black were not too different in age, but the general played tennis, did pushups, and virtually ran up hills in the Northeast; he could have been mistaken for a man in his thirties. Thompson, who would turn sixty-one in 1967, certainly looked his age, if not older, with his deep facial lines and skin weathered by tropical tanning and his paunchy waist jutting out over his usual khakis, which made him look like he still dressed for prep school.

The general wasn't a deep thinker or much of an emoter, other than yelling during the regular tennis game he demanded no matter where he traveled, but Black surely noticed that his old friend sometimes seemed so weary that nothing could cheer him up. "Sometimes the general would say to me, after a night at Jim's, 'Jim has been out here a long time, maybe too long,'" Horgan said.[15]

Even the silk business, which had always held Thompson's attention despite the battles with other companies and fights within his own firm, seemed to bore him. Tired of the basic silks, Thompson in the 1960s had begun making printed silks, and the prints proved even more popular with foreign buyers. This new art form, wrote Thompson's friend William Warren, had proven "therapeutic to take his mind off his recent difficulties," and he'd made himself extremely busy at work in 1966 and 1967.[16]

But despite the thrill of discovering a new form of silk printing, being in the shop—or, worse, in the company office, which Thompson had never enjoyed, even in the early days—had become a chore; the sales pitches and fake chumminess with wealthy clients were tiresome. When he saw his niece Martha, whom he loved and had invited to Bangkok for a long trip, back in America in 1966, Thompson seemed to be summing up his life, as if preparing for the end. When Thompson looked at her, she wrote, he paused as if he were taking a picture, as if "impressing an image of me on his mind forever."[17]

Black's perception of his friend's exhaustion was probably accurate. For years, resentment and sadness had been building in Jim Thompson, but most of the time he had kept this blackness at bay, either by having dinner parties virtually every night and allowing himself no alone time amid the constant work schedule and party chatter, or by channeling his frustration and anger into occasional bursts of rage at Thai leaders, the U.S. government, or even his own employees.

But by the mid-1960s, Thompson seemed unable to restrain himself any longer. It had become obvious that the United States was going to become deeply involved in the Vietnam War; it had become clear that Jim Thompson's liberal Thai friends were never coming back; and it seemed sure that Thompson was going to die alone, with no immediate family. In 1967, his ex-wife, Pat, appeared on the verge of death after a blood vessel burst at the base of her brain. They had not spoken much since their rapid marriage and divorce, but the news upset Thompson greatly, though he did not go to see her in the hospital in San Francisco before she died, since he did not want to run into the man she'd left him for.[18]

Pat's illness made Thompson wonder, more intensely, whether he'd made the right life decisions. "He would tell his sister, ask her, 'Why didn't I ever try to have a family?'" said Thompson's niece Ann Donaldson.[19]

Dinners at Thompson's house didn't always disintegrate into anger—Thompson was normally still the gracious and witty host he'd always been. But by 1967, any restraint Thompson once had—fear of being tarred as unpatriotic, concern about alienating old friends like Black—was gone. The previous year, he'd done one last favor for a friend in the Central Intelligence Agency, agreeing to meet a young operative who wanted to know about Laos and the Thai Northeast, but he'd kept it quiet, so as not to suggest he would help the CIA any more. "By this time, the American officials, the people in the CIA, a lot of them who before never believed Jim Thompson was a communist – because he wasn't—now they really did believe it," said one CIA operative who worked in Southeast Asia and knew Thompson.[20]

In 1967, rather than just discussing U.S. policy at his house or in private on trips to the Northeast with the general, Thompson met an American television camera crew, who followed him to his house, his weavers, and his shop. Thompson had given hundreds, maybe thousands, of interviews to journalists from newspapers, magazines, and radio and television stations.[21] In the past, he'd almost always stuck to a kind of informal script, taking the reporters to meet his weavers and to his house, telling the stock story of how he'd started his company, but this interview was different.

On the tape, Thompson told the camera crew, standing in front of the skyline of Bangkok, "Vietnam, I worry about that terribly." Jim Thompson wasn't a communist—he made that clear, telling the interviewer that once the United States was in Vietnam, it couldn't just back down. But, he said sadly, America should never have been there—not allied with the French, and certainly not now.[22]

In a long, revelatory letter he wrote in early 1967 to his old boss from New York, Arthur Holden, Thompson abandoned much of the restraint he showed when writing to his sister, a restraint that stemmed from a fear of the Thai authorities reading his mail. "The whole Vietnam affair seems very tragic," Thompson wrote to Holden, before the Vietnam War was publicly perceived in America as a great failure. "The Viet Cong would never have driven themselves to the lengths they go now if they had been allowed to settle down peacefully in an independent country at the end of [World War II.]"[23]

Thompson, said one of his close friends, had come to a realization that other liberal former OSS men understood by the 1960s: they had fought to rid the world of imperialism—Japanese and German and French, but also British and Dutch—and yet, by continuing their intelligence work into the 1940s and 1950s, they had actually mid-wifed a new era of imperialism. American imperialism.

Another former OSS officer named Edmond Taylor later wrote, sadly, "As the conscious servant of my country's consciously anti-imperialist aims in Asia, I had been unconsciously helping to enlarge the frontiers of our existing Pacific imperium."[24]

"Think about it," said Thompson's friend Philippe Baude. "You watch your time, your time is over, your era is disappearing in front of you, but you are still alive, and you know that you have been an engineer of change, but of change that wasn't what you wanted. There is a certain deep sadness in that."[25]

15

In the week before Easter Sunday of 1967, Jim Thompson seemed even more frantic than usual. He'd held a sixty-first birthday party: a dinner with his closest friends and then a massive celebration with employees from the silk company.[1] He had just moved his company into a new building on Suriwong Road, and his silk business was so busy that even though he'd agreed to celebrate Easter at a friend's cottage in the Cameron Highlands of Malaysia, he'd forgotten to get his papers in order before leaving Thailand—including a cholera shot and tax forms—but a sympathetic official at the airport allowed him to leave the kingdom.[2] He also apparently forgot to pack enough money for the trip.

Thompson's friend Andree Burrow, who also worked in the silk shop, warned him that it didn't make sense to travel when he was so tired and scattered. "Jim, you're really not in a fit state to travel," Burrow told him. "Each time you go to the Cameron Highlands something happens to you." On his last visit, he had stumbled into a hornets' nest and nearly gotten stung all over.[3] Thompson declined her advice.

Jim had traveled to the Cameron Highlands, 137 miles from the Malaysian capital of Kuala Lumpur, before, and he loved the highlands' lush hills and cool, almost frosty air; at over five thousand feet above sea level, the air was a stark change from the soup that passed for a sky in sea-level Bangkok, where the city actually sank a few feet every year into the marshy ground below it. After the British colonized Malaya, as it was then called, in the late nineteenth century, civil servants and businessmen turned the highlands into a hill-station respite from the summer heat of Kuala Lumpur; the temperature in the highlands rarely topped seventy-five degrees Fahrenheit.

By 1967, Malaya—now called Malaysia—was no longer a British colony, but the Tudor-style cottages and peaked roofs and manicured lawns of the highlands still resembled a kind of British country town stuck in the middle of Southeast Asia and surrounded by coconut palms, waterfalls, and small Hindu shrines decorated with garish pink and baby-blue statues of gods. Now the area attracted mostly middle-class Chinese families from Kuala Lumpur and Penang as well as tourists from Thailand and Singapore who believed the cool moist air had health benefits. But you could still sit down for a Sunday roast supper or a traditional afternoon tea with clotted cream and scones at one of the highlands' older lodgings, like Ye Olde Smokehouse inn, where servants offered tea on silver plates and blue and white china to guests sinking into overstuffed furniture that looked like it hadn't been changed since the early twentieth century. Indian workers picked tea leaves on the plantations dotting the highlands and tended the rose gardens in front of bungalows and the occasional Swiss-style chalet set back from the rutted, winding roads.

Though the highlands' homes might have resembled Brighton, outside the clusters of inns and houses, many parts of the highlands remained relatively wild in 1967. Now tour buses clog the highlands' roads, but in 1967 tigers still stalked its woods. Less than a decade earlier, over 250,000 Malayan and British troops had conducted a brutal counterinsurgency campaign in rural parts of the country against the Malayan communist guerrillas, and the insurgents had used some of the cottages in the highlands for wartime trials and summary executions.

The communist fighters, though defeated by government forces, would keep their campaign alive in the late 1960s. Groups of aboriginal people still lived in the highlands, practicing their traditional animist religion, hunting with poisoned darts, and residing in communal houses raised on stilts above the ground. Though locals had cut some footpaths through the dense jungle, many of the trails were narrow and difficult to follow, with deep and hidden ravines, and signs in the highlands warned trekkers never to travel alone. Hikers had been lost for days in the Cameron Highlands, though usually they were eventually found.

Those signs would mean little to Jim Thompson; he didn't usually pay much attention to signs, and he enjoyed walking by himself in northeastern Thailand, in the woods in Delaware, and on vacations. On a previous trip to the highlands, Thompson had gone hiking alone in the jungle. These walks were often the only time he had alone in months, since he spent nearly every waking hour in Bangkok at his shop or surrounded by people at his house.

Thompson had accepted an invitation for Easter weekend from his friends Dr. T. G. and Helen Ling, antiques collectors and dealers from Singapore, who owned a house in the highlands called Moonlight Cottage. Moonlight Cottage was a typically English-looking bungalow up a winding road on the top of the hill, with a white picket fence and surrounded on three sides by a steep drop off the mountain. Jungle paths overgrown with trees and small purple flowers snaked away from the cottage in several directions. Thompson's friend Connie Mangskau, an antiques dealer in Bangkok who'd known Thompson since just after World War II, decided to come as well.[4]

The trip from Bangkok to the highlands hardly proceeded smoothly, though with Thompson, who liked to stop along the way and hunt for art or interesting side trips, any vacation could be chaotic. When he and Connie Mangskau headed from Penang, a city in northern Malaysia, to the Cameron Highlands, their driver suddenly halted their car and ran out. He returned with a different driver and told them they had to go with the new driver and several other men in the car. When Connie Mangskau refused to ride with several strange men, possibly for fear of being kidnapped, the drivers backed off their proposal.[5] Later, though, two policemen who'd happened to witness Thompson's transfer in Penang said they saw nothing unusual that suggested a potential kidnapping plot.[6]

Once he arrived at Moonlight Cottage, Thompson still seemed unsettled and restless. On Easter Sunday morning, after attending church services, the Lings, Mangskau, and Thompson headed out for a picnic, but Thompson apparently wanted to cut the meal short and get back to the cottage as quickly as possible, an unusual rudeness for a man known for his elaborate courtesy.[7] He even started packing up all the food and items from the picnic before everyone had finished, and he hurried the rest of the group along rather than letting anyone enjoy a nap outside.

When they returned to the cottage, everyone except Thompson decided to take a nap. At around 3:30 p.m., Dr. Ling heard footsteps outside, crunching on the gravel path, and assumed that Thompson was leaving the cottage for a walk. A few minutes later, one of the servants at a nearby inn saw Thompson walking on one of the paths near Moonlight Cottage.

The Lings and Mangskau paid little attention to Thompson's leaving, since they knew he enjoyed trekking alone and he was an experienced hiker, going back to the jungle survival training he'd received in the OSS during the Second World War.[8] Later they would realize that Thompson had not taken his cigarettes with him, which seemed to suggest he wasn't planning any kind of long hike, since he could barely go an hour without a smoke. He also had not taken his passport, his gallstone pills, his jacket, or any other warm clothing.

When Thompson had not returned by nightfall, the Lings and Mangskau began to worry, though their fear was mitigated by knowing about Thompson's jungle skills. Just the day before, Thompson and Dr. Ling had hiked in the jungle and gotten lost, but Jim had found a stream and gotten them back to safety.[9] Still, by 7 p.m. on Easter, Dr. Ling called the Malaysian police.[10] Everyone stayed awake all night at Moonlight Cottage, keeping a vigil and expecting Thompson to return.

Henry Thompson, Jim's nephew, was standing in the brokerage firm where he worked when he saw the news, which flashed across the Dow Jones ticker. He immediately called his father, Jim's older brother. "He was surprised, but he wasn't as worried as he might have been, since he knew Jim could survive," said Henry.[11] When Thompson's sister Elinor, his closest relative, learned of his disappearance, she seemed inconsolable and quickly wanted to organize a family trip to Southeast Asia to help with a search; ironically, more of Thompson's family came to Thailand after he vanished than when he was still around.

Back in Bangkok, at the headquarters of Thompson's silk company, Charles Sheffield, Jim's top assistant, received a call from Malaysia informing him of Thompson's disappearance. When Sheffield told the employees the news, most burst out crying, and many simply could not work for days, they were so distraught; eventually, they came back to work, but the pressure of trying to maintain a happy face for customers at the silk shop proved impossible for some of the staff.[12] Some laid offerings at the spirit house outside the silk company offices, a means of praying for Thompson's return.

Thompson's friend Rene Burrow, hearing the news, remembered thinking, "Jim had simply walked out of our lives."[13] And at Thompson's residence, the houseboy Yee set the table for dinner that night anyway, though he'd heard of Thompson's disappearance; he simply couldn't believe that Thompson would actually be gone long; in fact, Yee continued setting the table for a dinner party for months on end, even though the master of the house never returned.

The Bangkok news media seemed to learn all at once—or at least, once one reporter learned that the most famous American in Asia had vanished and that a massive search party had begun combing the highlands the morning after Easter, every other newspaperman and broadcaster seemed to know. Within days of Easter Sunday, a mob of reporters had descended upon the Cameron Highlands, shadowing Malaysian police officials and repeatedly grilling the Lings and Connie

Mangskau for every detail of Thompson's last hours. Bangkok reporters called Sheffield constantly, while in the United States, Thompson's family members found themselves faced with a barrage of media inquiries they were unprepared to handle.

"It was really insane, the kind of media crush you think about today, not back then," said Denis Horgan.[14] The disappearance story featured in nearly every major international newspaper, as well as in *Newsweek, Time*, and other leading magazines. Graham Martin, who served as U.S. ambassador to Thailand and later as assistant secretary of state, told Thompson's brother-in-law that he'd answered literally hundreds of requests for comments about the Thompson case.[15]

By Monday, the Malaysian police had organized a massive search effort that included at least two hundred people hiking through the highlands in all directions, trained jungle search squads, and aboriginal trackers who knew the highlands better than anyone else.[16] They hunted for signs of a wounded man, a hit-and-run accident, a tiger mauling, an aboriginal animal trap that had snapped shut on a man, or a kidnapping. British army helicopters joined the hunt; Malaysian police used helicopters to fly low and look at the tops of trees.[17]

By Tuesday, two days after Thompson had vanished, nearly four hundred people were searching for him, the biggest rescue operation ever attempted in Malaysia.[18] The police alerted Interpol as well as the FBI, which took a close interest in the case.[19] Soon the search party expanded its area and was conducting a house-by-house search of the entire region around Moonlight Cottage. Thompson's silk company and several other businessmen friends put up a reward for any evidence that he was still alive.[20] Despite Thompson's long life in Thailand, none of his Thai friends or acquaintances went to Malaysia to join the hunt or help out in any way.

Still, even several days after he vanished, most of Thompson's friends could not believe the worst. Not long after the disappearance, Connie Mangskau returned to Bangkok, where she held her own sixtieth birthday party, which had been planned far in advance but which now felt like a wake. "I couldn't believe that he would just disappear like that. Not Jim. He had a strong sense of survival," Mangskau later told a reporter.[21]

Horgan was with General Ed Black, up in the Thai Northeast, when the general received a phone call from a friend the day after Easter informing him Thompson had not returned. "We're going to find Jim," General Black immediately told Horgan. "We're going there."[22] The army did not want Black leading an expedition to the Cameron Highlands; he held an important job in Thailand, Thompson was a civilian, and they probably did not want to link a vanished man with the U.S. armed forces in any way.

Black didn't pay much attention; on Thursday of the week that Thompson disappeared the general and Horgan flew to the Cameron Highlands, taking with them three military helicopters and a load of military search equipment.[23] When Black arrived, he informed the press and the local police, to their surprise, that he would be taking over the search effort. "I think the general just thought, 'This is my friend, he's gone, I'm going to do whatever is necessary to find him,' but it would really hurt him in his army career," said Horgan. "I don't think he even told the U.S. embassies in advance of what he was doing, and I'm sure they were extremely pissed."[24]

Years later, Black would tell *Life* magazine that the American embassies "showed a singular lack of interest in doing anything remotely active [about the Thompson case with him]. . . . They were completely unhelpful."[25]

But the general didn't seem to care what the embassies thought, and he probably also didn't mind having hundreds of reporters wanting to interview him. He strode around Moonlight Cottage, searching for clues himself; he interviewed the Lings, Mangskau, policemen, local businesspeople, and anyone else he could find. Then he and another of Thompson's friends hired their own aboriginal guides and trekked through the highland jungles themselves, finding nothing except some joss sticks and candles left by local mediums who'd been trying to get in touch with spirits that could help them to find Thompson.[26]

Black had Horgan climb up a local tower with his army radio equipment and oversee another group of searchers commanded by Black. They kept in contact by radio but found nothing. Then Black camped out at a local hotel to listen to stories from two men who were the first of an endless series of tipsters claiming to have information about Thompson that friends or relatives of the silk king could have for a price.[27]

Getting nowhere, Black finally went to the U.S. embassy in Kuala Lumpur, where the ambassador and some of his staff grudgingly offered him a briefing on the Thompson case. "They didn't want to tell us anything," said Horgan, but the U.S. ambassador in Kuala Lumpur did meet personally with the leader of Malaysia, Tunku Abdul Rahman, to ask for his assistance with the case.[28]

The Thai government didn't seem too interested in helping, either. An American lawyer in Bangkok, Charlie Kirkwood, was entrusted by Thompson's foreign friends, who'd put up the reward for him, with handling the reward money and sifting through tips. "Most of the information I was getting was people trying to extract a little bit of money on very flimsy evidence," said Kirkwood. "The Thais [government] didn't seem too eager to do anything at all. . . . They just stiff-armed me."[29]

On April 5, the Malaysian police officially called off their search for Thompson, even though the reward for information about him had doubled. "We have not found a single clue in the last nine days," one Malaysian police official told the Associated Press.[30]

Two days earlier, Black had given up his personal hunt for his friend, but he returned to Bangkok to plan a new approach for finding Thompson and to give as many media interviews as possible about the case.[31] When he returned to Bangkok, a more senior general, Horgan said, "read [Black] the riot act for doing this search for Jim Thompson—they told Black to just stay out of this." The general knew then, Horgan said, that he had damaged his career badly.[32] Indeed, after leading the Thompson search, Black was never promoted in the military again.

Two weeks later, Thompson's company hired a man named Dick Noone, one of the most accomplished jungle fighters in the world, to continue the hunt.[33] In all the searches for Thompson, no hunter boasted more experience than Noone; his report would prove the most authoritative and so would spark the most speculation about where Thompson had vanished to.

Backed by his own team of aboriginal trackers—Noone spoke Malaysian aboriginal dialects—Noone conducted another exhaustive foot search of many miles around Moonlight Cottage, before concluding, "If Jim were still in the jungle, I'm sure we would have found him."[34] When some locals argued that an animal might have killed Thompson and dragged him somewhere, Noone shot down that theory, saying that he and the aboriginal trackers would have seen some signs of an animal mauling.

Santokh Singh, a senior Malaysian policeman in the area, later told Martha Galleher, one of Thompson's favorite nieces, essentially the same thing, saying, "Your uncle wasn't lost in the jungle or attacked by animals" or the police would have found him.[35] Instead, most of the Malaysian police believed that Thompson had been kidnapped and then taken away from the highlands, though no one ever sent any ransom note.[36]

Once Black and the Malaysian police gave up, at least for the time being, the search actually got larger—and weirder. Local businesspeople in the highlands consulted a prominent temple medium, who put himself into a trance and assured them that Thompson was still alive. He was just the first of a number of psychics, jungle experts, and other publicity seekers who descended on the highlands.[37] Other local psychics pulled out dousing sticks and crystal balls and even sacrificed a white rooster in attempts to divine information about the silk king.[38]

In Bangkok, one prominent Jesuit priest claimed he'd found a spot on the map where Thompson was hiding.[39] Even Ed Black, not much inclined to mysticism, consulted several respected spirit mediums during his time in the highlands. One Malaysian police official tried to keep track and recorded that over 110 local spirit mediums had come to the area to make predictions about Thompson's whereabouts.[40]

But they were pushed aside by a much bigger magic man. Thompson's sister Elinor, inconsolable, decided she had to hire her own psychic. Other members of the Thompson family had begun their own efforts to find out what had happened to their relative, and Martha Galleher made the quest to find Jim her lifelong great white whale. She hounded American officials, including Secretary of State Henry Kissinger, and years later, in her seventies, wrote a self-published book about her uncle's case, still trying to track down aging U.S. diplomats who might have some information.[41]

But Elinor had known Jim the best, and after coming to Bangkok in May 1967 she proved willing to try anything to find clues about her beloved brother; even her husband, James Douglas, an unsentimental man who had served as secretary of the air force under Eisenhower, could not dissuade her. So, since the Thompson family had plenty of money, she hired the best. As Thompson's friend William Warren recounted, she paid a "substantial financial arrangement" to a man named Peter Hurkos, a fifty-five-year-old psychic from the Netherlands who claimed to have developed magical powers after falling off a ladder and to have used his extrasensory perception to solve twenty-seven murders in seventeen countries, including the famous Boston Strangler case.[42] (Unfortunately, the man Hurkos fingered in the strangler case turned out to be innocent.)

Hurkos never avoided publicity, and like a stage magician, he traveled with a beautiful young female assistant, in this case a blond woman in a miniskirt named Stephany Farb. The strangler case, despite his error, had elevated him into the top tier of psychics, far from the crystal ball–gazing fakirs and palm readers who told fortunes at country fairs. Hurkos became friends with Hollywood celebrities and was called in by many desperate families to help them find missing or murdered sons and daughters.[43]

Arriving in Asia, Hurkos first traveled to Bangkok, where he visited Thompson's house and declared that he felt negative energy in the silk king's dining room.[44]

Denis Horgan was given the job of escorting Hurkos in the Cameron Highlands, but the psychic did not seem to need much time on the ground. He stayed less than one full day in the highlands, where he first walked around Moonlight Cottage "as if trying to catch a scent," Warren wrote.[45] Hurkos then put himself into a kind of trance and began mumbling incoherently, and his lovely assistant translated his mutterings into a report.

Hurkos, out of his trance, then returned to Bangkok and confidently declared what he'd seen in his vision: once Thompson had walked away from Moonlight Cottage, a man came up to him, and after they had walked together for half a mile, the other man grabbed Thompson, put a cloth over his face to drug him, and then flew him out of Malaysia on an airplane that landed in Cambodia, where he was being held prisoner.

Philip Rivers, a Malaysian resident who had closely researched the Thompson case, noted that there was no airstrip nearby where someone could have landed to spirit Thompson away in a plane.[46] Also, Thompson's friend Warren noted that since neither Thailand nor the United States had diplomatic ties with Cambodia, it was conveniently hard to prove or disprove Hurkos's assertion.[47] Several officials at the U.S. embassy in Bangkok apparently did send cables back to Washington, attesting to Hurkos's powers and asking the State Department to find a neutral nation to approach Cambodia's government and, on the advice of a psychic, persuade the Cambodians to begin a hunt for a missing American.

The content of these cables, which turned on the psychic's mumblings, Warren noted, "was probably without precedent at the embassy"—surely an understatement. When no other country would take up Hurkos's charge to search Cambodia for the missing silk king, Hurkos left Asia, angrily claiming that he would go directly to President Lyndon Johnson with the matter.[48] Whether he ever tried remains unknown; Johnson's detailed presidential papers do not record any interactions with the psychic or his blond assistant.

Though Black and Horgan believed they'd gotten only the bare minimum of cooperation from the U.S. embassy in Bangkok, and several of Thompson's relatives would also later complain of embassy stonewalling, one group of American officials in Bangkok closely followed the Thompson case. Very soon after Thompson's disappearance became known, the CIA station in Bangkok, and soon the FBI as well, took an intense interest.

One man who had access to Thompson's large classified personnel file at the agency archives said that because Thompson had been involved in intelligence work in the past, because some in the agency believed he was still involved, and because many outsiders were convinced that, true or not, he was still running intelligence operations in 1967, the agency's leadership felt it had to take on his case.[49] Some agency officials believed that whether or not Thompson remained involved in intelligence, and even though he had publicly criticized the CIA, the fact that so many people in Asia believed he might have been kidnapped or killed by some enemy of the agency made it CIA business.

Other longtime CIA operatives worried that someone in the agency was actually responsible for the disappreance of Thompson, a major American critic. Joseph Lazarsky, who was working for the CIA at that time in Jakarta and who, like Thompson, had served in the wartime OSS, sent cables throughout the agency trying to find out any information about Thompson's disappearance. He found that within the agency, many operatives believed that Thompson had been killed and that Thai officials knew what happened. Thompson's old friend Campbell James, another longtime CIA operative, also tried to track down information about Thompson's whereabouts through the agency and found that many operatives seemed to believe that Thompson's disappearance was somehow connected to the transformation of his political beliefs, though he never concluded for sure that the agency was behind his disappearance.

Robert Jantzen, the CIA station chief in Bangkok, closely followed every report and decision being made in the embassy on the Thompson case, essentially serving as the point man. Jantzen himself traveled down to the Cameron Highlands to conduct his own quiet search for Thompson, accompanied by several aides, and Jantzen sent out an all-points bulletin to all station chiefs for any CIA information about Thompson.

The agency had other sources of leads on Thompson, too: while Noone, the jungle expert, reported to Thompson's silk company, he also allegedly made another, private report to the agency.[50] Yet, even more than forty years after Thompson's disappearance, the CIA refuses to comment publicly about Thompson.

The FBI, which had launched a lengthy investigation into Thompson in the early 1950s, also tracked his disappearance closely, as declassified records later showed. The bureau conducted its own investigation of the possible rationales for Thompson's disappearance, interviewing his associates and friends, some of whom also told the bureau that Thompson's political views and activities might have put him in danger with senior Thai officials.[51]

Though Jantzen had been a personal friend of Thompson's, the silk king's relatives found they could not get much information out of most agency operatives, or other American officials, about the case. When Thompson's niece Ann Donaldson visited Bangkok, the U.S. ambassador, she said, brushed off any questions she had about how Thompson vanished, preferring to talk only about the distribution of his estate. Donaldson found Jantzen even cagier, refusing to tell her almost anything. "I still think the CIA knew about what had happened to Jim, but Jantzen wasn't going to tell me," she said.[52] She wound up convinced that the CIA had played a role in his disappearance.

Martha Galleher met with senior State Department officials but found that they avoided nearly every question she had. And when Thompson's relatives traveled to Malaysia in May 1967, the CIA station chief in Kuala Lumpur told them, "I can assure you that your brother is not buried in this country." When pressed, the station chief did not offer any more information about Jim Thompson.[53]

16

Ed Black, Connie Mangskau, Charles Sheffield, and Thompson's other friends continued to launch new search-and-rescue schemes, even as outside interest had waxed and then waned. At a meeting in December 1967 led by Black, a group of Thompson's friends and army men in Thailand concluded that the silk king had probably been "kidnapped and held incommunicado against his will."[1] They offered a new reward, and his friends also planned to rescue Thompson by parachuting a Nepalese mercenary into the Cambodian town where some intelligence operatives and psychics believed Thompson was being held. The gurkha did sneak into the Cambodian town but found no sign of the missing silk king.[2]

Several months later, Black traveled again to Malaysia, where he met with the senior Malaysian police investigators on the Thompson case; by then they had concluded that Thompson had been approached by someone he knew just outside Moonlight Cottage and then been taken against his will, probably by a highly disciplined group of attackers.[3] Since Thompson had been grabbed without any of his medications, he might well have died during a kidnapping, the Malaysian investigators believed.

Black himself, in a private memorandum sent to the U.S. ambassador, surmised that it was unlikely Thompson had perished from an accident, given the extensive search for him by so many experienced trackers. When friends asked Black whether Thompson, depressed and exhausted, might have killed himself, the general—and most of Thompson's relatives—always adamantly denied it was a possibility.

Thompson, said his nephew Henry, could be lonely or sad, but he had never given any indication that he wanted to kill himself. "He was at a professional dead-end then, he'd lost a lot of friends, he felt isolated, he didn't have many people to lean on . . . but he just wasn't the type of person who'd kill himself."[4]

But others were not so sure that Thompson, if not wishing to kill himself, hadn't at least wanted to somehow escape his life. Muriel Dewar was a woman who'd worked for the overseas arm of Thompson's silk company and had become a close friend of his. "Jim's tiredness was part psychological and part physical," she wrote to Thompson's niece Martha Galleher. "He could have decided to take the moment to slip quietly away to walk in the jungle" and essentially make a new life for himself as someone other than the silk king.[5]

Later in her life, Connie Mangskau came to believe something similar: that Thompson might have considered trying to vanish in order to fashion himself a new life somewhere else in the world, or that he was considering it, hurt himself, and never made it back to the cottage

Ultimately, a higher reward, a new search, more pressure by Ed Black, and all the connections of the Thompson family in American high society and government could not turn up Jim Thompson. Though Thompson's servants had for months kept preparing the house as if the silk king could return at any moment, and the company, while continuing to prosper, had put off any formal succession planning while employees waited for the boss to potentially return, by 1968 Thompson's friends and business partners had accepted that he'd probably never return.

Some still believed, as Thompson's friend Rene Burrow said, "that one day Jim would just come walking back into his house with a 'hello there,' just like that,"[6] but in 1974, seven years after he had vanished in the Cameron Highlands, Thompson's family had him declared deceased for legal purposes. Yet the myth of the silk king did not end there, as many in Bangkok, Delaware, and Washington expected it would. Thompson's silk business actually expanded, becoming a prominent global fashion company; his house turned into one of the top tourist attractions in Thailand; and his story was captured in a Thai miniseries and in a continuing string of high-profile magazine articles. Friends, adventure hunters, former CIA agents, and people who'd simply been to his house once in Bangkok and left entranced by his story continued to search for him.

In Bangkok, younger acquaintances of Thompson styled their lives on his, consciously or unconsciously, and one of his admirers actually moved into the Thompson house as a kind of caretaker of the legend.[7] The most devoted among the searchers traded letters, phone calls, and ultimately, e-mails with theories and clues about Thompson's life and disappearance.

William Warren, an old friend of Thompson's, continued to receive phone calls all the time from reporters thinking up new stories on the silk king or commemorating the anniversary of his vanishing. People continued to report Thompson sightings: tourists supposedly saw him in Tahiti, wearing a disguise; old acquaintances glimpsed him in rural Cambodia; another mystic believed he was living in another part of Cambodia, smoking opium; others claimed he'd dyed his hair, become a mystic, and was telling fortunes at a temple in another part of Malaysia.[8]

All these searches and hunts did not deliver a final answer to the mystery of Jim Thompson's disappearance. But given all the evidence that has been amassed, it is possible to construct a speculative answer. Though Warren believed he could have hurt himself in an accident and perished in the Malaysian jungle, nearly every seasoned investigator who examined the case, from jungle fighter Dick Noone to senior Malaysian police official Santokh Singh, concluded it was unlikely that Thompson had met with an accident or some kind of animal attack in the jungle, since they had found no torn clothes, bloodstains, body parts, or any other remnants of Thompson in the area around Moonlight Cottage.[9]

General Black, too, eventually concluded it was highly unlikely that Thompson's body was still in the Malaysian jungle somewhere. Philip Rivers, a longtime Malaysia resident who studied the case, noted, "They [the Malaysian police] thoroughly searched not only throughout the entire area . . . but also along trails through the adjacent jungle into Perak and the lowlands," a wide radius of area in which Thompson's body could have lain.[10] Noone further insisted that if Thompson's body had fallen into a hole of some sort, his experienced aboriginal trackers would have noticed it; other hikers who'd gotten lost in the highlands almost always eventually were found.

Other experienced Malaysian detectives, Rivers notes, tracked the case far beyond the Cameron Highlands to Penang, a city four hours away by car, and even to Singapore, at the tip of peninsular Malaysia, and to Sarawak, on the adjacent island of Borneo.[11] Unlike the Thai police, Malaysia's elite police force, Rivers found, made the Thompson investigation its highest priority. The Malaysian police ruled out the possibility that a criminal gang had kidnapped Thompson in order to demand a ransom; gangs often targeted wealthy people in Malaysia—often Malaysian Chinese businesspeople—but no one ever came forward to ask for a ransom for Thompson, even though his friends and business acquaintances publicly offered sizable sums for any information about him.[12]

While Thompson clearly suffered from bouts of depression and had grown weary of U.S. policy in Southeast Asia and of many aspects of his life in Thailand, it also seems very unlikely that he committed suicide or somehow vanished in order to escape his life. As much as he might complain about his life; as much as he sometimes hated hosting people every night at his house; as sad as he could be about his gallstones, pneumonia, and other ailments that were diminishing the frenetic pace of his life; and as bitter as he had become at both the Thai and U.S. governments, Jim Thompson still, even on his worst days, enjoyed enough of the role of the silk king that he would never want to give it up.

After all, said his nephew Henry, if he'd really been so tired of hosting guests in his house every night or telling his stories over and over, he could have organized fewer parties, taken more vacations, and entertained fewer foreign dignitaries. If he'd really wanted to get out of his life, he could have slowed down, Henry said.[13] But Jim Thompson didn't—and few of his other relatives or friends saw signs that his depression was morphing into suicidal tendencies. His friend Warren wrote, "Thompson was never particularly noted for concealing his feelings—indeed, he had a reputation for expressing them rather freely and openly, even when they concerned quite personal matters," yet never, in his final weeks, did Thompson tell his sister, his close friends in Bangkok, or his regular doctor, with whom he was quite intimate, that he'd had any suicidal thoughts.[14]

The CIA closely monitored the Thompson case, conducted its own private hunt for the silk king, and still seems unwilling to share its results, and it immediately emerged, to many of Thompson's friends, as a possible culprit.[15] The agency, over the years, has masterminded numerous operations to kill foreign leaders, foreign operatives, and even whole foreign armies, but ordering the assassination, or even the kidnapping, of an American citizen would be a whole different matter. When in early 2010 the Obama administration authorized the CIA to kill Anwar al-Awlaki, a radical Islamist cleric living in Yemen who holds U.S. citizenship, the episode turned into a major media story, and the *New York Times* called such a decision to authorize the killing of a U.S. citizen an "extraordinary step"[16]— one that could result in a serious legal challenge against the Obama White House.

In his time, Jim Thompson was certainly as famous as the cleric, and yet in the late 1960s, before the revelations of Watergate, the CIA's secret proxy war in Laos, and scandals like Iran-Contra, the agency still operated with far less government oversight. The media, too, prior to the downhill slide of the war in Vietnam and the Nixon White House's attacks on the press, tended to be highly quiescent, failing to seriously probe power—and unable to quickly transmit information around the world the way it can in today's Internet era. Congress, highly deferential to the executive branch before the

Watergate era, rarely questioned the agency on its operations and allowed the CIA to prosecute the secret war in Laos for years without seriously questioning how and why the United States was spending its money in that tiny country. Compared to 2010, if the agency had wanted to get rid of an American citizen, it would have been far easier for it to do so with less questioning from other parts of the government or from the American media. After all, the CIA had for years conducted other destructive clandestine programs, such as MK-ULTRA, a covert human research program in the United States in which the agency tested subjects' brain functions through sleep deprivation, beatings, and the surreptitious administration of drugs. Only with the investigative efforts of the congressional Church Committee in 1975 did many of the agency's abuses come to light.

Jim Thompson had, in many ways, turned against the CIA; he had, according to some CIA officers, embarrassed the agency by criticizing it and even mocking it, and his friends still working in the U.S. government worried that his impertinence might one day rebound against him, though they usually imagined Thompson's critiques would hurt his business or cost him any remaining access to U.S. embassy officials—not get him kidnapped or killed. Would Thompson's offenses have merited such a brutal response? Robert Jantzen, the station chief in Bangkok, genuinely enjoyed Thompson's company and his wife volunteered at Thompson's home. And Thompson still had fans in other parts of the agency, though few would have spoken his name publicly, for fear of being tarred by association.

Still, the agency would not have been sorry to see him gone and to finally bury the legend of the silk king. But to coordinate a kidnapping operation in Malaysia, a country that was not the closest of American allies, in order to make Jim Thompson vanish, would have been a risky operation for the agency. Some of Thompson's relatives, furious and frustrated by the stonewall treatment they received from many American officials, did not believe that the CIA was responsible for his disappearance. And if Thompson had engineered his own disappearance in order to carry out some secret intelligence mission while technically being "dead," then eventually, over the years, as other CIA operatives retired and some of the files on the Cold War were declassified (though Thompson's CIA personnel file remains classified), the details of that mission would probably have come out, or some of Thompson's collaborators would have told their story in public. But they never did—and the possibility that the agency, which had become increasingly furious at Thompson, would have trusted him on a mission where he engineered his own "disappearance" in order to carry out some top-secret CIA mission seems extremely implausible.

The Thai intelligence agencies, and the Thai government—at least, in its official capacity—probably did not get rid of Jim Thompson. The relationship with Washington was critical to the Thais, and despite many government officials' disdain for Jim Thompson, an official policy, an official plan to vanish the silk king, could have reverberated badly against Bangkok. And if, as a policy, the Thai military or intelligence agency had decided to get rid of the silk king, taking care of the mission in a neighboring country, and one extremely touchy about foreigners intruding on its sovereignty, seems unlikely. After all, in 1967 Thailand was still far from being a democracy, and if senior officials, as a matter of policy, had wanted to get rid of Jim Thompson, they had had many chances to do so while he was in Thailand.

While the Thai government in 1967 still harbored some fear of Pridi Banomyong—who, having lived in exile for years in China (and later in France), still represented an example of Thai democracy—Pridi posed no real threat to the Thai leadership in the late 1960s. Pridi might still blast the military leadership on radio broadcasts into Thailand, or pen essays on Thai politics that would eventually make their way, samizdat-style, into the hands of intellectuals in Bangkok, but Pridi no longer posed any real military threat, the kind the generals feared, to the leaders in Bangkok. If Jim Thompson had wanted to embark on a secret mission to meet Pridi—which was highly unlikely, since the silk king had not been in contact with Pridi in years—the Thai generals might have noticed, but they wouldn't have taken real steps to stop it. And Pridi himself always denied that he'd ever had anything to do with Jim Thompson's disappearance.[17]

But just because the Thai government, as a matter of policy, was not going to get rid of Jim Thompson did not mean that he was safe from the many enemies he had accrued in Bangkok after years of commercial competition and antagonism between himself and the royal family and other Thai elites. For years, Thompson had intimated to friends and relatives that he was being watched not only by the Thai police but also by his many business competitors. By 1967, after all, the silk industry had become a major business in Bangkok; Thompson faced over 150 other silk firms, and some of his own former employees had left his shop to start their own companies, engendering at times a bitter, hateful rivalry.

The silk industry continued to expand, and the Thai government and tourism ministry had started exhaustively promoting Thai silk. Many entrepreneurs in Bangkok could see the potential for growth, especially with so many more tourists coming to Thailand. Many government officials, seeing how General Sarit's wife had built a silk company—though ultimately her firm failed and had to sell off all the fancy equipment it purchased—had considered starting their own silk firms, and nearly every tailor in the central business district seemed to offer his own silk clothing.

At that time—and, to some extent, still today—the skyscrapers, banks, and late-model European and Japanese sedans of Bangkok concealed a developing city with weak institutions and even weaker laws, a kind of hollow edifice in which the structures of the industrialized world had been implanted over a political culture that remained personalized, familial, and almost tribal. In 1967—as, too often, today—the Thai police investigated the cases they wanted to investigate and avoided those that might involve prosecuting powerful, well-connected, and rich Thais. A well-placed bribe could all but ensure that the police did not look too closely at even a serious crime.

So, for a relative pittance, businessmen in Bangkok, or simply any angry person, could hire trained killers for an assassination, including some who operated not only in Thailand but also in neighboring countries, and who, unlike Thai officials, wouldn't worry about the diplomatic ramifications of a kidnapping or an execution attempt in Malaysia. Only a year and a half earlier, in October 1965, another prominent foreigner living in Bangkok, Darrell Berrigan, who worked as editor of the English-language daily *Bangkok World*, had been brutally murdered—shot through the back of the head with one bullet and left to die, face down, in the backseat of his car.[18]

The Berrigan murder shows how easy it was to kill someone in Bangkok at that time and that foreigners were not immune from the violence that too often was the first resort of jilted lovers or ambitious businessmen who did not trust the law to handle their problems. "If you wanted to get rid of someone in business in Thailand, you could," said one longtime Bangkok resident. "For a lot of people trying to settle disputes, they found it a lot easier, and less messy, than going to the police or to court."[19]

Perhaps Jim Thompson fell prey to a similar setup. He had not accumulated jealous lovers, like Berrigan, who was reportedly murdered by a former boyfriend, but if the silk king's business had failed, it would have benefited other silk companies enormously. And though business rivals could have hired an assassin in Bangkok, by organizing a kidnapping—and potential murder—outside the country, they would draw attention even further away from them.

"Ed Black was convinced, finally, that Thompson was killed in a murder for hire organized in Bangkok," said Thompson's niece Ann Donaldson. "Most of us wound up thinking the same thing."[20] Indeed, after concluding his investigations, Black believed that Thompson had been kidnapped by business rivals back in Bangkok, since no one had emerged to ask for money, the norm in a kidnapping for profit.[21]

Still, whether any Thai officials directly had a hand in the disappearance of the silk king, in many ways the two governments profited from his vanishing, which is probably why Bangkok officials offered Black and others little assistance in their search. By the late 1960s, Thailand was becoming a more open place, with university students in Bangkok and some intellectuals publicly criticizing the military regime for its political repression and involvement in the Vietnam War.

By the early 1970s, this rumble of dissent would explode into violent, bloody protests, first in 1973, when the Thai military gunned down at least ninety prodemocracy protesters in the streets of Bangkok. But in the mid- and late 1960s, when this dissent still had not crested, the government in Bangkok certainly did not look kindly on foreigners adding to the criticism of the regime, even if the government was not in the habit of kidnapping Americans.

After leaving the army, Denis Horgan stayed in Bangkok, where he landed a job editing the *Bangkok World*, the daily paper where Berrigan had once worked. Horgan soon found that without his U.S. Army uniform, the Thai authorities treated him a lot differently: they pressured the paper to tone down its reporting and opinions. He discovered that foreigners who spoke out too openly about the Thai military's abuses would find their visas unable to be renewed, and he learned that the Thai government was developing as little tolerance for meddlesome foreigners as for its own domestic critics.

Then again, many of Thompson's relatives, after researching his case, still came back to the American government. "I don't think the Thai government was exactly sorry that Jim wasn't around anymore," said Thompson's niece Ann Donaldson, who also traveled to Bangkok to investigate the disappearance of her uncle. "It was a hassle taken off of their hands, the most famous foreigner there, who'd now become a critic, suddenly gone. It was like a blessing for them . . . as much as for the CIA."[22]

Some of Thompson's friends and acquaintances saw the same motives in the American government's view of the silk king's disappearance. If the best-known private citizen in Southeast Asia was hosting visiting dignitaries and delivering harsh verdicts on U.S. policy, that wasn't exactly going to help the White House and the American embassy in Bangkok to convince increasingly skeptical reporters or congressional representatives and senators that Washington should invest even more heavily in the Indochina war. Now that Thompson was openly airing his views on major U.S. television stations, he'd become even more of an irritant.

Of course, several senior U.S. government officials assured Thompson's family that Washington had spared no effort to find the silk king, but few family members, including Donaldson, believed them. "When I met with people from the embassy, they were not helpful, the ambassador just wanted to talk about Thompson's will. . . . I got the sense some of them were kind of relieved. . . . I never trusted their response," she said.[23] Even General Black, who up until the time of Thompson's disappearance had been a by-the-books military man trusting of executive authority, now became increasingly doubtful of the information he was receiving from Washington. As Ed Black told his wife, Cobey, "If they [the U.S. embassy in Bangkok] really were so upset about [Thompson's disappearance], why didn't they do more?"[24]

By 1967, Willis Bird no longer had any interaction with Jim Thompson. The foreigner community in Bangkok had grown large enough that the two men could easily avoid each other, and Bird now tended to socialize, if at all, with his wife's extended family and with associates from his business and intelligence operations rather than with the international jet-set crowd who came to Thompson's house.

Bird had become convinced that the Vietnam War would turn out poorly for the United States, but unlike Jim Thompson, he didn't feel any need to publicly denounce the war—Bird had none of the public fame of Thompson, so any statement would have gotten little notice—and instead had long ago realized the commercial opportunities of the conflict.

Bird gave no interviews, except an occasional one about doing business in Thailand, and since he'd never been a major aficionado of Thai culture—for relaxation, he dabbled in herbal medicine or just watched television—the urbanization of Bangkok and the growth of American-style restaurants, supermarkets, and bars barely bothered him.

Bird himself stayed away from the brothels, but he had never held the Thais up as any kind of model and had never seen himself as there to preserve anything, so when parts of their capital turned into sprawling red-light areas, and the new American-built tarmac cut through villages in the Northeast, Bird felt little disappointment.

"Bird saw all these changes as progress and good business—why would he want to stop it?" said Jesse Henry, a friend of Bird's. For the foreigners who mourned a past idyllic Thailand, Bird had only contempt and disdain for their romanticism. "Bird thought that by then [the mid-1960s], Thompson had become kind of lost," said Henry.

"[Bird was] never invested in Thailand the same way as Thompson, never tried to be accepted like a Thai or claimed he was like a Thai."[25]

Mostly, Willis Bird kept to himself, unless he had business to take care of. The Thai leaders and the agency men would come to him when they needed help or connections or advice about how to handle the latest coup in Bangkok. "Bird was the opposite of someone like Jim Thompson; he was private, he didn't want to be public, he didn't get anything out of it [doing things publicly]," Henry continued. "He'd learned that to survive in Thailand you had to become more like the Thais—not confront people in public, but behind their back, make your allies quietly, then use them against your enemies—what you did in public didn't matter much."[26]

Well into the late 1960s and early 1970s, Thai leaders still turned to Bird for counsel about delicate political matters, trooping into the television room of his Bangkok house for an audience. Bird was still advising senior Thai generals, helping to arrange business deals for them in Thailand and Laos, and assisting them in making CIA contacts. His old allies from the Narasuan Committee, like Phao, might be gone, but the Thai military and police could still use a man who would introduce them to the right American intelligence figures or help to move money in and out of the country without much notice, a man who knew how to keep a secret and had few qualms about some of the brutal methods employed by the Thai government.

Bird had stepped back from direct involvement in the twilight war in Laos, but he'd kept his hands in, at least indirectly. Bird's brother-in-law, Bill Lair, managed the training of the Thai Special Forces who fought in Laos and the buildup of assistance to Vang Pao from his base in Thailand, but Lair grew increasingly uncomfortable with the Americanization of the Indochina war, the buildup to larger battles on open terrain rather than Hmong-led guerrilla tactics. Still, Lair stayed on with the twilight war from his base in northeastern Thailand, until eventually, in the early 1970s, the American pullout from Indochina essentially rendered him useless to the CIA.[27]

And Bird's son, Willis Bird Jr., half Thai and half American and fluent in Thai, had always worshiped his father, seeing how Bird's intelligence work had put him at the center of Thai political intrigue. With the elder Bird stepping back from Laos, Willis Jr. went into intelligence himself, assisting one U.S. military intelligence officer working in Thailand to build relationships with senior Thai generals and, ultimately, Hmong fighters.

"Because of who his father was, when I dealt with Billy [Bird Jr.], I would find the hilltribes; they saw him and it was like he was a hero to them," said the U.S. military intelligence officer.[28] And when Vang Pao's fighters ultimately had to flee Laos in the wake of the American defeat in Indochina, Willis Jr. helped arrange for many their safe passage into Thailand, with some of the fighters actually living on his compound in northern Thailand.[29]

Just because Bill Bird had cut his ties with Jim Thompson didn't mean he could avoid the spectacle of Thompson's vanishing. To Bird, Thompson's growing bitterness and alienation in Thailand proved an ideal cautionary tale. Thompson, Bird told friends, had lost sight of who he was and had left himself with no allies at all: no Thai allies and few American allies.

Thompson, Bird would say, had convinced himself he could be almost Thai, trusting that his Thai friends and allies would protect him as they would another Thai, but in reality, he'd always be a foreigner in Thailand, no matter how many Buddha sculptures he preserved, silk weavers he employed, or monks he hired to perform ceremonies at his store. Bill Bird had no such illusions about Thailand, and no such ideals, and he thought that Thompson, whom he'd trusted as savvy and well connected back in the 1940s, had become a fool.

"Everyone thought Thompson was so smart about Asia, but in the end, what he was—he was just naive," said Willis Bird Jr. "My father couldn't believe this guy had gotten so famous and he was still so naive about Thailand."[30]

Unlike Jim Thompson, Willis Bird survived into old age in Thailand; he died in 1991, by which time Thailand finally seemed to be building a democracy and some political stability and Bangkok had grown into a city of some six million people. By the end, Bird no longer played a direct role in Thai politics, and he sometimes seemed to miss the cycle of coups and countercoups and palace intrigue of the 1950s and 1960s. But he'd survived.

He survived the exile of his patron Phao, the rise of Phao's enemies, the establishment of Thai companies competing for Bird's import-export business, and the hatred of many people at the U.S. embassy in Bangkok. He survived, in the mid-1970s, the withdrawal of the United States from Vietnam and Laos, which severely reduced the intelligence operations being run out of Bangkok. He survived his own business competitors employing some of the same hardball tactics against him, his own employees occasionally sneaking company ideas and secrets out the back door, and his own challenges when powerful government officials wanted their share of the export-import business. But it hadn't ruined him.

"My father was not naive," said Bird's son. "He never convinced himself he was anything more than an American living in Thailand, a guest who could be tossed out at any time, even if the Thais seemed to need him. So, if they turned on him, he expected it and wasn't surprised."[31] His father, said Willis Jr., never let down his guard.

Epilogue

When Jim Thompson vanished, most of his friends assumed that if he never returned, his legend would eventually fade and his story would be largely forgotten. Other foreigners had disappeared in Thailand, and Thompson was not the first man to wander into a jungle and never be seen again. Other intelligence agents had tried, or failed, to transform parts of the world in America's image.

But the story didn't fade and the legend didn't die: Thompson's combination of mystery, power, idealism, glamour, and, eventually, failure, transfixed one generation after the next and led to continued interest in what happened to the silk king. Thompson's legend grew, at least among many people in Southeast Asia, within the CIA and among a group of amateur sleuths who treated the Thompson case like a miniature version of the theories surrounding the assassinations of John and Robert Kennedy.

Today, more than four decades after Thompson disappeared, sleuths continue to follow supposed leads that they think might lead them to his body or to him still alive—though if he were alive, he would be over one hundred years old by now. Thompson's niece Martha

Galleher made the quest to find him her life's work, hounding Henry Kissinger, the former king Sihanouk of Cambodia, and virtually any U.S. government official she could find. Ultimately, well into her seventies, she self-published a rambling account of her decades of tracking her uncle, including the endless array of people who seemed eager to avoid her.

Many private investigators and amateur searchers still try to solve the puzzle of what happened to Thompson; they even occasionally meet to tramp through the Cameron Highlands, no longer a quaint English-style country village but now a built-up, somewhat tacky resort area catering mostly to local tourists from Kuala Lumpur and to Chinese tour groups. Some of the investigators want to exhume bodies from the highlands to examine the bones of unidentified bodies there with the latest DNA techniques; others continue to follow the lives of Thompson's surviving family members, much as Kennedy watchers followed Teddy, John Jr., or Caroline.

And within the CIA, which resolutely refuses to reveal information about Thompson's spying career—information I had to dig out myself—his name still evokes a kind of fascination among older agency employees and retirees. The agency's own classified internal publication has examined the Thompson case, relying upon agency files, and at informal gatherings of old agency Asian hands, little time goes by before the Thompson case is discussed.

Even at the headquarters of Thompson's silk company, now located in one of the Bangkok exurbs that sprang up as the Thai capital expanded into a megacity, some of the oldest Thai employees, those who knew "Nai Jim" personally, still gather occasionally to reminisce about the earlier days of the company, about their old boss, and about the way Bangkok was before traffic and pollution turned it into a *Blade Runner*-esque urban apocalypse. A few of the Thai employees, many of whom possess strong beliefs in the supernatural, believe that Thompson could still return to Bangkok. "You never know," said one longtime employee of the silk company. "Maybe he wandered off on purpose, maybe he wants to surprise us by coming back."

Though by law Thompson was officially declared dead seven years after his disappearance, which allowed his family to handle his estate and his will, his legacy remains powerful. His priceless Asian art collection, fought over after his disappearance by his family, the Thai government, and a private foundation in Thailand, now appears in his house in Bangkok, which has been turned into a museum and has become one of the most popular tourist attractions in Bangkok.[1]

Thompson's company, now known as Jim Thompson: The Thai Silk Company, did not disappear with him, either. Building on Thompson's unique eye for color and design, the heirs to his company built it into a larger silk empire, with more stores in Thailand and other parts of Asia, and selling all over the world.[2] (Thompson's U.S. subsidiary, Thaibok, was purchased by famed designer Jack Lenor Larsen, who credited Thompson's silk stylings as one of his prime inspirations.)

Thompson's silk company stayed true to his original vision of social welfare, though he might have blanched at how large the corporation had become, since he wanted, in a way, to encourage a small cottage industry in Thailand, like the types of artisans who'd made Italy famous. It was an idea ahead of its time: in the early 2000s, after the Asian financial crisis of the late 1990s had decimated the Thai economy, heavily dependent on low-end manufacturing for export, the incoming prime minister, a man named Thaksin Shinawatra, launched a plan to build up small artisanal microenterprises in villages and towns across Thailand.

Ultimately, Thailand increasingly became known as a global fashion and design capital. Revived by Thompson, Thailand's silk industry has continued to expand, and by 2010 it employed some 350,000 families in Thailand.[3] Everyone from the queen of Thailand to the flight attendants on Thai Airways International now dons Thai silk outfits as a point of national pride, and Thompson's legend has become an established part of the story of the industry.

The broader political conditions that in the 1940s made Southeast Asia a center of the new American mission of democratizing the world, and then in the 1960s and 1970s made Southeast Asia a center of the Cold War, have also changed dramatically. As Thompson had long predicted, the Vietnamese, whom he'd praised as the toughest fighters and most industrious workers in Asia, eventually defeated not only France but also the United States in Hanoi's quest for sovereignty and national unity. The U.S. collaboration with France in Vietnam, and then America's own battle there, cost the United States enormously in global prestige.

Like Jim Thompson, many former OSS, CIA, and State Department personnel who, in the days after World War II, had admired the Vietnamese and seen them as nationalists more than communists grew so disillusioned with American policy that they quit government service and became prominent critics of the Vietnam War. By the end of the Vietnam War, too, the CIA was mutating from the freewheeling, largely unmonitored days of Thompson, Bird, and Wild Bill Donovan to a more risk-averse and typical federal bureaucracy, one that operated with greater oversight but also seemed unable to make major intelligence breakthroughs.

After the final withdrawal of American diplomats from Saigon in 1975, Washington all but forgot about Southeast Asia, and with the warming of relations between the United States and the Soviet Union, and then the collapse of the Berlin Wall, many of the old ideological conflicts that pitted men like Thompson against men like Bird seemed to vanish. Though the United States had spent hundreds of millions of dollars supporting the Hmong in the twilight war in Laos, as the communists gained ground, Washington all but abandoned the Hmong, while years of American bombing had left tiny Laos as one of the most ordnance-littered nations in the world, with much of the land still unsafe to walk today and the minimal infrastructure that existed before the war totally decimated.[4] (Today, Laos remains one of the poorest countries in Asia, in part because of the misrule of its communist leaders but also because of the destruction of the war.)

By the early 1970s, journalists and congressional hearings had blown open the secret war, which was no longer much of a secret and for which Congress increasingly balked at paying the price. Most of the original men who'd hatched the secret war in Laos had moved on, been transferred to other jobs, or, like Bill Bird, aged and begun to retreat from political intrigues. The towns and villages of Laos returned to being the sleepy backwaters they had been before the Indochina conflict. The idea that Laos once upon a time was a central front in a global struggle seemed laughable to many young Americans—though soon the United States would become deeply involved in another faraway landlocked nation that before 2001 seemed so peripheral to American interests that the State Department struggled to find anyone who spoke the local languages of Afghanistan.

With the U.S. government generally ignoring their onetime Hmong allies at the end of the Vietnam War, it was left to individual CIA-affiliated pilots and other agency men and women to try to help the Hmong flee Laos before the communist government could take reprisals against them. Over 250,000 Hmong fled to Thailand, usually crossing the border by foot; Vang Pao and some of his top lieutenants were flown to Thailand by agency-affiliated pilots.[5]

The Hmong refugees remained in Thai camps, with many ultimately departing for the United States, where they were finally granted refugee status, though they found adapting to America far harder than previous immigrant groups like Italians or Chinese.[6] For those Hmong who could not make it out of Laos, the end of the war did deliver harsh reprisals, with the Lao communist government allegedly organizing detentions, torture, and even massacres of Hmong who remained in the country.[7]

That willful U.S. ignorance of Indochina continued well into the 1990s, when America—and its veterans—began to make peace with Vietnam and the war itself and Washington started to again pay greater attention to Asia. The United States reestablished relations with Vietnam in 1995, and in 2000 President Bill Clinton visited Hanoi, where he was mobbed by young Vietnamese like some kind of rock star.[8]

Today, America is Vietnam's second-largest trading partner, and the two countries have developed close strategic and security ties, based partly on a shared fear of a rising China—exactly the kind of shared interests between the United States and Vietnam that Thompson and other early OSS operatives had had in mind.[9] In fact, though the Vietnamese government today is communist, in many respects it has come to view the relationship with America the way Thompson had anticipated: a relationship of mutual benefit, of protection from Vietnam's old enemy, China, and of growing cultural and business ties.

Unlike the United States, Thailand benefited enormously from the Vietnam War. The vast American spending during the war built up Thailand's physical infrastructure, sparked trade ties between the two countries, and helped to establish the country as a major tourism destination. Under a series of authoritarian but economically liberal governments, Thailand in the 1970s, 1980s, and early 1990s developed one of the most high-powered economies in the world.

The country grew so rapidly that in one generation, many Thai families leapfrogged from living in traditional teakwood houses and farming for staple crops like rice as they had for centuries to living in air-conditioned condominiums, driving late-model Toyota pickup trucks, and assembling computer parts in high-tech factories. Even after the Asian financial crisis of the late 1990s slowed Thailand's economic ascent, by 2010 Bangkok boasted a per capita income of some fourteen thousand dollars, putting it on par with some of the less affluent European capitals.

Of course, not everyone in Thailand was thrilled by the legacy of the Cold War and the American alliance. Decades of U.S. backing for authoritarian Thai leaders, starting with Jim Thompson's nemesis Phibul, left Thailand with a stunted political culture and weak institutions. And if, in Thompson and Bird's day, Thailand had managed to hold itself together despite Thompson's warnings that the venal, dictatorial, and conservative Thai autocrats would eventually do great harm, in recent years Thailand has been unable to overcome the legacy of its past.

Since the 1970s, Thailand has stumbled toward true democracy, but each step forward has triggered a regressive backlash, and today Thailand staggers from election to violent street protest to coup, seemingly unable to establish lasting democracy. That lack of real democracy has hurt the country badly: it lurches from one autocrat to the next, even though it boasts many educated people and is clearly ready for democracy, despite the doubts in the past of men like Bird. Without solid democracy, coups, street riots, and other violent means of changing governments still rule in Bangkok.

• • •

Nearly all the other players in Jim Thompson's story today are dead, though some of Thompson's younger relatives and friends do still survive. Wild Bill Donovan died in 1959, one of the last of the intelligence men of an era before the public, and Congress, had such mistrust of the national intelligence agency. Jim's sister Elinor Douglas, his closest family confidante, is dead, keeping inside her the personal and professional secrets of her brother, a man she both loved and clearly envied. Irena Yost's husband, the famed diplomat Charles, died in 1981. Irena herself passed away in 2006. Pridi Banomyong, the father of Thai democracy, died in exile in France in 1983, having not set foot in Thailand since 1949.

As Thailand has democratized, Pridi's reputation has slowly been rehabilitated, and today Bangkok boasts an institute dedicated to his memory in addition to the university he founded, Thammasat, generally considered one of the two finest universities in the country. Still, says his son Sukprida, Pridi in many ways died a broken man, embittered that he could never return home and furious at the United States, his onetime ally, for totally abandoning him.[10]

By the 1970s, with his old ally Phao long gone, his other Thai intelligence contacts losing influence, and the CIA becoming more constrained and cautious, Willis Bird found himself less and less in demand for advising Thai political leaders and for executing off-the-books operations for the U.S. government.[11] Always a player, with few hobbies other than work, Bird resented no longer being on the inside of political maneuvering, and as he aged he made politicians or intelligence officers who still came to soak in his wisdom wait for long periods to see him.

"When Thai politicians or anyone else would come to see him, he'd make them wait to speak with him until he was through watching his favorite television show; they'd see him in the next room, but he clearly would watch the whole show before coming out," remembered one intelligence officer who worked closely with him.[12]

By the 1980s, Bird was mostly retired, and his son took over some of his intelligence work. Bird died in 1991. To this day, most Thais have no idea of how powerful an influence off-the-books intelligence operations like the Narasuan Committee had on the trajectory of their country's development.

Though most of the characters in this book had passed away by the time I began my research, their intimate circles often had not. And yet every trip to Thailand, every phone call to Thompson's and Bird's friends in America, seemed tinged with sadness and loss, a sentiment I could rarely shake. As I tracked down the circles of relatives and friends of Jim Thompson and Willis Bird, I felt I was watching these last remnants of the post–World War II era fading away.

When I met with foreigners who had lived in Bangkok for decades, a community where the survivors all knew one another, I sometimes felt like I wanted to videotape the sessions, since I never knew if they could be repeated—the memories so vastly different from the megacity that moved at a frantic pace, never stopping, in the streets below their apartments or outside their Bangkok cottage windows.

I would interview a person only to find that on my next trip to Bangkok he or she had passed away or was no longer well enough to speak with me. More than once, I was only days too late to speak with someone who'd lived through Jim Thompson's time, or I slurped plates of rice noodles and sour orange soup at a Bangkok food court with a longtime expatriate and then never saw him again, his e-mail and phone no longer working.

One man sent me faxes from his Bangkok hospital bed, promising to meet me in a month or two, full of stories about doing business in the Thai capital in the chaos just after the Second World War. For nearly a year, I traded faxes with him in the hospital, but we never met. Finally, his longtime companion faxed me to tell me that he was no longer well enough even to correspond.

It was not only these longtime expatriates who were fading from the scene. As I traveled to Thai villages and, in Bangkok, into the sheltered estates of royals and the Thai wealthy, I saw an earlier, genteel generation of Thais who themselves seemed bewildered by the rapid development of their country, which had made them, almost as much as me, strangers in their homeland.

In one villa in the Bangkok suburbs, where servants greeted me at the door and then pattered upstairs, an elderly Thai man, a former diplomat, sat amid classical Thai temple paintings and models of Italian violins. He seemed more befuddled than I was, even angry, with how much Thai society had changed, far more than the changes in the United States over recent decades—not just the noise, light, and sound of Bangkok's megamalls but the confrontational, even angry attitude of Thai youth, in a culture that historically had revered quiet, tact, and nonconfrontation.

Of course, this anger and confrontationalism could be seen as courage, the strength of young Thais to stand up for themselves, for their politics, and for their country. But there was little place in that country for this man anymore, and like many of my interviewees he seemed to want to drag out the conversation as long as possible; his servants offered me more cups of tea, more plates of papaya, more tiny cookies. Though he remained in fine physical health, the former diplomat rarely left his villa on a gated estate. Like Jim Thompson, he no longer belonged.

Yet even as I watched an era fade, I saw in many of the foreigners I met in Thailand and Laos, and in my young Thai friends who'd come of age in the era of street protests against Thai dictators, much of the same idealism that drove Jim Thompson. With faster, more regular trans-Pacific flights, a global news cycle, and modern communications technology, many more young people in the West are drawn to travel or to live as expatriates, not only in Thailand but also in ever more remote places like Laos or Zambia. Certainly, if they stay abroad for any extended amount of time, young Americans confront many of the same questions and paradoxes that plagued Jim Thompson throughout his life: Can you ever really fit into a foreign place and a foreign culture? Will you necessarily lose touch with the values, the ideas, the everyday activities of your home? Can you really ever remake your life, change who you are?

My Thai friends, who'd grown up in the 1970s, 1980s, and early 1990s, believed, as Jim Thompson once had, that democracy was finally was coming to the kingdom. The economic crisis of the 1990s and early 2000s and the angry violent politics that roiled Bangkok in 2010, leading to bloody battles in the city, came as a bitter disappointment to them. I still saw the idealism I'd known when I had moved to Thailand in the late 1990s. I saw it in a Thai friend who taught basic skills to commercial sex workers in some of the grittiest districts of Bangkok; I saw it in an acquaintance who brought most of his salary as a photographer home to his extended family in the poorer parts of the Northeast, where drought had ruined whole farms.

Yet that idealism often seemed to be crumbling. Friends who'd worked as investigative reporters, started nonprofits, or led street rallies quit them to go work in banking, take over the family business, or move to Australia or the United States for their studies. "Now it's time to make money," I heard from many of them, as the country, in the 2000s, turned away from some of the hard work of building a democracy and, led by a corporate tycoon–turned–prime minister, set about consuming and spending, often beyond its means.

Just as in America, a price would eventually be paid for this recklessness, but for now, many of my Thai friends seemed to be enjoying a kind of abdication of responsibility, and when the military took power again in 2006, many young middle-class Bangkok residents, some of whom had protested dictatorships in the past, threw flowers on the soldiers and snapped photos of the young army men with their cell phone cameras.[13]

At some of the places in the city where Jim Thompson had played a large role, his presence was still celebrated, but the nuances of his life, the bitterness at the end, had been tastefully removed, leaving a hazy glow. At the Jim Thompson House, the gloriously preserved museum, well-trained guides in stunning silk skirts paraded foreign tourists through Thompson's rooms of antiques and paintings, describing the old silk king's dinner parties, collecting, and trips upcountry but never venturing into any of the topics that got him in trouble: the politics, the intense arguments, the anger at the Thai government, the ailments, the clashes with his family, the personality that allowed him to sell anything to anyone.

I took the tour myself, several times, to get a feeling for the house. It was still stunning, but sterile. And as I wandered behind the tour guide from room to room, I couldn't help remembering what one of Thompson's old friends had said: "The house was beautiful, but it didn't change that much if you went night after night—the food there really wasn't so great, really, it was just street food. But when you'd been there at night with Jim Thompson, in your memory, it was the greatest night of your life."[14]

Acknowledgments

This book could not have been written without the generous assistance and wise advice of many people.

Ralph Boyce and Joshua Glazeroff read drafts of the manuscript and offered insightful comments. My mother, my first writing teacher, read the manuscript and gave her own unique thoughts, and my father contributed invaluable legal counsel as well as support.

Shelby Leighton and Doris Duangbudda contributed important research and analysis. Susan Strange helped enormously at the National Archives, as did Larry McDonald and John Taylor, who passed away during the writing of the book. Bruce Reynolds shared his knowledge of Thailand in the Second World War. The OSS Society helped me get in touch with surviving members of Jim Thompson's OSS class, and Andrew van der Plaats generously shared earlier interviews with Thompson's friend Alexander MacDonald. Christopher Goscha provided me with copies of the diaries of Tao Oun. James Frasche allowed me to view the papers of his father, Dean.

The archivists at St. Paul's School in New Hampshire, Princeton University, the University of Pennsylvania, the Delaware state archives, Cornell University, the Lyndon Baines Johnson Library and Museum, the Pridi Banomyong Institute, and the Thai national archives helped me to find key documents. Songpol Kaoputumtip, William Klausner, Michael Montesano, Philip Rivers, and many other scholars offered their insights into Thompson and his era in U.S.-Thai relations.

At John Wiley & Sons, editor Eric Nelson shepherded the book to its final form and shaped it into a far better piece of writing. My agent, Heather Schroder, of International Creative Management, provided encouragement throughout the process, feedback, and the initial shape of the draft. I'd also like to thank copyeditor Judith Antonelli and Wiley production editor Kimberly Monroe-Hill.

Research for the book relied on the help of many people. Hope Anderson generously lent me the master tapes and transcripts from her documentary, *Jim Thompson, Silk King*. Bill Booth and the rest of the Jim Thompson Company arranged for me to interview current and former employees, opened their archives to me, and sat with me for hours answering questions about Jim Thompson. William Warren, author of the previous Thompson biography, *The Legendary American*, met with me in his Bangkok home and discussed his work and experiences with Thompson. Ann Donaldson, Robin Graves, Andrews Reath, Tom Donaldson, and other members of Thompson's family shared their memories and written records of their uncle. Willis Bird Jr. and Virginia Bird generously answered all my questions about their father.

Charles Burwell, Jack Lenor Larsen, Murray Fromson, Harold Stephens, Kit Young, Anne Tofield, Ethan Emery, Lily Tuck, Diane Baude, Philippe Baude, Jackie Ayer, Christine Rangsit-Cameron, Campbell James, Greg Davis, Jesse Henry, Rene Burrow, Carolina Barrie, Cobey Black, and other friends of Thompson's sat for lengthy discussions. Denis Horgan offered his perspective as a young army officer who knew Thompson and Ed Black at the time. William vanden Heuvel excavated his diaries from the 1950s to help me understand the era of Bill Donovan in Thailand, as did Rolland Bushner, Phillip George, and Prok Amaraond.

Siddhi Satevsila and other Free Thai veterans sat with me for hours explaining the Free Thai role during World War II. Barry Broman provided me with a copy of his interviews of many Thompson friends and relatives. Several Central Intelligence Agency veterans offered critical confidential advice, information, and material.

Dr. Jeffrey Magaziner gave his counsel and wonderful bedside manner throughout the process, and his assistance helped to restore my health somewhat. I also thank my family and friends for bearing with me throughout the writing of this book.

Most generously, Henry Thompson, the nephew and heir of Jim Thompson, opened his home to me, provided me with his uncle's letters, shared with me time lines of his uncle's life, and filled in gaps in my understanding of Jim Thompson's life, friends, and times.

Throughout it all, Caleb remained the joy and love in my life. Whenever I felt down, I could always get a hug from him, and a reminder: "Let's go!"

Notes

Preface

1. Christina Klein, *Cold War Orientalism: Asia in the Middlebrow 1945–1961* (Berkeley: University of California Press, 2003).

Chapter 1

1. Denis Horgan, interview by author, West Hartford, CT, March 2007.
2. Benedict R.O.G. Anderson, *In the Mirror: Literature and Politics in Siam in the American Era* (Ithaca, NY: Cornell University Press, 1985), pp. 22–23.
3. "Holder of the Kingdom, Strength of the Land," *Time*, May 27, 1966.
4. Horgan, interview.
5. Rene Burrow, phone interview by author, April 2007.
6. Rene Burrow, unpublished memoirs, p. 45.
7. William Warren, *Jim Thompson: The House on the Klong* (Singapore: Dider Millet Publishers, 2007), pp. 3–34.
8. Horgan, interview.
9. Ibid.

10. Ibid.
11. Ibid. William Warren, interview by author, Bangkok, July 2007. Henry Thompson, interview by author, Oyster Bay, NY, March 2007.
12. Horgan, interview.

Chapter 2

1. On the dates of Thompson's various jobs in the military: "Officer Qualification Report," U.S. Army file, March 1942, National Archives II.
2. JT to Mary Thompson, May 1941, private collection of Henry Thompson (JT's nephew).
3. On Jim's applying for officer candidate school: Henry Thompson, interview by author, Oyster Bay, NY, March 2007.
4. Letter to JT, February 4, 1942, Arthur Holden collection, Cornell University Library.
5. JT to Mary Thompson, November 10, 1942, and September 12, 1943, Thompson collection.
6. JT to Miss Norman, April 1941 and September 1941, Holden collection.
7. JT to Mary Thompson, November 10, 1942, Thompson collection.
8. Henry Thompson, interview.
9. Jane Scott, phone interview by author, February 2007.
10. Ann Donaldson, interview by author, New York, September 2007.
11. Edward Longacre, *From Union Stars to Top Hat: A Biography of the Extraordinary General James Harrison Wilson* (Mechanicsburg, PA: Stackpole Books, 1972), pp. 260–285.
12. Ibid., pp. 270–285.
13. Mary Thompson, unpublished memoir, pp. 43–48.
14. Ibid., pp. 23–39.
15. Henry Thompson, interview.
16. JT to Mary Thompson, March 20, 1942, Thompson collection.
17. Henry Thompson to JT, October 9, 1943, Thompson collection.
18. Franklin C. Wells to JT, February 19, 1943, Holden collection.
19. JT to Arthur Holden, January 1943, Holden collection.
20. Ibid.
21. Henry Thompson, interview.
22. JT to Mary Thompson, June 9, 1943, Thompson collection.
23. Henry Thompson, interview.
24. "Patricia Maury-Thraves Is Married to Capt. James Thompson in Virginia," *New York Times*, June 30, 1943.

25. JT to Arthur Holden, May 1943, Holden collection.
26. JT to Mary Thompson, May 1943, Thompson collection.
27. Ibid.
28. JT to nephew Henry Thompson, February 11, 1967, private collection of Tom Donaldson; Cobey Black, interview by author, Honolulu, June 2007.
29. Elizabeth McIntosh (former OSS employee), interview by author, Reston, VA, February 2007.
30. War Department memo, December 4, 1943, National Archives, Ref Off-Br-WEF-Ph 79075.

Chapter 3

1. W. Thomas Smith, *Encyclopedia of the Central Intelligence Agency* (New York: Facts on File, 2003), p. 106.
2. Elizabeth McIntosh, interview by author, Reston, VA, February 2007.
3. Anthony Cave Brown, *The Last Hero: Wild Bill Donovan* (New York: Vintage Books, 1984), p. 155.
4. Ibid., pp. 177–178.
5. Quoted in Thomas F. Troy, *Wild Bill and Intrepid: Donovan, Stephenson, and the Origin of CIA* (New Haven, CT: Yale University Press, 1996), p. 21.
6. Brown, *The Last Hero*, p. 173.
7. Richard Harris Smith, *OSS: The Secret History of America's First Central Intelligence Agency* (Guilford, CT: Lyons Press, 2005), p. 13.
8. David Bruce, quoted in ibid., p. 3.
9. Smith, *OSS*, p. 4.
10. Ibid., pp. 5–10.
11. Catherine Bodenstein, interview by author, Los Angeles, February 2007.
12. Quoted in Smith, *OSS*, p. 5.
13. Alexander MacDonald, *Bangkok Editor* (New York: Macmillan, 1949), pp. 2–4.
14. Ibid.
15. Dilworth Brinton to his family, September 12, 1945, private collection of the Brinton family.
16. Smith, *OSS*, p. 26.
17. McIntosh, interview.
18. Quoted in Smith, *OSS*, p. 27.
19. Quoted in Brown, *The Last Hero*, p. 298.
20. Smith, *OSS*, p. 306.

21. Ibid, pp. 307–309.
22. McIntosh, interview.
23. Smith, *OSS*, p. 15.
24. Ibid., p. 78.
25. Brown, *The Last Hero*, p. 533.
26. Joseph Lazarsky, interview by author, Middleburg, VA, December 2006.
27. Smith, *OSS*, p. 175.
28. Henry Thompson, interview by author, Oyster Bay, NY, August 2007.

Chapter 4
1. Jacques Snyder (OSS colleague of JT's at OSS training), e-mail to author, July 13, 2003.
2. John Bottorff (OSS colleague of JT's at OSS training), e-mail to author, July 13, 2003.
3. Ibid.
4. JT to Mary Thompson, March 1944, private collection of Henry Thompson.
5. Edwin Black, résumé, 1979, private collection of Cobey Black.
6. "Adjusted Service Rating Card for James HW Thompson," August 15, 1944, National Archives II.
7. Arthur Layton Funk, *Hidden Ally: The French Resistance, Special Operations, and the Landings in Southern France, 1944* (New York: Greenwood Press, 1992), pp. 58–62.
8. John Rosenfield, interview by author by phone, August 2006.
9. "Far East Orientation School Report. Subject: Major James HW Thompson," January 27, 1945, National Archives II.
10. William vanden Heuvel, interview by author, New York, April 2007.
11. Funk, pp. 77–78.
12. Ibid., pp. 118–120.
13. Federal Bureau of Investigation, "Case of James Harrison Wilson Thompson," June 19, 1953, National Archives II.
14. "Efficiency Report," August 8, 1945, National Archives, W-OSS-PERS-5.
15. Henry Thompson, interview by author, Oyster Bay, NY, June 2007.
16. Kenneth Landon, diary entry, September 1945, Kenneth Landon collection, Wheaton College Library.
17. On the 1932 revolution and its aftermath: Paul Handley, *The King Never Smiles: A Biography of Thailand's Bhumibol Adulyadej* (New Haven, CT: Yale University Press, 2006).
18. Vichitvong Na Pombhejara, *Pridi Banomyong and the Making of Thailand's Modern History* (Bangkok: Ruankaew, 2001), pp. xiv.

19. Pridi Banomyong, Chris Baker, and Pasuk Phongpaichit, *Pridi by Pridi: Selected Writings on Life, Politics, and Economy* (Seattle: University of Washington Press, 2001), p. 83.
20. Landon, diary entry, Landon collection.
21. Vichitvong, *Pridi Banomyong*, p. 163.
22. Richard Harris Smith, *OSS: The Secret History of America's First Central Intelligence Agency* (Guilford, CT: Lyons Press, 2005), p. 292.
23. S. Dillon Ripley, "Incident in Siam," *Yale Review*, Winter 1947, pp. 262–273.
24. Henry Thompson, interview by author, Oyster Bay, NY, December 2006.
25. Dorothy Woodman, "Soldier and Statesman: Phibul and Pridi," *Asian Horizon*, Summer 1948, pp. 9–22.
26. Frank Darling, *Thailand and the United States* (New York: Public Affairs Press, 1965), pp. 3–32.
27. Landon, diary entry, Landon collection.
28. Vichitvong, *Pridi Banomyong*, p. 165.
29. Woodman, "Soldier and Statesman."
30. Ibid.; Edgar Snow, "Secrets from Siam," *Saturday Evening Post*, January 12, 1946; see also Wimon Wiriyawit, *Free Thai: Personal Recollections and Official Documents* (Bangkok: White Lotus Press, 1997), pp. 6–30.
31. Nicol Smith and Blake Clark, *Into Siam: Underground Kingdom* (Indianapolis: Bobbs-Merrill, 1946), p. 19.
32. "Thailand: Ally in Secret," *Newsweek*, September 3, 1945.
33. Piya Chakkaphak, Siddhi Savetsila, and other Free Thai veterans, interviews by author, Bangkok, July 2007.
34. Woodman, "Soldier and Statesman."
35. Sharon Karr, *Traveler of the Crossroads: The Life of Adventurer Nicol Smith* (Jacksonville, OR: Log Cabin Manuscripts, 1995), p. 232.
36. George C. Chalou, ed., *The Secrets War: The Office of Strategic Services in World War II* (Washington, DC: National Archives and Record Service, 1992), pp. 328–354.
37. William Donovan, "Our Stake in Thailand," *Fortune*, July 1955.
38. Smith and Clark, *Into Siam*, pp. 33–34; see also Wimon, *Free Thai*, pp. 71–75.
39. Tran van Dinh, interview by author, Washington, DC, November 2006.
40. Alexander MacDonald, *My Footloose Newspaper Life* (Bangkok: Post Publishing Company, 1990), p. 97.
41. Kenneth Landon, diary entry, October 1945, Landon collection.

42. Wimon, *Free Thai*, pp. 27–28.
43. "Thailand's Aid to US Told by OSS," *Washington Post*, September 9, 1945.
44. Ripley, "Incident in Siam."
45. Karr, *Traveler of the Crossroads*, p. 236.
46. MacDonald, *My Footloose Newspaper Life*, p. 97.
47. Richard Kelly, "Mission to Bangkok," *Blue Book*, December 1946.
48. Ripley, "Incident in Siam."
49. Dilworth Brinton to his family, September 12, 1946, private collection of the Brinton family; see also Leigh Williams, *Jungle Prison: Twenty Years in Siam* (London: Andrew Melrose Publishing, 1941), pp. 30–31.
50. Brinton to his family, September 12, 1945, Brinton collection.
51. Henry Thompson, interview.
52. Charles Burwell, interview by author, Millwood, VA, July 2006.
53. JT to Mary Thompson, February 1946, Thompson collection.
54. Ann Donaldson, interview by author, New York, September 2006.
55. Henry Thompson, interview by author, Oyster Bay, NY, August 2006; Ann Donaldson, interview by author, New York, April 2007.
56. Landon, diary entry, October 1945, Landon collection.

Chapter 5

1. Alexander MacDonald, *Bangkok Editor* (New York: Macmillan, 1949), pp. 4–5.
2. John Rosenfield, interview by author by phone, December 2006.
3. Elizabeth McIntosh, interview by author, Reston, VA, November 2006.
4. E. Bruce Reynolds, "The OSS and American Intelligence in Postwar Thailand," *Journal of Intelligence History*, Winter 2002, p. 30.
5. Arlene Neher, "Prelude to Alliance: The Expansion of American Economic Interest in Thailand during the 1940s" (master's thesis, Northern Illinois University, 1980), p. 14.
6. Dilworth Brinton to his family, October 21, 1945, private collection of the Brinton family.
7. Neher, "Prelude to Alliance," pp. 23–27.
8. Kenneth Landon to Margaret Landon, December 22, 1945, Kenneth Landon collection, Wheaton College Library.
9. Neher, "Prelude to Alliance," p. 124.
10. Frank Darling, *Thailand and the United States* (New York: Public Affairs, 1965), p. 42.
11. Reynolds, "The OSS and American Intelligence," pp. 22–23.

12. Edwin Stanton, *Brief Authority: Excursions of a Common Man in an Uncommon World* (New York: Harper and Row, 1956), p. 165.
13. Neher, "Prelude to Alliance," p. 29.
14. MacDonald, *Bangkok Editor*, pp. 9–10.
15. Harold Martin, "They Love Us in Siam," *Saturday Evening Post*, April 24, 1948; see also Neher, "Prelude to Alliance," p. 121.
16. Bill Young, interview by author by phone, March 2006.
17. William Warren, *Chronicles of American Business in Thailand* (Bangkok: American Chamber of Commerce, 2006), p. 28.
18. S. Dillon Ripley, "Incident in Siam," *Yale Review*, Winter 1947, p. 274.
19. Neher, "Prelude to Alliance," p. 97.
20. Henry Thompson, interviews by author, Oyster Bay, NY, January and March 2007; Rosenfield, interview.
21. Stephen Sysko, interview by author by phone, March 2006.
22. Sukprida Banomyong, interview by author, Bangkok, July 2007.
23. Rolland Bushner, interview by author by phone, February 2007.
24. Ann Donaldson, interview by author, New York, August 2006
25. *Foreign Relations of the United States*, volume 6 (Washington, DC: Government Printing Office, 1945), pp. 1388–1389.
26. *The OSS and Ho Chi Minh: Unexpected Allies in the War against Japan* (Lawrence: University Press of Kansas, 2009), p. 315.
27. Dixee Bartholomew-Feis and Daniel Fineman, *A Special Relationship: The United States and Military Government in Thailand, 1947–1958* (Honolulu: University of Hawaii Press, 1997), p. 18.
28. Philippe Baude, interview by author by phone, February 2007.
29. Robert Trumbull, "Bangkok Is 'Home' for Exiled Rebels," *New York Times*, January 26, 1949.
30. Bushner, interview.
31. Oun Sananikone, translated by John B Murdoch, *Lao Issara: The Memoirs of Oun Sananikone* (Ithaca, NY: Cornell University Press, 1975), pp. 9–10.
32. Thompson briefing on secret control, May 31, 1946, National Archives II; see also Reynolds, "The OSS and American Intelligence," p. 35.
33. Thompson briefing.
34. Willis Bird Jr., interview by author, Chiang Mai, Thailand, July 2007; Willis Bird funeral volume, 1991, private collection of Bird family.
35. Carole Bird, interview by author by phone, February 2007.
36. Willis Bird Jr., interview.
37. Ibid.; Maochun Yu, *OSS in China: Prelude to Cold War* (New Haven, CT: Yale University Press, 1997), pp. 188–189.

38. Willis Bird to friends, 1947, private collection of Willis Bird Jr.
39. Neher, "Prelude to Alliance," p. 50.
40. Willis Bird to friends.
41. Marsh Thomson, interview by author by phone, June 2007.

Chapter 6
1. James Thompson, "Report on the Siamese Case," May 13, 1946, National Archives II, File ZMM 482, State Department Archives.
2. E. Bruce Reynolds, "The OSS and American Intelligence in Postwar Thailand," *Journal of Intelligence History*, Winter 2002, p. 37.
3. Thompson, "The French Case," May 13, 1946, National Archives II, File ZMM 482, State Department Archives.
4. Thompson, "Report on the Siamese Case."
5. Reynolds, "The OSS and American Intelligence," pp. 40–41.
6. JT, cable to Don Garden, September 10, 1946, National Archives II, RG 226, Box 9, Entry 108C.
7. Ibid.
8. JT, cable to Don Garden, May 1, 1946, National Archives, RG 226, Box 9, Entry 108D.
9. Ibid.
10. Rayne Kruger, *The Devil's Discus* (London: Cassell, 1964), p. 96.
11. Chris Baker and Pasuk Phongpaichit, *A History of Thailand* (Cambridge: Cambridge University Press, 2005), p. 142.
12. Rolland Bushner, interview by author by phone, January 2007.
13. Reynolds, "The OSS and American Intelligence," pp. 40–42.
14. Jim Thompson, "The Situation in Indochina," briefing report, 1946, U.S. Army Military History Institute, OSS files.
15. JT, cable to Don Garden, October 17, 1946, National Archives II.
16. Reynolds, "The OSS and American Intelligence," p. 43.
17. Martha Galleher, *The Missing Thai Silk King* (Baltimore: self-published, 2007), p. 76.
18. JT to Elinor Douglas, November 22, 1948, private collection of Tom Donaldson.
19. Rolland Bushner, interview by author by phone, April 2007.
20. JT to Elinor Douglas, November 22, 1948, and October 25, 1949, Donaldson collection.
21. Henry Thompson, interview by author, Oyster Bay, NY, June 2007.
22. Ann Donaldson, interview by author, New York, September 2006.
23. Henry Thompson, interview.
24. Ibid.

25. Willis Bird Jr., interview by author, Chiang Mai, Thailand, July 2007.
26. Lynne Joiner, *Honorable Survivor: Mao's China, McCarthy's America, and the Persecution of John S. Service* (Annapolis, MD: Naval Institute Press, 2009).
27. Carole Bird, interview by author by phone, March 2007.
28. Bill Lair, interview by author by phone, September 2007.
29. Willis Bird Jr., interview; Harold Martin, "They Love Us in Siam," *Saturday Evening Post*, April 24, 1948, pp. 180–182.
30. Lair, interview.
31. Reynolds, "The OSS and American Intelligence," p. 43.
32. Willis Bird funeral volume, 1991, private collection of the Bird family.
33. Kempton Jenkins, interview by author, Washington, DC, February 2007.
34. Kruger, pp. 103–104.
35. Daniel Fineman, *A Special Relationship: The United States and Military Government in Thailand, 1947–1958* (Honolulu: University of Hawaii Press, 1997), p. 20.
36. Baker and Pasuk, *A History of Thailand*, p. 142.
37. Alexander MacDonald, "The Two Kings and I," MacDonald Papers, private collection of Andrew Van Der Plaats.
38. Wanthani Phanitchakun, *Neung satawan Suphasawat* (Bangkok: Amarin Press, 2000), p. 563.
39. David van Praagh, *Thailand's Struggle for Democracy: The Life and Times of MR Seni Pramoj* (Teaneck, NJ: Holmes and Meier, 1996), p. 108; Kruger, pp. 108–109.
40. Alexander MacDonald, *Bangkok Editor* (New York: Macmillan, 1949), p. 57.
41. Rolland Bushner, interview by author by phone, October 2006.
42. Kruger, pp. 108–109.
43. JT, cable to Don Garden, September 7, 1946, ZMM 633, State Department Archives.
44. Fineman, *A Special Relationship*, p. 21.

Chapter 7
1. On the Marshall mission: Jay Taylor, *The Generalissimo: Chiang Kaishek and the Struggle for Modern China* (Cambridge, MA: Harvard University Press, 2009).
2. Andrew Roth, "Fact and Fiction in Siam," *Nation*, December 25, 1948, p. 725.

3. Robert Blum, *Drawing the Line: The Origins of American Containment Policy in Asia* (New York: W. W. Norton, 1983), p. 108; National Security Council, "A Report to the President on the Position of the United States with Respect to Asia," December 30, 1949, Harry S. Truman Library.

4. Blum, *Drawing the Line*, p. 109.

5. JT, cable to Don Garden, September 23, 1946, National Archives II.

6. JT, cable to Don Garden, October 17, 1946, National Archives II.

7. Arlene Neher, "Prelude to Alliance: The Expansion of American Economic Interest in Thailand during the 1940s" (master's thesis, Northern Illinois University, 1980), p. 95.

8. Quoted in ibid., p. 216.

9. Ibid., p. 231.

10. Blum, *Drawing the Line*, p. 214.

11. Alexander MacDonald, *Bangkok Editor* (New York: Macmillan, 1949), pp. 148–149.

12. Ibid., pp. 152–155.

13. Ibid., p. 149.

14. Rolland Bushner, interview by author by phone, March 2007.

15. Neher, "Prelude to Alliance," p. 249.

16. Judith A. Stowe, *Siam Becomes Thailand: A Story of Intrigue* (Honolulu: University of Hawaii Press, 1991), p. 240.

17. Thak Chaloemtiarana, *Thailand: The Politics of Despotic Paternalism* (Ithaca, NY: Cornell University Press, 2007), pp. 26–27.

18. Stowe, *Siam Becomes Thailand*, p. 240.

19. Daniel Fineman, *A Special Relationship: The United States and Military Government in Thailand, 1947–1958* (Honolulu: University of Hawaii Press, 1997), p. 37.

20. Thak, *Thailand*, p. 31.

21. Geoffrey Thompson, *Front Line Diplomat* (London: Hutchinson, 1959), p. 200.

22. Alexander MacDonald, *My Footloose Newspaper Life* (Bangkok: Post, 1990), pp. 122–123.

23. Thak, *Thailand*, p. 31.

24. MacDonald, *Bangkok Editor*, p. 154.

25. Alexander MacDonald, "The Two Kings and I," MacDonald Papers, private collection of Andrew van der Plaats.

26. Rayne Kruger, *The Devil's Discus* (London: Cassell & Company, 1964), pp. 116–117.

27. Vichitvong Na Pombhejara, *Pridi Banomyong and the Making of Thailand's Modern History* (Bangkok: Ruankaew, 2001), pp. 260–261.

28. Neher, "Prelude to Alliance," p. 237; Vichitvong, *Pridi Banomyong*, pp. 242–243.

29. MacDonald, *Bangkok Editor*, p. 161.

30. Paul Handley, *The King Never Smiles: A Biography of Thailand's Bhumibhol Adulyadej* (New Haven, CT: Yale University Press, 2006), p. 88.

31. MacDonald, *Bangkok Editor*, p. 126; Roth, "Fact and Fiction in Siam," p. 725.

32. Fineman, *A Special Relationship*, pp. 20–45.

33. MacDonald, *Bangkok Editor*, p. 178; William Warren, *Chronicles of American Business in Thailand* (Bangkok: American Chamber of Commerce, 2006), p. 135.

34. Virginia Thompson, "Governmental Instability in Siam," *Far Eastern Survey*, August 25, 1948, p. 185; Percy Wood, "Yankee Editor Feels Wrath of Siamese Rulers," *Chicago Daily Tribune*, April 29, 1949, p. 17.

35. Campbell James, interview by author, Newport, RI, March 2007.

36. Dorothy Woodman, "Soldier and Statesman: Phibul and Pridi," *Asian Horizon*, Summer 1948, pp. 20–21.

37. Doris Russell, interview by author, Bangkok, April 2007.

38. Alfred W. McCoy, *The Politics of Heroin in Southeast Asia* (New York: Harper, 1973).

39. William Stevenson, *The Revolutionary King: The True-Life Sequel to The King and I* (London: Constable and Robinson, 2001), p. 119.

40. Frank Darling, *Thailand and the United States* (New York: Public Affairs Press, 1965), pp. 114–115.

41. Thak, *Thailand*, pp. 84–85; Joseph Lazarsky, interview by author, Middleburg, VA, November 2006.

42. E. Bruce Reynolds, "The OSS and American Intelligence in Postwar Thailand," *Journal of Intelligence History*, Winter 2002, p. 46; "Police Describe How Four Men Met Death Yesterday," *Bangkok Post*, March 6, 1949.

43. Thak, *Thailand*, p. 62.

44. JT to Elinor Douglas, March 7, 1949, private collection of Andrews Reath.

45. Henry Thompson, interview by author, Oyster Bay, NY, March 2007.

46. William Warren, *The Legendary American: The Remarkable Career and Strange Disappearance of Jim Thompson* (Boston: Houghton Mifflin, 1970), pp. 80–88.

47. Ibid, p. 87.

48. Neher, "Prelude to Alliance," p. 234.

49. Ibid., p. 236.
50. Campbell James, interview by author, Newport, RI, August 2007.
51. JT to Elinor Douglas, November 14, 1948, Reath collection.
52. Neher, "Prelude to Alliance," p. 239.
53. Ibid., p. 366.
54. Blum, *Drawing the Line*, p. 199.
55. Kempton Jenkins, interview by author, Washington, DC, August 2007.
56. Neher, "Prelude to Alliance," pp. 239–240; Virginia Thompson and Richard Adloff, *The Left Wing in Southeast Asia* (New York: William Sloane, 1950), pp. 51–52.
57. Fineman, *A Special Relationship*, p. 10.
58. MacDonald, *Bangkok Editor*, p. 202; Stevenson, *The Revolutionary King*, p. 117.
59. *New York Times*, August 31, 1949, p. 12; Roth, "Fact and Fiction in Siam," p. 725.
60. Neher, "Prelude to Alliance," p. 94; Fineman, *A Special Relationship*, p. 57.
61. Fineman, *A Special Relationship*, pp. 87–88.
62. Neher, "Prelude to Alliance," p. 28.
63. Ibid., p. 240.
64. Ibid., pp. 213–214.

Chapter 8
1. "The Story of Thai Silk," *Holiday Time in Thailand*, May–June 1985, pp. 7–12.
2. Jackie Ayer, interview by author by phone, January 2007.
3. Susan Conway, *Thai Textiles* (London: British Museum, 1992), pp. 43–50. Also, Jane Puranananda, *The Secrets of Southeast Asian Textiles: Myth, Status, and the Supernatural* (Bangkok: River Books, 2007), pp. 23–56.
4. Ibid, pp. 43–44.
5. Jane Puranananda, ed., *Through the Thread of Times: Southeast Asian Textiles* (Bangkok: Jim Thompson Foundation, 2004), pp. 45–74.
6. Conway, *Thai Textiles*, p. 157.
7. Susan Conway, interview by author by phone, September 2007.
8. Mary Cable, "The Silk of Thailand," *Atlantic Monthly*, January 1966, p. 107.
9. John Rosenfield, interview by author by phone, December 2006.
10. Jackie Ayer, interview by author by phone, December 2006.
11. William Klausner, *Thai Culture in Transition: The Collected Writings of William J. Klausner* (Bangkok: Siam Society, 1997), p. 18.

12. Ibid., p. 7.
13. Ibid., pp. 7–10.
14. Frank Darling, *Thailand and the United States* (New York: Public Affairs Press, 1965), p. 116.
15. Thak Chaloemtiarana, *Thailand: The Politics of Despotic Paternalism* (Ithaca, NY: Cornell University Press, 2007), pp. 84–85.
16. Darling, *Thailand and the United States*, p. 116.
17. Willis Bird Jr., interview by author, Chiang Mai, Thailand, July 2007.
18. Willis Bird to Bill Donovan, December 20, 1947, William J. Donovan collection, U.S. Military History Institute.
19. Willis Bird Jr., interview; Greg Davis, interview by author, Washington, DC, March 2007; Siddhi Savetsila, interview by author, Bangkok, July 2007.
20. Virginia Bird, interview by author, Chiang Mai, Thailand, July 2007.
21. "Siamese Requests for Arms through Willis H. Bird," March 4, 1949, Central Intelligence Agency.
22. *Foreign Relations of the United States: Asia and the Pacific, 1951* (Washington, DC: U.S. Government Printing Office, 1951), pp. 1633–1634.
23. Willis Bird to Police General Phao Sriyanond, December 2, 1953, private collection of Willis Bird Jr.
24. Vichitvong Na Pombhejara, *Pridi Banomyong and the Making of Thailand's Modern History* (Bangkok: Ruankaew, 2001), pp. 247–248.
25. Rayne Kruger, *The Devil's Discus* (London: Cassell, 1964), pp. 138–139.
26. Ibid.
27. Geoffrey Thompson, *Front Line Diplomat* (London: Hutchinson, 1959), pp. 55–71.
28. Edwin Stanton, *Brief Authority: Excursions of a Common Man in an Uncommon World* (New York: Harper and Row, 1956), pp. 224–225.
29. Alexander MacDonald, *Bangkok Editor* (New York: Macmillan, 1949), pp. 218–219.
30. "The Heaviest Fighting," *Siam Nikorn*, February 27, 1949.
31. Stanton, *Brief Authority*, pp. 222–225.
32. Sukprida Banomyong, interview by author, Bangkok, July 2007.
33. MacDonald, *Bangkok Editor*, p. 222.
34. Ann Donaldson, interview by author, New York, March 2007.
35. Henry Thompson, interview by author, Oyster Bay, NY, September 2007.
36. Donaldson, interview.
37. JT, cable to Don Garden, July 24, 1946, National Archives II.
38. Confidential CIA source, interview by author, Washington, DC, March 2007.

39. Sompong Sucharitkul, interview by author by phone, January 2008; confidential CIA source, interview.

40. Martha Galleher, *The Missing Thai Silk King* (Baltimore: self-published, 2007), p. 38.

41. JT, cable to Don Garden, August 9, 1946, National Archives II.

42. Richard Harris Smith, *OSS: The Secret History of America's First Central Intelligence Agency* (Guilford, CT: Lyons Press, 2005), pp. 338–340.

43. Ibid.

44. JT to Elinor Douglas, April 15, 1951, private collection of Andrews Reath.

45. William J. Donovan, "Our Stake in Thailand," *Fortune*, July 1953, pp. 94–95.

46. Rene Burrow, interview by author by phone, September 2006.

47. Philippe Baude, interview by author by phone, February 2007.

48. William Warren, *The Legendary American: The Remarkable Career and Strange Disappearance of Jim Thompson* (Boston: Houghton Mifflin, 1970), pp. 62–65.

49. Charles Burwell, interview by author, Reston, VA, March 2007.

50. Rene Burrow, interview by author by phone, March 2007.

51. Warren, *The Legendary American*, pp. 62–65.

52. Henry Thompson, interview by author, Oyster Bay, NY, March 2007.

53. Rene Burrow, unpublished memoirs, p. 19; Warren, *The Legendary American*, pp. 62–65.

54. Francis and Katharine Dranke, "Jim Thompson and the Busy Weavers of Bangkok," *Reader's Digest*, October 1959, pp. 232–233.

55. Warren, *The Legendary American*, pp. 62–66.

56. Jorges Orgibet, *From Siam to Thailand* (Bangkok: Kofco, 1982), pp. 28–29.

57. Doris Russell, interview by author, Bangkok, July 2007; Ruth Gerson, interview by author, Bangkok, July 2007.

58. Greg Davis, interview by author, Arlington, VA, January 2007.

59. Elizabeth McIntosh, interview by author, Washington, DC, December 2006; also, "The Two Kings and I," private papers of Alexander MacDonald, collection of Andrew van der Plaats.

60. Russell, interview; Willis Bird Jr., interview; Greg Davis, interview.

61. Jesse Henry, interview by author, Bangkok, July 2007.

62. Ramphai to Willis Bird, June 5, 1949, private collection of Willis Bird Jr.

63. Virginia Bird, interview.

64. E. Bruce Reynolds, "The OSS and American Intelligence in Postwar Thailand," *Journal of Intelligence History*, Winter 2002, p. 48.

65. Bill Young, interview by author by phone, April 2007.
66. Willis Bird funeral volume, 1991, private collection of the Bird family.
67. Willis Bird Jr., interview.
68. Reynolds, p. 48.
69. Willis Bird Jr., interview.
70. Dennis Horgan, interview by author, West Hartford, CT, December 2006.
71. Jesse Henry, interview by author, Bangkok, July 2007; also Davis, interview.

Chapter 9

1. Edwin Stanton, "Spotlight on Thailand," *Foreign Affairs*, October 1954, pp. 79–80.
2. Daniel Fineman, *A Special Relationship: The United States and Military Government in Thailand, 1947–1958* (Honolulu: University of Hawaii Press, 1997), pp. 91–92.
3. Ibid., p. 173.
4. Timothy Castle, *At War in the Shadow of Vietnam: US Military Aid to the Royal Lao Government, 1955–1975* (New York: Columbia University Press, 1993), pp. 12–13.
5. Fineman, *A Special Relationship*, p. 135.
6. Jesse Henry, interview by author, Bangkok, July 2007.
7. Dennis Warner, *The Last Confucian: Vietnam, Southeast Asia, and the West* (New York: Angus and Robinson, 1964), pp. 236–237.
8. Ibid.
9. Kobkua Suwannathat-Pian, *Thailand's Durable Premier: Phibun through Three Decades, 1932–1957* (New York: Oxford University Press, 1995), pp. 206–207; Francis Belanger, *Drugs, the U.S., and Khun Sa* (Bangkok: Duang Kamon, 1989), pp. 92–93.
10. Christopher Goscha, *Thailand and the Southeast Asian Networks of the Vietnamese Revolution* (London: Curzon Press, 1999), pp. 184–185.
11. Ibid., p. 186.
12. Ibid, pp. 192–193.
13. E. Bruce Reynolds, "The OSS and American Intelligence in Postwar Thailand," *Journal of Intelligence History*, Winter 2002, p. 41.
14. JT to Elinor Douglas, May 1949, Reath collection.
15. U.S. Department of State, cable from Saigon to Washington, August 23, 1950.
16. Ibid.
17. Ronald MacMillan, "Office of Strategic Services Memorandum to James R Murphy re: The Hastings Matter," January 29, 1946, File ZM-002-1228, National Archives II.

18. James Murphy, "Recommendations in the Hastings Matter," Office of Strategic Services memo, December 26, 1945, File ZM-002-1228, National Archives II.
19. Augur Magruder, "Dispatch Augur Magruder from Taylor," Office of Strategic Services cable, December 14, 1945, National Archives II.
20. Cable from Saigon to Washington, August 23, 1950.
21. Anond Srivardhana, e-mails to author, September 2002; Bill Lair, interview by author by phone, January 2007.
22. Jesse Henry, interview by author, Bangkok, September 2006.
23. Fineman, *A Special Relationship*, p. 135.
24. Thomas Lobe, *United States National Security Policy and Aid to the Thailand Police* (Denver, CO: University of Denver Press, 1977), pp. 23–25.
25. Robert Lee Scott, *Flying Tiger: Chennault of China* (New York: Doubleday, 1959), p. 23.
26. Ibid., pp. 201–222.
27. William Leary, *Perilous Missions: Civil Air Transport and CIA Covert Operations in Asia* (Washington: Smithsonian Institution Press, 2002), pp. 1–7.
28. On the early days of CAT: Felix Smith, *China Pilot: Flying for Chennault during the Cold War* (Washington, DC: Smithsonian Institute Press, 1995); Scott, *Flying Tiger*, p. 278.
29. Leary, *Perilous Missions*, pp. 69–71.
30. Ibid., pp. 44–47.
31. Ibid., p. 112.
32. Peter Dale Scott, *Drugs, Oil, and War: The United States in Afghanistan, Colombia, and Indochina* (Lanham, MD: Rowman and Littlefield, 2003), pp. 188–189.
33. Willis Bird Jr., interview by author, Chiang Mai, Thailand, July 2007.
34. Ibid.
35. Francis W. Belanger, *Drugs, the US, and Khun Sa* (Bangkok: Duang Kamol, 1989), pp. 86–87.
36. Fineman, *A Special Relationship*, p. 141.
37. Richard Gibson, interview by author, Washington, DC, September 2006.
38. Willis Bird Jr., interview by author, Chiang Mai, Thailand, July 2007.
39. William vanden Heuvel, interview by author, New York, September 2006.
40. Jesse Henry, interview by author, Bangkok, September 2006.
41. "Battle of Bangkok," *Time*, July 9, 1951.

42. Ibid.
43. Chris Baker and Pasuk Phongpaichit, *A History of Thailand* (Cambridge: Cambridge University Press, 2005), pp. 144–146.

Chapter 10
1. Rolland Bushner, interview by author by phone, March 2007.
2. William vanden Heuvel, interview by author, New York, August 2006. Also, Kempton Jenkins, interview by author, Washington, DC, January 2006.
3. Robert Lee Scott, *Flying Tiger: Chennault of China* (New York: Doubleday, 1959), p. 282.
4. Timothy Castle, *At War in the Shadow of Vietnam: US Military Aid to the Royal Lao Government, 1955–1975* (New York: Columbia University Press, 1993), p. 10.
5. Daniel Fineman, *A Special Relationship: The United States and Military Government in Thailand, 1947–1958* (Honolulu: University of Hawaii Press, 1997), pp. 141–149.
6. Ibid., pp. 215–216.
7. Ibid., pp. 240–242.
8. Thak Chaloemtiarana, *Thailand: The Politics of Despotic Paternalism* (Ithaca, NY: Cornell Southeast Asia Program 2006), p. 57.
9. Jesse Henry, interview by author, Bangkok, March 2007.
10. Fineman, *A Special Relationship*, pp. 141–145.
11. William vanden Heuvel, interview; Fineman, *A Special Relationship*, pp. 206–210.
12. William Donovan, "Our Stake in Thailand," *Fortune*, July 1955, pp. 94–95.
13. Greg Davis, interview by author, Arlington, VA, August 2006.
14. Confidential CIA source, interview by author by phone, December 2006.
15. Confidential CIA source, interview by author by phone, November 2006.
16. Martha Galleher, *The Missing Thai Silk King* (Baltimore: self-published, 2007), pp. 75–77.
17. U.S. State Department, "James Harrison Wilson Thompson Executive Order 10422," September 4, 1953.
18. Galleher, *The Missing Thai Silk King*, p. 54.
19. Confidential State Department source, interview by author, Washington, DC, December 2007.
20. Rene Burrow, interview by author by phone, August 2007.

21. Federal Bureau of Investigation, "James Harrison Wilson Thompson: Loyalty of the Employees of the United Nations and Other Public International Organizations," report, June 22, 1953, File FD-204.

22. Ibid.

23. Burrow, interview; Philippe Baude, interview by author by phone, August 2007.

24. Philippe Baude, interview by author by phone, March 2007; see also Galleher, *The Missing Thai Silk King*, pp. 67–68.

25. Galleher, *The Missing Thai Silk King*, pp. 63–64.

26. JT to Elinor Douglas, April 16, 1951, private collection of Andrews Reath.

27. JT to Elinor Douglas, February 25, 1951, Reath collection.

28. William vanden Heuvel, interview by author, New York, November 2006.

29. Philippe Baude, interview by author by phone, June 2007.

30. Campbell James, interview by author, Newport, RI, February 2007; Murray Fromson, interview by author, Los Angeles, June 2007.

31. Rene Burrow, interview by author by phone, March 2007; William Warren, interview by author, Bangkok, July 2007.

32. Surindr Supasavasdebhandu, interview by author, Bangkok, July 2007.

33. *Eastern Sun* (Singapore), March 30, 1967.

34. Ann Donaldson, interview by author, New York, September 2006; Christina Klein, *Cold War Orientalism: Asia in the Middlebrow Imagination, 1945–1961* (Berkeley: University of California Press, 2003), p. 222.

35. William Warren, *The Legendary American* (Boston: Houghton Mifflin, 1970), p. 62.

36. William Booth, interview by author, Bangkok, July 2007.

37. Henry Thompson, interview by author, Oyster Bay, NY, February 2007.

38. Jackie Ayer, interview by author by phone, March 2007.

39. Anne Tofield, interview by author, August 2007; Jackie Ayer, interview by author by phone, July 2007; William Booth, interview.

40. Jackie Ayer, interview.

41. Klein, *Cold War Orientalism*, pp. 103–104.

42. Warren, *The Legendary American*, pp. 64–65.

43. Warren, interview.

44. Warren, *The Legendary American*, pp. 90–91.

45. Surindr, interview.

46. JT to Elinor Douglas, January 2, 1953, Reath collection.

47. Charles Burwell, interview by author, Leesburg, VA, March 2007.
48. Ibid.
49. Henry Thompson, interview by author, Oyster Bay, NY, September 2007.
50. Surindr, interview.
51. Warren, *The Legendary American*, p. 72.
52. William Warren, interview.

Chapter 11
1. Mary Cable, "The Silk of Thailand," *Atlantic Monthly*, January 1966, pp. 107–110; James H. W. Thompson and Niphon Nimboonchaj, *6 Soi Kasemsan II: An Illustrated Survey of the Bangkok Home of James H. W. Thompson* (Bangkok: Siva Phorn, 1959).
2. Rene Burrow, unpublished memoirs, pp. 48–49.
3. William Warren, *The Legendary American* (Boston: Houghton Mifflin, 1970), pp. 105–114.
4. "Thai Silk's the Thing," *Asia Magazine*, March 22, 1964, pp. 8–9.
5. Rene Burrow, interview by author by phone, February 2007; Ethan Emery, interview by author by phone, August 2007.
6. Franie Phillips, "James Thompson: The Host with the Most," *Bangkok World Sunday Magazine*, February 19, 1967, pp. 2–3.
7. Burrow, interview; Ethan Emery, interview by author by phone, April 2007.
8. Burrow, unpublished memoirs.
9. William Warren, interview by author, Bangkok, July 2007.
10. Burrow, interview.
11. JT to Elinor Douglas, March 3, 1966, private collection of Andrews Reath.
12. Henry Thompson, interview by author, Oyster Bay, NY, March 2007.
13. JT to Elinor Douglas, July 27, 1958, Reath collection.
14. Philip George, interview by author, New York, November 2006.
15. Jackie Ayer, interview by author by phone, January 2007.
16. Ying Charuvan, interview by author by phone, January 2007.
17. Ibid.; Ying Charuvan, unpublished memoirs.
18. JT to Elinor Douglas, April 1, 1956, Reath collection.
19. JT to Elinor Douglas, October 30, 1956, Reath collection.
20. William Booth, interview by author, Bangkok, December 2006; Thai Silk Company, "Annual Ordinary Meeting Report, Thai Silk Company, 1958."
21. JT to Elinor Douglas, April 23, 1955, Reath collection.

22. JT to Henry Thompson, September 2, 1955, Reath collection.
23. Philippe Baude, interview by author by phone, March 2007.
24. Chris Baker and Pasuk Phongpaichit, *A History of Thailand* (Cambridge: Cambridge University Press, 2005), pp. 102–142.
25. Ibid., pp. 148–149.
26. Ibid., p. 162.
27. David Lyman, *Yesteryear—Bangkok in 1956: What Life Was Like When AMCHAM Thailand Was Born* (Bangkok: Tilleke and Gibbins, 2006), pp. 41–46.
28. William Klausner, *Thai Culture in Transition* (Bangkok: Siam Society, 1998), pp. 42–46; Prok Amaranand, interview by author, Bangkok, July 2007.
29. Baude, interview.
30. Denis Horgan, interview by author, West Hartford, CT, August 2006; Cobey Black, interview by author, Honolulu, June 2007; Benedict Anderson, *In the Mirror: Literature and Politics in Siam in the American Era* (Ithaca, NY: Cornell University Press, 1985), pp. 22–23.
31. Daniel Fineman, *A Special Relationship: The United States and Military Government in Thailand, 1947–1958* (Honolulu: University of Hawaii Press, 1997), pp. 232–233.
32. Henry Thompson, interview.
33. Mervyn Brown, *War in Shangri-La: A Memoir of Civil War in Laos* (London: I. B. Tauris, 2001), pp. 181–195.
34. William Leary, "Supporting the Secret War: CIA Air Operations in Laos, 1955–1974," *Studies in Intelligence*, Winter 1999–2000.
35. Dwight D. Eisenhower, *Waging Peace, 1956–1961: The White House Years* (New York: Doubleday, 1965), p. 609.
36. Evan Thomas, *The Very Best Men: The Daring Years of the CIA* (New York: Simon and Schuster, 1995), pp. 279–281.
37. "Person of the Year: John F. Kennedy," *Time*, January 5, 1962.
38. Timothy Castle, *At War in the Shadow of Vietnam: US Military Aid to the Royal Lao Government, 1955–1975* (New York: Columbia University Press, 1993), p. 27.
39. Ibid., pp. 52–53.
40. Leary, "Supporting the Secret War."
41. Willis Bird Jr., interview by author, Chiang Mai, Thailand, July 2007.
42. George Tanham, *Communist Revolutionary Warfare: From the Viet Minh to the Viet Cong* (Santa Barbara, CA: Praeger, 2006), pp. 73–74.
43. Marsh Thomson, interview by author, Bangkok, July 2007.
44. Leary, "Supporting the Secret War," p. 75.

45. Philippe Baude, interview by author by phone, March 2006.
46. JT to Elinor Douglas, December 19, 1960, Reath collection.

Chapter 12
1. JT to Elinor Douglas, November 11, 1961, private collection of Andrews Reath.
2. JT to Elinor Douglas, March 19, 1966, Reath collection.
3. Rene Burrow, unpublished memoirs, p. 76.
4. JT to Elinor Douglas, April 17, 1962, Reath collection; see also JT to Elinor Douglas, August 1, 1964, Reath collection.
5. Burrow, unpublished memoirs, p. 54.
6. I. J. Talbot, "City Man Spins Riches in Thai Silk Industry," *Wilmington News Journal*, February 25, 1964, p. 23; Martha Galleher, *The Missing Thai Silk King* (Baltimore: self-published, 2007), p. 74.
7. Rita Reif, "From Khaki to Thai Silks by a Profitable Twist of Fate," *New York Times*, September 12, 1966; Arlette Cykman, interview by author, Pattaya, Thailand, July 2007; "Millions from the Mulberry Bush," *Time*, July 16, 1965.
8. Mary Cable, "The Silk of Thailand," *Atlantic Monthly*, January 1966, pp. 107–108; William Booth, interview by author, Bangkok, July 2007; Cykman, interview.
9. "Jim Thompson Opens New Headquarters," *Bangkok Post*, March 18, 1967.
10. Henry Thompson, interview by author, Oyster Bay, NY, March 2007; Booth, interview; Surindr Supasavasdebhandu, interview by author, Bangkok, July 2007.
11. Surindr, interview.
12. Ibid.
13. Khunying Niramol Kasemsart, interview by author, Bangkok, July 2007.
14. William Warren, interview by author, Bangkok, July 2007.
15. Praphan Liewchalermvong, interview by author, Bangkok, July 2007.
16. Surindr, interview.
17. William Booth, interview by author, Bangkok, March 2007.
18. Philippe Baude, interview by author by phone, January 2007.
19. Ibid.
20. Surindr, interview.
21. Ethan Emery, interview by author by phone, February 2007; Warren, interview.
22. Emery, interview.
23. Campbell James, interview by author, Newport, RI, April 2007.

24. Rene Burrow, interview by author by phone, January 2007; Murray Fromson, interview by author, Los Angeles, June 2007.

25. Keyes Beech, "'Good American' Gets Ugly Deal in Thailand," *Chicago Daily News*, November 13, 1962.

26. Ibid.

27. Christine Rangsit-Cameron, interview by author by phone, January 2007.

28. Beech, "'Good American.'"

29. JT to Dhanit Yupo, October 8, 1962, Siam Society collection, Bangkok; William Warren, *The Legendary American* (Boston: Houghton Mifflin, 1970), pp. 122–123.

30. JT to Elinor Douglas, October 14, 1962, Reath collection.

31. Warren, *The Legendary American*, p. 126.

32. JT to Dhanit Yupo, October 8, 1962, Siam Society collection.

33. Warren, *The Legendary American*, pp. 127–128.

34. JT to Jean Gordon, October 17, 1962, Elizabeth Lyons collection, University of Pennsylvania Museum.

35. Warren, interview; Marsh Thomson, interview by author, Bangkok, July 2007.

36. Thomson, interview.

37. Campbell James, interview by author, Newport, RI, March 2007; JT to Elinor Douglas, October 29, 1962, Reath collection.

38. JT to Elinor Douglas, October 14, 1962, Reath collection.

39. Burrow, unpublished memoirs, p. 72.

40. Ibid., p. 78.

41. Murray Fromson, interview by Hope Anderson, *Jim Thompson, Silk King*, DVD, 2000.

42. Christine Rangsit-Cameron, e-mail to author, March 2007; Burrow, unpublished memoirs, p. 71.

43. JT to Jean Gordon, October 17, 1962, Lyons collection.

44. Ann Donaldson, interview by author, New York, September 2006.

45. Burrow unpublished memoirs, p. 71.

46. Christine Rangsit-Cameron, interview by author by phone, April 2007.

47. Christine Rangsit-Cameron, interview by author by phone, February 2007; Henry Thompson, interview.

48. Robin Graves, interview by author, Dedham, MA, September 2006.

49. Henry Reath, interview by author by phone, September 2006.

50. Harold Stephens, interview by author, Bangkok, March 2007.

51. JT to the Frasche family, August, 1966, private collection of James Frasche.

Chapter 13

1. Evan Thomas, *The Very Best Men: The Daring Years of the CIA* (New York: Touchstone, 1995), pp. 183–184.
2. John Reed, interview by author, Washington, DC, September 2006; Jane Jantzen, interview by author by phone, August 2006.
3. John Prados, *Lost Crusader: The Secret Wars of CIA Director William Colby* (Oxford: Oxford University Press, 2003), p. 170.
4. Ibid., p. 171.
5. Campbell James, interview by author, Newport, RI, March 2007.
6. Thomas, *The Very Best Men*, p. 184.
7. Thomas Powers, *The Man Who Kept the Secrets: Richard Helms and the CIA* (New York: Alfred A. Knopf, 1979), pp. 98–99.
8. Prados, *Lost Crusader*, pp. 170–172.
9. Joseph Lazarsky, interview by author, Middleburg, VA, September 2006; see also Thanh-Dam Truong, *Sex, Money, and Morality: Prostitution and Tourism in South-East Asia* (London: Zed Books, 1990), p. 179.
10. Truong, p. 179.
11. Alexander Caldwell, *American Economic Aid to Thailand* (Lexington, MA: Lexington Books, 1974), pp. 171–172.
12. Marsh Thomson, interview by author, Bangkok, July 2007.
13. Caldwell, *American Aid*, pp. 171–172. Also, George Visknins, "United States Military Spending and the Economy of Thailand, 1967–1972," *Asian Survey*, May 1973, pp. 441–450.
14. Chris Baker and Pasuk Phongpaichit, *A History of Thailand* (Cambridge: Cambridge University Press, 2005), p. 149.
15. "Holder of the Kingdom, Strength of the Land," *Time*, May 27, 1966.
16. U.S. embassy in Vientiane, Laos, to U.S. State Department, Foreign Service dispatch, July 11, 1958, National Archives II, 851j.2553.
17. "Probe Told of Dispute on Laos Aid," *Washington Post*, March 25, 1959.
18. Jack Landau, "Ex-Aide Pleads Guilty to Laos Fraud Charge," *Washington Star*, February 15, 1963.
19. "Foreign Aid Corruption in Laos Stirs Reform," *Los Angeles Times*, June 15, 1959, p. 8; U.S. Agency for International Development, "USAID Operations in Laos: Congressional Committee on Government Operations Seventh Report (Washington, DC: U.S. Government Printing Office, 1959), p. 22.
20. Sterling Seagrave, *Soldiers of Fortune: The Epic of Flight* (New York: Time-Life Books, 1982), p. 154.
21. Willis Bird Jr., interview by author, Chiang Mai, Thailand, July 2007.

22. Timothy Castle, *At War in the Shadow of Vietnam: U.S. Military Aid to the Royal Lao Government, 1955–1975* (New York: Columbia University Press, 1993), pp. 2–65.

23. Keyes Beech, "How Uncle Sam Fumbled in Laos," *Saturday Evening Post*, April 22, 1961, p. 28.

24. William Leary, "CIA Air Operations in Laos, 1955–1974," *Studies in Intelligence*, Winter 1999–2000, p. 71.

25. "Memorandum for the Record: Background Information on Air America Inc., Udorn," March 9, 1973, Air America archives, University of Texas.

26. Christopher Robbins, *Air America* (New York: G. P. Putnam's Sons, 1979), pp. 21–25.

27. Ibid., p. 108.

28. Ibid., p. 35.

29. Castle, *At War in the Shadow of Vietnam*, p. 80.

30. Ibid., p. 81.

31. For more on the Hmong casualties, see Jane Hamilton-Merritt, *Tragic Mountains: The Hmong, the Americans, and the Secret Wars for Laos, 1942–1992* (Bloomington: Indiana University Press, 1999).

32. Symington Hearings, part 3, p. 712; "Rapid American Military Buildup in Southeast Asia," *Congressional Record* 112 (August 30, 1966), 89 1st sess., parts 5–6.

33. Daniel Fineman, *A Special Relationship: The United States and Military Government in Thailand, 1947–1958* (Honolulu: University of Hawaii Press, 1997), p. 262.

34. Seymour Topping, "The Twilight War in Laos," *New York Times*, January 24, 1965; "Senator Fulbright's NBC Interview," *Congressional Record* 112 (October 4, 1966), parts 16–20.

35. JT to Elinor Douglas, November 3, 1960, private collection of Andrews Reath.

36. Bird, interview.

37. Bill Lair, interview by author by phone, August 2006.

38. Bird, interview.

Chapter 14

1. Roger Warner, *Shooting at the Moon: The Story of America's Clandestine War in Laos* (South Royalton, VT: Steerforth Press, 1996), pp. 349–350.

2. Denis Horgan, interview by author, West Hartford, CT, January 2007.

3. Ibid.

4. Ibid.

5. Paul Battersby, "Border Politics and Broader Politics of Thailand's International Relations in the 1990s: From Communism to Capitalism," *Pacific Affairs*, Winter 1998–1999, pp. 473–488.

6. Louis E. Lomax, *Thailand: The War That Is, the War That Will Be* (New York: Random House, 1967), p. 40.

7. JT to Elinor Douglas, February 11, 1967, private collection of Andrews Reath.

8. Horgan, interview.

9. Alfred McCoy, *The Politics of Heroin in Southeast Asia* (New York: Harper and Row, 1972), pp. 144–146.

10. Ibid., p. 277.

11. Ibid., p. 278.

12. Horgan, interview.

13. William Warren, interview by author, Bangkok, July 2007; Horgan, interview.

14. Warren, interview.

15. Horgan, interview.

16. William Warren, *The Legendary American* (Boston: Houghton Mifflin, 1967), p. 135.

17. Martha Galleher, *The Missing Silk King* (Baltimore: self-published, 2007), p. 78.

18. JT to Elinor Douglas, March 12, 1967, Andrews Reath collection.

19. Ann Donaldson, interview by author, New York, September 2006.

20. Campbell James, interview by author, Newport, RI, March 2007.

21. Warren, *The Legendary American*, pp. 138–139.

22. Hope Anderson, *Jim Thompson, Silk King*, DVD, 2000.

23. JT to Arthur Holden, February 3, 1967, private collection of Henry Thompson.

24. Edmond Taylor, *Awakening from History* (London: Chatto and Windus, 1971), pp. 354–355.

25. Philippe Baude, interview by author by phone, January 2007.

Chapter 15

1. William Warren, *The Legendary American* (Boston: Houghton Mifflin, 1970), p. 140.

2. Ibid., p. 16.

3. Rene Burrow, unpublished memoirs, p. 56.

4. Joanna Cross, interview by author, Bangkok, January 2007.

5. Warren, *The Legendary American*, p. 18.

6. Philip Rivers, e-mails to author, June 2010.

7. Mark Jenkins, "The Saga of the Thai Silk King," *Princeton Alumni Weekly*, May 6, 1987.

8. Elizabeth McIntosh, interview by author, Arlington, VA, September 2006.

9. Cross, interview.

10. Noel F. Busch, "The Jim Thompson Mystery," *Reader's Digest*, Asian edition, 1969, pp. 17–20.

11. Henry Thompson, "In the Matter of James H. W. Thompson," testimony to the Office of the Register of Wills for New Castle County, Delaware, June 10, 1974.

12. Surindr Supasavasdebhandu, interview by author, Bangkok, July 2007.

13. Burrow, unpublished memoirs, p. 60.

14. Denis Horgan, interview by author, West Hartford, CT, January 2007.

15. Martha Galleher, *The Missing Silk King* (Baltimore: self-published, 2007), p. 145.

16. Rivers, e-mail.

17. Ibid.

18. Robert Sam Anson, "The Mystery of the Thai Silk King," *Life*, May 1984, p. 78.

19. Rivers, e-mail.

20. Thai Silk Company, "Reward Notice for Mr. Jim Thompson," April 1, 1967.

21. Pira Sudham, "A Day in the Life of Jim Thompson," *Bangkok Post*, July 15, 1979, p. 20.

22. Horgan, interview.

23. Thai Silk Company, "Trip Report Compiled by Denis Horgan," April 1967.

24. Horgan, interview.

25. Anson, "The Mystery of the Thai Silk King."

26. Thai Silk Company, "Memorandum for Record: Gen Black Trip to Malaysia," April 1967.

27. Thai Silk Company, "Itinerary 20 Mar–4 April for Brigadier General Edwin Black," April 5, 1967.

28. Warren, *The Legendary American*, p. 150.

29. Charlie Kirkwood, interview by author by phone, March 2006.

30. "Malaysian Police Call off Search for Jim Thompson," *Bangkok World*, April 5, 1967, p. 1.

31. "US General Ends Search in Malaysia for 'Silk King,'" Reuters, April 3, 1967.

32. Horgan, interview.

33. "Jungle Expert Joins Search for American in Malaysia," Reuters, April 22, 1967.

34. Busch, "The Jim Thompson Mystery," p. 21.

35. Galleher, *The Missing Silk King*, p. 116.

36. "Malaysian Police Believe Jim Thompson Kidnapped," Associated Press, April 28, 1967.

37. "Thompson: Official Search Called Off," *Bangkok Post*, April 5, 1967, p. 1.

38. Rivers, e-mail.

39. "A Walk in the Jungle," *Time*, April 7, 1967.

40. Rivers, e-mail.

41. Galleher, *The Missing Silk King*, pp. 35–174.

42. Warren, *The Legendary American*, pp. 174–175; see also Louis Kraar, "Espionage, Intrigue, Politics Cloud the Thompson Case," *Time*, May 5, 1967, p. 14.

43. Warren, *The Legendary American*, pp. 174–175.

44. William Warren, "Is Jim Thompson Alive and Well in Asia?" *New York Times Magazine*, April 21, 1968, pp. 109–110.

45. Warren, *The Legendary American*, p. 179.

46. Rivers, e-mail.

47. Warren, "Is Jim Thompson Alive," pp. 109–110.

48. Ibid.

49. Confidential CIA source, interview by author by phone, March 2006; Thompson, "In the Matter of James H. W. Thompson," pp. 24–25.

50. Richard Hughes, "Richard Hughes' Column," *Far Eastern Economic Review*, September 3, 1981, p. 33; confidential CIA source, interview.

51. Retired FBI source, interview by author, Washington, DC, March 2006.

52. Ann Donaldson, interview by author, New York, September 2006.

53. Jane Jantzen, interview by author by phone, March 2006.

Chapter 16

1. United States Army Support, "Memorandum for Record: Mr. James HW Thompson," Bangkok, December 12, 1967.

2. Robert Sam Anson, "The Mystery of the Thai Silk King," *Life*, May 1984, pp. 70–78.

3. Ed Black to James Douglas, June 24, 1968, private collection of Thai Silk Company.

4. Henry Thompson, interview by author, Oyster Bay, NY, March 2006.

5. Martha Galleher, *The Missing Thai Silk King* (Baltimore: self-published, 2007), p. 206.

6. Rene Burrow, interview by author by phone, February 2007.
7. William Booth, interview by author, Bangkok, July 2007.
8. Galleher, *The Missing Silk King*, p. 206.
9. Ibid., p. 143.
10. Philip Rivers, e-mail to author, July 2010.
11. Ibid.
12. William Warren, *The Legendary American* (Boston: Houghton Mifflin, 1970), pp. 246–248.
13. Henry Thompson, interview by author, Oyster Bay, NY, September 2006.
14. Warren, *The Legendary American*, pp. 249–252.
15. Ann Donaldson, interview by author, New York, September 2007.
16. Scott Shane, "US Approves Targeted Killing of American Cleric," *New York Times*, April 6, 2010.
17. Sukprida Banomyong, interview by author, Bangkok, July 2007.
18. Peter Jackson, "An American Death in Bangkok: The Murder of Darrell Berrigan," *GLQ: A Journal of Lesbian and Gay Studies* 5, no. 3, 1999, pp. 361–411.
19. Jesse Henry, interview by author, Bangkok, July 2007.
20. Ann Donaldson, interview by author, New York, September 2006.
21. Edwin Black, "Memorandum for Ambassador Bell," April 2, 1967, private collection of Thai Silk Company.
22. Ann Donaldson, interview by author, New York, October 2007.
23. Ibid.
24. Cobey Black, interview by author, Honolulu, June 2007.
25. Henry, interview.
26. Ibid.
27. Roger Warner, *Shooting at the Moon: The Story of America's Clandestine War in Laos* (South Royalton, VT: Steerforth Press, 1996), p. 395.
28. Greg Davis, interview by author, Arlington, VA, May 2007.
29. Willis Bird Jr., interview by author, Chiang Mai, Thailand, July 2007.
30. Ibid.
31. Ibid.

Epilogue
1. Docents at Jim Thompson House, interviews by author, Bangkok, July 2007; Probate Admission of the Will of James H. W. Thompson, Register of Wills Office, New Castle County, DE, November 25, 1974; "Silk Man's Home to Keep His Art," *New York Times*, July 8, 1968, p. 44.

2. William Booth, interview by author, Bangkok, July 2007.

3. Ibid.

4. See Jane Hamilton-Merritt, *Tragic Mountains: The Hmong, the Americans, and the Secret War for Laos, 1942–1992* (Bloomington: Indiana University Press, 1999).

5. Marsh Thomson, interview by author, Bangkok, July 2007.

6. On the Hmong struggles: Anne Fadiman, *The Spirit Catches You and You Fall Down* (New York: Farrar, Straus and Giroux, 1997).

7. For more on the issues related to the Hmong and human rights, visit www.hmongihrw.org.

8. Alejandro Reyes, "From Our Correspondent: After the Visit," *Asiaweek*, November 22, 2000.

9. On the current U.S.-Vietnam relationship and modern Vietnam: Bill Hayton, *Vietnam: Rising Dragon* (New Haven, CT: Yale University Press, 2010).

10. Sukprida Banomyong, interview by author, Bangkok, July 2007.

11. Willis Bird Jr., interview by author, Chiang Mai, Thailand, March 2007.

12. Greg Davis, interview by author, Washington, DC, December 2006.

13. Thai academics, interviews by author, Bangkok, October 2006.

14. Rene Burrow, interview by author by phone, March 2007.

Index

262